William Williams

Goldsmith's Deserted Village, Cowper's Task (book III, the Garden) and, The de Coverley Papers (from the Spectator)

William Williams

Goldsmith's Deserted Village, Cowper's Task (book III, the Garden) and, The de Coverley Papers (from the Spectator)

ISBN/EAN: 9783337182892

Printed in Europe, USA, Canada, Australia, Japan

Cover: Foto ©ninafisch / pixelio.de

More available books at **www.hansebooks.com**

ENGLISH LITERATURE SERIES.

GOLDSMITH'S DESERTED VILLAGE,

COWPER'S TASK,

(BOOK III., THE GARDEN)

AND

THE DE COVERLEY PAPERS,

(FROM THE *SPECTATOR*).

EDITED WITH

LIVES, NOTES, INTRODUCTORY CHAPTERS AND
EXAMINATION QUESTIONS.

BY

WILLIAM WILLIAMS, B.A.,

*Head Master Collingwood Collegiate Institute, Author of " Goldsmith's
Traveller" and "Gray's Elegy."*

COMPRISING IN ONE VOLUME

ALL THE SELECTIONS IN LITERATURE PRESCRIBED FOR UNI-
VERSITY MATRICULATION, FIRST (GRADE C.) AND SECOND
CLASS TEACHERS' CERTIFICATES, AND THE HIGH
SCHOOL INTERMEDIATE EXAMINATION.

Toronto:
CANADA PUBLISHING COMPANY.
1881.

CONTENTS.

GENERAL INTRODUCTION.

THE eighteenth century, as regards the history of poetry, may be conveniently divided into three periods. The first embraces almost half the century, while the artifi_cial school of Pope and his admiring imitators bore undisturbed sway within the domain of the Muses; the second is a period of barrenness and transition, during which the sentimental school of Darwin and Hayley spread out in vain their viands of luscious sweets to regale the sated appetites of their guests, and when a few voices, led by Thomson, Gray, and Collins, were gently heralding in the dawn of a brighter day; in the last, poetry, under the hand of Cowper, the real, if unconscious, founder of a new school, broke entirely loose from the conventional artificiality of the early part of the century, and returned in a manner to the old sources of inspiration, at which had drunk the great masters of English verse— Chaucer, Spenser, and Shakespeare.

The Augustan age, a term frequently employed to denote the supremacy of Pope in poetry and Addison in prose, possessed but little that could call forth and develope a true poetic spirit. Prior to the Revolution, literary men had formed a distinct class; but, with the introduction of responsible parliamentary government, it was united with, or rather absorbed into, the political.

Hence, literature, instead of being an honored profession, became merely an instrument to be employed for the pleasure of the Court, or for the assistance of political intrigue. The atmosphere in which it was thus compelled to live, and the menial purposes it was obliged to serve, dwarfed its growth, narrowed its sympathies, chilled its heart, and degraded its tone. Yet the new relation it occupied was not without its advantages. It was one of the received opinions of the time that the Government should assist struggling genius, and that a certain proportion of the means at its control should be devoted to this purpose. During the reign of Anne, both Whigs and Tories —Somers and Montague on the one side, Harley and St. John on the other—did more to assist literature than any other English statesmen have ever done. The system may have had its abuses ; but it cannot be denied that the brilliant outburst of poetic and prose writings of this age was fostered, if not created, by the pensions, appointments, and professional promotions which were conferred by the Government on Newton, Addison, Swift, Steele, Prior, Rowe, Congreve, Parnell, and many others. With the accession of the House of Hanover all this was changed. George I. possessed none of the qualities that made his mother one of the most brilliant women in Europe. Walpole, his minister, was likewise totally devoid of literary tastes. The management of party was his aim. In this he spent the large sums at his control, and to attain this end he employed the patronage of the Government. If he used literary men, it was for the same purpose, and the rewards he gave were the wages of party libel or political vituperation. The inevitable result was social degradation, literary drudgery, and the most wretched poverty. Steele died in neglect, Savage wandered home less and starving through the streets of London, Johnson spent thirty years in penury, and Thomson was deprived of a small place in Chancery, his sole means of support. Queen Caroline, it is true, exerted her influence in favor of many men of merit, and drew from obscurity some well worthy of her patronage—as Butler, Sherlock, and Secker. The suddenness of the change from social consideration to contempt, from pensions and sinecures to garrets and hack-work, threw a class of men that had been taught to look up to the Government for support, entirely upon their own resources. At this time the reading public was small, and its tastes low. Little work could be found, except political pamphleteering, that promised any remuneration, so that such as determined to follow letters were doomed, with few exceptions, to drudging for booksellers, at such a pittance as they chose to dole out to their starving toilers. In the Court and in political circles the state of public morality was exceedingly low. The reaction against the deep earnest Puritanical austerity had reached its intensity, and the opposition current which was already beginning to set in, soon after rose to such impetuous violence, that it bore down in its mighty wave many of the customs and fashions of society, and revolutionized the moral condition of England. In this grand transformation, not only the religious life of the people was renewed, but its literature likewise felt the regenerating power ; and the old poetic spirit of the nation once more burst forth, and broke away entirely from the modish bonds which had so long held it in polished chains. But this was not suddenly accomplished. Great national changes seldom are. There was a long period during which this elegant mode was rising to perfection ; nor did it instantly pall upon the taste. Society for a time humbly worshipped the diamond image it had set up. For the first two generations of the century this state of affairs continued. The lower classes were brutal and ignorant ; the higher were profligate, irreligious, and sentimental. The pulpit no longer, except in rare instances, sought to inculcate the deep experimental piety of the Commonwealth, but contented itself with seeking to instil a love for morality, and to enforce the precepts of natural religion. The sermons were lectures on the authenticity of Christianity, and the system of religion of that period could have as well been founded on the writings of Socrates or Confucius as on the Gospel of Christ. The wave of Deism which had overflowed from France had inundated the entire land. Men had become rationalistic as well as sceptical. They did not look deep into the foundation upon which all truth rests. They sought rather to adapt truth to their own capacity, and to their own conventional standard. It was not the firm foundation, but the imposing visible structure that they valued. It was not the purity within, but the polish without that they admired. In this temper of mind we could not expect that the poetry they relished would be that which touched the heart or stirred the soul, but that which could dazzle the understanding, and sparkle in its own extrinsic brilliancy ; not that which revels in the description of Nature, but that which boasts that it can scan the mind ; not that which creates, but that which explains and justifies creation. It was not a creative period. Men were yet scarcely beginning to investigate for new truth, but only to doubt and defend. Their ideas were neither lofty nor deep. They did not rise into the sublime heights of metaphysical abstraction, nor had they yet learned to dive into the hidden mysteries of scientific investigation. To understand society, to enjoy life as they found it, to be thorough men of the world, was their highest ideal of the aims of life. It was, forsooth, an age of prosaic common sense, of social conventionality, literary elegance, and polished superficiality. " In literature, in art, in speculation, the imagination was repressed ; strong passions, elevated motives, and sublime aspirations were replaced by critical accuracy of thought and observation, by a measured sobriety, and good sense. We find this alike in the prose of Addison, in the poetry of Pope, and in the philosophy of Hume. The greatest wit and the most original genius of the age was also the most intensely and the most coarsely realistic."

French tastes and modes of thought had been transplanted into English soil with the return of Charles II., and were now bearing abundant fruit. Dryden, the chief poet of his time, catered to those tastes, and his strong rugged genius did much to popularize the fashions that prevailed at Court. But it must not be forgotten that though his writings are inspired by influences from beyond the Channel, they are nevertheless truly English, and, as such, were the direct and regular offspring of the poetical productions of the preceding age. The Elizabethans and their successors, in the prodigality and grandeur of their genius, had mainly kept in view the expression of the profusion of lofty ideas that rushed upon their brain, pay-ing comparatively little attention to the manner in which those ideas found utterance. The vehemence of the pas-sion that wrought within their breast, and the multitude of visions that pressed for utterance, both from the grand and stirring scenes of their own time and of the by-gone Middle Ages which lay in rich and yet ungathered harvest before their warm and lively fancy, poured down in such richness that it was impossible for them to break in the language to poetry, and they fell frequently into caprice of thought as well as obscurity of expression, and neglected that polish and elegance which adorns and gives duration to art. To this there came a natural reaction. To add form and finish, to give clearness to language and plain-ness to thought, to adapt poetry to the expression of the affairs of life, to describe man, not as a creature of pas-sion, but as a social and intellectual being, such was the task of Dryden and his successors.

Poetry now lost that singleness of aim which charac-terized it in the hands of the Elizabethans, and adapted itself to the metrical expression of all the varied interests of human life. In Blackmore's *Creation* and Prior's *Solo-mon* we have imitations of the epic taste of stronger gene-rations. " In Swift are seen the feuds and bitterness of party government ; in Pope and Parnell, the current theo-logical and moral speculations ; the peace and commer-cial advance under wise Walpole are embodied in the di-dactic verse of Dyer and Grainger, Somerville and Thom-son ; Watts marks the beginning of the religious change of which Cowper represents the maturity. The influences of nature on poetry reappear in Gray, Warton and Burns ;

foreign travel yields its first fruits in Goldsmith; Gay gives pictures from common life, viewed from the side of sentiment, Crabbe under the influence of social economy. Nor are traces of the more general currents affecting politics and manners absent, although these cannot be so individually specified." In the wider range of subjects to which poetry was thus applied, obscurity, conceits and affectation gave place to simplicity and clearness. Thus far great praise is due to the poets of this age. But they could not follow their new system in moderation. Men never can. New ideas must be carried to extremes. And so it was here. Soon form became everything, and it subdued within its rigid bonds, not merely the language and the versification, but the sentiments likewise. The whole tone of society was also artificial, so literature and society, by their mutual action and reaction upon each other, tended to further the same end. Uniformity, symmetry, and consequent mediocrity, became all the fashion. Poetry contained no lofty flight of imagination, no strong passion, no deep emotion. It was a sort of regular and modulated prose. From prose, indeed, it differed chiefly in form. Its matter was the same, its purpose, too, to systematize and clearly expound human knowledge and the concerns of life—was also similar.

The poetry of this period was even more crystallized in form than in sentiment. However the poets may have differed in other respects, they uniformly agreed to seek for the greatest perfection in the form of their verse—that is to say, perfection according to their standard. The character of the poetic line has greatly varied in the history of English poetry. With Chaucer and his followers, it was

not deemed necessary to regard an exact number of regularly accented syllables as the only essential of good verse ;
much the same manner was observed with our Elizabethans, after them it was the fashion to glory in the
ruggedness of the verse. Then came the practice of
making the line smooth, regular and exact in its syllables,
and harmoniously varied in the pauses of the different
lines. Much was accomplished in the bold and vigorous
style of Dryden, but the fulness of the art was attained
by Pope. A host of other poets of less note likewise
caught his method, till

" Every warbler had his tune by heart."

In this respect many of them were no mean imitators, if,
indeed, they did not frequently rival the skill and facility of their master. As the aim was to be witty and
sparkling, so was it to set out that wit in the most pointed
and elegant language, in the most correct and brilliant form.
In truth, it not unfrequently appears that the thought was
a secondary consideration to the smoothness and epigrammatic beauty of the couplet.

Polish and brilliancy may dazzle, but can never do more
than please the ear and eye. Alone they can have little
lasting effect on the heart. Hence we are prepared to find
that this artificiality in poetry could not endure, and more,
that such an unnatural state of society could not be perpetual. There soon became manifest an evident desire
to return to the nature and natural emotion which had
been the informing spirit of early English poetry.

The pioneer of the new taste, at least, in subject and
mode of treatment, was Thomson, whose *Seasons* (1726-30)

exhibit in their rich melody and felicity of description an ardent love of nature, though yet in artificial dress. Almost simultaneously came Dyer's *Grongar Hill* and *Evening Walk* (1727). Then nearly twenty years elapsed before the description of nature received a further impetus from the skyey fancy and melting pathos of Collins (1746), and from the elegant and elaborate verse of Gray (1747—57). The next step, that in which we meet with the first simple daylight landscape, where the human figure and the aspects of nature are united in such a manner as to delight us, not as moralizations, but as pictures, is taken in the poems of Oliver Goldsmith. The publication of Percy's *Reliques* (1763), a collection of English ballads wherein the old spirit, the openness and freshness of life, the warm expression of human passion and that simplicity which is the highest grandeur, dwelt in rich plenitude, found in the chilled heart of the nation a cordial reception, and called forth such desires as could no longer be satisfied with tinsel and unreality. The attention of both poets and readers was turned to the older poetry of the language. Study gave rise to admiration, and admiration to imitation. A new school of criticism that was about this time founded by the Wartons, which received its inspiration from romantic rather than from classical sources, and on which the Middle Ages wrought almost as effectually as Greek and Roman literature did on Collins and Gray, fostered the same course of feeling. The public, too, had grown tired of art, and gladly welcomed a return to simplicity and nature· Nor was this retarded by pushing the old-school principles to extremes, as was done by Darwin and Hayley, whose poetry resembles polished metal, bright and shining, but cold, hard and lifeless.   The change was first perceptible in the sentiments, and later it affected also the structure of the verse.   A new class of subjects were chosen, and, consequently, a different mode of treatment was adopted. Instead of the reflective came the descriptive, and in lieu of the didactic, the tale and lyrical narrative.

While these tendencies were making gradual but constant progress, there came over England a ferment of religious enthusiasm that spread its leaven throughout almost the entire nation, and gave an impulse that carried them rapidly forward to the most important results.   The lethargy and indifference of the clergy, the ignorance and brutality of the lower orders, had awakened a concern for the spiritual interests of the nation in the breasts of some of the more devout and zealous of the ministers of the Established Church.   Instead of preaching the old doctrines of theoretical morality, which for many years had appeared to be almost the only function of the pulpit, these men began to insist upon the vital importance of experimental religion.   The enthusiasm which they aroused took a deep hold on the middle and lower classes of the nation, and produced the most momentous results both within and without the Establishment—results which brought back the heart of the nation, vastly raised the standard of public morality and set on foot instrumentalities and agencies for the uplifting and cleansing of the people, which are still bearing the noblest fruit, and which are now embodied in the frame-work of society throughout the world.   This great movement, which, at first, was wholly within the national church, was afterwards, in part, severed from it.   Those who separated from the Church assumed the name of Methodists, while the term Evangelicism was employed to indicate the movement within its pale. To the latter, Cowper, as well as his friend and protector, Mr. Newton, belonged. Cowper did not commence in earnest to write poetry till he was fifty-five years old, twenty-three years after his conversion—two facts important to be remembered. He then undertook it simply that he might have some occupation for his mind. He had not kept up his reading in literature and poetry, which had never been extensive ; hence, when he began to write, he stood almost alone, and was not greatly influenced either by poetic theories or poetic practice. Nor had he, indeed, the remotest idea of inaugurating a new school of poetry, though he evidently felt himself impelled to seek for matter and expression in a different field from that cultivated by Pope, who appeared to him to have '' made poetry a mere mechanic art." The real source of his inspiration was the religious movement of the time, of which he is the grand and devoted exponent in the poetic life of the country. The change which has been described as gradually coming over the poetic taste and production of the century received a powerful impetus from the upward movement in morality, which had long been coming on as a natural reaction to the irreligion and vice of the period succeeding the Restoration, and which already for many years had been permeating and transforming the nation. Cowper, the lonely hermit of the Ouse, united these two—the rising moral and religious purity of the people, and their renewed love for nature, passion, and imagination in poetry—into one noble pean of song. The task was his to gather into one the converging streams of moral and poetic progress that arose from the quiet return from speculation and doubt to faith and practice, and from the artificial gloss with which society had been veneered to the warmer ebullition of human passion, and the genuine love of simple nature. Speaking of the part borne by Cowper, a writer in *Blackwood's Magazine* (June, 1871) has well said :—

" It was the re-birth of poetry in England—the first bold departure from the well-worn channel in which all poetical compositions had flowed for many years. Cowper, in this new work, served himself suddenly heir to the old poets of greater ages, and to the homely vigorous English which they had not found too common for their handling. He cast aside the worn-out moulds, threw the traditions of Pope's and Dryden's era to the winds, and caught the old perennial stream from the fountain at which it flowed brightest and most full. When we think of it, it is impossible to over-estimate the courage and even hardihood of this step. Every poetical influence had been setting one way during the entire century. Cowper, at the end of that century, a man with no impulse of youth to help him, no new enthusiasm to animate him, deliberately set his face against it and turned the tide. All the smoothness of versification, the artificial melody of rythm in which his generation had delighted, and in which he too, himself, had imitated the other songsters of the age, he put aside to make his new venture. It was entirely new though it was so old. England had fancied herself to have outlived the lofty melody of blank verse. She discovered now that the old strain was her favorite—that it could charm her ear as well as rouse her soul. She found out that nature was as sweet as it had been in the days of Milton, the English fields as fair, the rural sights and sounds as fresh and tender. This worn-out sick man growing old, half frantic, half madman, half recluse, drew the veil from her eyes and threw open to her a new, sweet, dewy, fragrant world. It is difficult for us even to imagine the surprised delight with which the nation felt the sweetness of this new voice, which was so familiar, so homelike, so unpretending. After all, the shade of the Throckmorton elms, the woodman on his way to the forest, the pheasant's nest perched on the hillside, the post-boy, light-hearted wretch! twanging his horn across the bridge, were a thousand times more near the heart than the outpouring of a poet's malice, the impalation of a Sporus or a Sappho. Nobody had thought of it up to that moment; but when the moment came, all England saw it with that sudden enlightenment which is like inspiration. All through the conventional ages, the period in which poetry had been a thing of wits and coffee-houses, the production of a class, full of allusions and assaults which only that class could appreciate, Shakespeare and Milton had still been read in the silent corners, in those depths of the national heart which criticism and its artificial standard did not reach; and, lo, these secret worshippers of the old gods rose up with a thrill of delight to greet the new light which carried in it all the marks of divinity which they could not recognise in its predecessors."

CHRONOLOGICAL PARALLEL.

A.D.	ENGLISH HISTORY AND LITERATURE.	LIFE OF GOLDSMITH.	LIFE OF COWPER.
1728	Pope's *Dunciad.* Percy *b.* Thos. Warton *b.*	Born, November, 10th	
1729	Congreve *d.* Steele *d.*		
1730	Colley Cibber, Poet Laureate. Burke *b.*	Family leave Pallas for Lissoy.	
1731	Defoe *d.*	Sent to Miss Delap.	Born, Nov. 26th.
1733	Priestley *b.*		
1734		To school to Byrne.	
1735	Beattie *b.* Pope's *Moral Essays.*		
1736	Porteous Riots.	To Rev. Mr. Griffin's.	
1737	Gibbon *b.* Green *d.*		Loses his mother. To school at Market Street.
1739	War declared against Spain	To Rev. Mr. Campbell's.	To Mrs. Disney's house.
1741	Walpole resigns.	To Rev. P. Hughes'.	To Westminster School.
1743	Pelham takes office.		
1744	Pope *d.*		
1745	Pretender's Rebellion.	Enters Trin. College.	
1747		His father dies.	
1748	Thomson *d.* Peace of Aix-la-Chapelle.		Entered at the Middle Temple.
1749		Takes his B.A.	
1750	Dr. Johnson's *Rambler.*	At home.	
1752	Chatterton *b.* Bishop Butler *d.* *The Adventurer* started.	Tutor at Mr. Flinn's. Starts out to study law. To Edinburgh to study medicine.	
1753	The *World.*		First attack of despondency (or 1754)
1754	Crabbe *b.* Fielding *d.*	To Leyden. Travels.	Called to the Bar.
1756	War against France.	Returns to Eng. and.	His father dies.
1757	Seven years' War begins. Whitehead, Poet Laureate.	Teaches for Dr. Milner. Writes for *Monthly Review.*	
1758	Dr. Johnson's *Idler.*	Fails at examination.	
1759	Quebec taken. Burns *b.*	*Life of Voltaire.* *Inquiry. The Bee.*	Removes to the Inner Temple.
1760	George III. Poems of Ossian. Churchill's *Rosciad.*	Writes for *British Mag.* and *Public Ledger.*	
1761	Richardson *d.*	*Citizen of the World.*	
1762	Bute Premier. *N. Briton.*	*Life of Beau Nash.*	
1763	Literary Club founded. Grenville Ministry.		Confined at St. Alban's.
1764	Horace Walpole's *Otranto.*	*History of England. Traveller.*	

CHRONOLOGICAL PARALLEL.

A.D.	ENGLISH HISTORY AND LITERATURE.	LIFE OF GOLDSMITH.	LIFE OF COWPER.
1765	Rockingham takes office. Young *d.* Percy's *Reliques.*	*Experimental Philosophy.*	Inmate of Mr. Unwin's, at Huntingdon.
1766	Mosaic Ministry.	*Vicar of Wakefield. Collection of Essays.*	
1767			Settles at Olney.
1768	Sterne *d.* Grafton takes office	*Good-Natured Man.*	
1769	Letters of Junius.	*M.B.* at Oxford. *Roman History.*	
1770	North succeeds Grafton. Wordsworth *b.*	*Deserted Village. Life of Parnell. Life of Bolingbroke.*	
1771	Walter Scott *b.*	*Haunch of Venison. English History.*	
1772	Coleridge *b.*		
1773	Francis Jeffrey *b.*	*She Stoops to Conquer*	Deranged, third time.
1774	Southey *b.* Lord Clive *d.* Warton's *English Poetry* Vol. I.	Death, 4th April; buried, 9th April. *Retaliation. Animated Nature.*	
1775	American War begins.		
1776	Smith's *Wealth of Nations.*		
1779	Garrick *d.*		*Olney Hymns.*
1782	North succeeded by Rockingham; he by Lord Shelburne.		First volume of Poems.
1783	Peace of Versailles.		
1784	Dr. Johnson *d.*		
1785			*The Task.*
1786	Burns' Poems.		Leaves Olney for Weston Underwood.
1787			Deranged, fourth time.
1789	Dr. Darwin's *Loves of the Plants.* French Revolution.		
1791	Rev. J. Wesley *d.*		*Translation of Homer.*
1792			Again deranged.
1794	Gibbon *d.*		Pension of £300.
1795	Warren Hastings acquitted.		Removed to Norfolk.
1796	Macpherson *d.*		Death of Mrs. Unwin.
1798	Wordsworth's *Lyrical Ballads.*		
1800	Moore's *Anacreon.*		Death, at Dereham, April 25th.

LIFE OF GOLDSMITH.

WHEN the assembled wits had decided to place the best epitaph upon Dryden's tomb that had ever been chiselled, Atterbury exclaimed, "'Dryden' is enough; they who know his works, want no more, they who do not know them, would not be enlightened by the most eloquent eulogy." True as these words are of Dryden, they are even more applicable to Goldsmith. As we read his works, his character gradually unfolds itself with each successive page, and we become familiar with the virtues, the weaknesses and the foibles of our author. In one part or other of his writings, he has left us a complete autobiography of himself, drawn by a faithful, yet gentle hand. We smile and sympathize, or admire and love, as we meet, on every page, a genial, easy, and unceasing flow of good humor, good sense, and good feeling; as we see, in all the characters he has sketched, his own artless benevolence and fitfulness, his kindness and waywardness, or trace in their blunderings and buffetings, the mischances, ludicrous scenes, or laughable mistakes of his own life

The Goldsmiths were a respectable, but unthrifty race, whose "hearts were in the right place, but whose heads seemed to be doing anything but what they ought." Accordingly the Rev. Charles Goldsmith, Oliver's father, married very young and very poor, and so was obliged for some years to "pray and starve" on forty pounds a year, in a small rural curacy at Pallas, a remote hamlet in the county of Longford, in Ireland. It was here that

Oliver, the second son of a family of four sons and two daughters, was born, on the 10th of November, 1728. While he was yet a child, his father was presented to the rectorship of Kilkenny West, in Westmeath, worth £200 a year. The family consequently exchanged the antique mansion and lonely wilds of Pallas for an elegant rectory situated on the busy high-road leading to Lissoy. Here, Oliver spent his boyhood days, here, he received his early education, and these are the scenes which, in the delightful strains of his *Deserted Village*, he has embalmed in our language forever. When only about three years old, he was sent to an old lady's private school to learn his letters. At the end of four years, she pronounced him a dunce, and passed him over to the hands of the village schoolmaster, Thomas (or, as the boys had it, Paddy) Byrne. Byrne, educated for a teacher, had enlisted in the army, served abroad in Queen Anne's time, and risen to the rank of quarter-master. On his return from service, he had engaged to drill the urchins of Lissoy in reading, writing and arithmetic ; but, like many a teacher whose knowledge is limited, yet whose tongue is ready, he gilded over his deficiencies by entertaining his wondering scholars with an exhaustless fund of stories. Besides his facility in story-telling, he was an enthusiastic admirer of the ancient Irish bards, whom he fancied he could imitate. Such a tutor was just the person to produce deep and lasting impressions on the imaginative mind of young Oliver who, before he was eight years of age, had begun to scribble verses of poetry. Some of these lines coming under the notice of his mother, she readily perceived that her son was a poetical genius, and from that time urged upon his father the necessity of giving the lad an education befitting his abilities. The expense of educating his eldest son, Henry, had so straitened the father's narrow income, that he had determined to put Oliver to a trade ; but the mother's earnest solicitations won the day, and it was decided to give him a University education. Hence, on his recovery from a severe attack of small-pox, he was placed under the care of the Rev. Mr. Griffin, of Elphin. One evening while here, a number of young people assembled at his uncle's for a dance, and the fiddler, turning Oliver's short clumsy figure and pock-marked face into ridicule, called him " Æsop." This was too much for his sensitive nature, and stopping short, he replied : " Heralds proclaim aloud this saying—See Æsop dancing and his monkey playing." This repartee raised him greatly in the estimation of his friends, several of whom—especially his uncle, the Rev. Thomas Contarine—contributed means to place him in a school possessing advantages superior to those afforded at Elphin. He was therefore removed to a school kept by the Rev. Mr. Campbell, at Athlone, and, after two years, transferred to one at Edgesworthstown, under the supervision of the Rev. Patrick Hughes. He does not appear to have been distinguished at any of these schools—except, indeed, by his easy, idle disposition, and blundering manners. No favorite with the teacher, he was the leader in the sports of the playground, and never hindmost in any school-boy prank.

With this preparation he was sent up to Trinity College, Dublin. He was now in his seventeenth year, eccentric, idle and thoughtless. His sister having married a wealthy gentleman, named Hodson, her father deemed it a point of honor to furnish her with a suitable dowry, and, acting on this impulse, so embarrassed the family circumstances, that it was found impossible to give Oliver the same advantages as his brother, Henry. He accordingly entered College, as a sizar. This menial condition, as might be expected, was very galling to the proud spirit of young Oliver ; yet, while enduring indignities, in order to enjoy the advantages of the institution, he neglected his studies, quarrelled with his tutor, received a public reprimand for joining in an attack on a bailiff, violated the college rules by giving a supper and dance to some of his city friends, won an exhibition of thirty shillings, and was turned to the foot for playing buffoon in his class.

While he was at Dublin his father died, leaving the family very poorly provided for, so that Oliver's situation became still more painful. To relieve his necessities he occasionally wrote songs, sold them for five shillings each, and then squandered the money. However, by the aid of his uncle, he was enabled to remain at college till he took his degree in 1749. He then returned home, and spent three years, partly with his mother, who had taken a small cottage at Ballymahon, and partly with his brother-in-law, Hodson, at Lissoy. He was now twenty-one, and it became necessary to decide on some profession. His friends urged him to enter the church. After some difficulty his objections were withdrawn, and he began to qualify himself for Orders. The time for his ordination came. He presented himself to the bishop, dressed in scarlet breeches, and was, in consequence, rejected. He then became tutor in a wealthy family, but threw up the situation in a dispute over a game of cards. On receiving his wages he bought a fine horse, and set out for Cork, intending to sail for America ; but after six weeks he returned home on a wretched nag and without a penny in his pocket. Next he determined to study law. His friends provided him with a purse of fifty pounds, with which he set out for London, but on his way he met an old acquaintance at Dublin, who took him to

a gambling house and stripped him of his money. At
the suggestion of Dean Goldsmith, of Cloyne, a distant
relative, he then determined to study physic. His trust-
ing friends again subscribed the funds, and he set out for
Edinburgh, where he arrived in the autumn of 1752.
Here he remained for eighteen months, studying, riding
into the Highlands, gambling, singing Irish songs, or
telling Irish stories. At the end of that time, he persuaded his good uncle, Contarine, to furnish him with
funds to complete his medical studies at the University of
Leyden. For Leyden he forthwith left Edinburgh. On
arriving at this famous University, he recommenced his
studies and his gambling. What progress he made in
the former is uncertain, but, by the latter, he soon lost
the last shilling of the £33, with which he had left Scotland. His friend, Ellis, lent him a few pounds with which
to return to Paris, but he generously spent the whole, in
purchasing some costly tulip roots for his affectionate
uncle. Penniless and proud, he now determined to make
a tour of the Continent on foot, and so with one spare
shirt, a flute, and a guinea, he set out on his journey,
visiting France, Germany, Switzerland and Italy. In
the story of the " Philosophic Vagabond," in the *Vicar of
Wakefield*, he has given us some delightful reminiscences
of his experiences in these wanderings,

" Remote, unfriended, melancholy, slow,"

in which he made those observations upon the peculiar
characteristics of the various countries and their inhabitants, which he has, in his own easy, graceful style,
recorded for the delight of all future ages, in the *Traveller*. At Padua he remained for some months. Here, it
is probable, his medical studies were resumed, and from
this University, he tells us, he received his medical degree.

His generous uncle, whose slender remittances had never entirely ceased, died about this time, and the wanderer was compelled to seek his native shore. So after a year of roaming about on the Continent, he landed at Dover in 1756.

"Without friends, recommendation, money, or impudence," he arrived in London. Here, his flute had no attractions, nor could his philosophy supply his wants. He was compelled to seek other employment. He tried to turn his medical knowledge to advantage, but without avail. He then became a strolling-player, but his face and figure soon drove him from the boards. Next, he is found pounding drugs in a chemist's laboratory near Fish Street. Through the friendship of Dr. Sleigh, an old fellow-student, he was enabled to commence the practice of physic in Bankside, Southwark, but his patients were chiefly among the poorest and humblest classes of society. To eke out the miserable pittance thus received, he began to do some hack-work for the booksellers. A few months later, and we find him usher in a school kept by Dr. Milner, at Peckham. His bitter experiences in this situation, he has left us in a lively sketch in the sixth number of the *Bee*, and in the history of "George Primrose." While thus employed, Mr. Griffiths, proprietor of the *Monthly Review*, being in need of increased writers in order to cope with the opposition which he now met from the *Critical Review* under the able conduct of Dr. Smollett, engaged Goldsmith for a year, at a small regular salary, with board and lodging. Irksome as the slavery of an usher had been, the vassalage of the bookseller and his critical wife was still more unbearable. At the end of five months, the engagement was broken off. After some further occasional and ill-paid contributions to various Reviews, he returned in deep want to Dr. Milner's, and took charge of the school during the Doctor's illness. He next received a medical appointment in the service of the East India Company. To raise money for the expected voyage, he set to work to write a treatise to be entitled *An Inquiry into the Present State of Polite Learning in Europe;* but before it was completed the appointment had been cancelled. He then presented himself for examination as hospital mate. The suit of clothes in which he appeared had been secured by writing four articles for Griffiths' *Monthly Review.* He failed at the examination, and pawned the unpaid clothes to relieve his landlady's distress. The *Life of Voltaire* was written at this time, to pacify the demand of Griffiths for the return of the suit of clothes and the books he had reviewed.

In 1759, appeared the *Inquiry*, a work of little value now-a-days, but which, to the grace and charm of its style, added much that then commanded public attention.

This was the age of periodicals, and Goldsmith must needs have his. The *Bee* first appeared on the 6th of October, 1759. It was to be issued every Saturday, and the price was three pence. It was filled with essays in great variety, penned in Goldsmith's neat and elegant style, but it failed to charm the public of the day; and its short career of eight weeks closed on the 29th of November. Whilst publishing the *Bee*, Goldsmith had been writing for other periodicals, the *Busy Body* and the *Critical Review.* He soon after became an important contributor to the *British Magazine* and to the *Public Ledger.* The series of letters which appeared in the latter was afterwards republished under the title of the *Citizen of the World.* These letters, purporting to be addressed by a Chinese traveller to his friends at home, contain some lively and humorous sketches of English society, and have been " justly praised, for their fresh original perception, their delicate delineation of life and manners, their wit and humor, their playful and diverting satire, their exhilarating gaiety and their clear and lively style."

Two other anonymous works were published about this time, *The Life of Beau Nash*, and *The History of England in a Series of Letters from a Nobleman to his Son*. The latter became exceedingly popular, and was attributed in turn to Lords Chesterfield, Orrery and Lyttleton.

It was during these years that Goldsmith became acquainted with several of the distinguished literary characters of the time. Dr. Percy, renowned for his collection of English ballads, had some years before introduced himself to Goldsmith while the latter sat " writing his *Inquiry* in a wretched, dirty room in which there was but one chair, and when he, from civility, offered it to his visitor, was obliged himself to sit in the window." He managed to bring about a meeting between Goldsmith and the great literary autocrat of the period, Dr. Johnson. Among his acquaintances also, were now the distinguished painters, Hogarth and Reynolds. At the house of Reynolds, he was introduced to more notable company than he had yet been accustomed to meet ; and on the formation of the Literary Club in 1763, he was invited to become one of its members. This club which was suggested by Reynolds, originally consisted of Johnson, Burke, Beauclerc, Nugent, Bennet Langton, Hawkins, Chamier, Reynolds, and Goldsmith. Its meetings were held once a week at the Turk's head inn, in Gerrard street, Soho, and its conversations exercised no little influence on the literature of the time. But though Goldsmith's circumstances were now greatly improved, life seems to have still been a struggle with him. Sometimes he revelled in plenty, but oftener was pining in want. One morning in the winter of 1764, he sent for Dr. Johnson, to come to him immediately, as he was in trouble. Johnson sent him a guinea, and as soon as he was dressed called to see him. He found that Goldsmith had changed the guinea, and procured a bottle of Madeira, over which he was disputing with his landlady who had that morning arrested him for arrears of rent. Johnson replaced the cork, and begged his friend to calm himself and consider how the money was to be obtained. The latter thereupon produced a novel upon which he had been engaged. After glancing over the manuscript, Johnson perceived that the work possessed rare merit, went out, and sold it to a bookseller for £60, brought back the money, and the rent was paid. The novel which thus passed into the hands of the publisher, but which lay unprinted for upwards of two years, was the *Vicar of Wakefield*. Goldsmith was not yet known to the public as an author, and the bookseller had probably made his bargain, depending largely on the judgment of Johnson. Soon all this was to be changed, for he was to have a reputation of his own, that would not only warrant the publication of the *Vicar*, but give his future productions a ready popularity.

In 1764, the *Traveller* was published, and Goldsmith was at once recognised as a poet of genuine worth. The ablest critics of the day joined in lauding the poem as worthy of a high place amongst our English classics, and Johnson, under whose fostering care it had been completed, introduced it to the public by a kindly notice in the *Critical Review*. And it well deserved all the praise it received. Its outward form, its polish, and the correctness of its versification, are after the manner of the time. It has not all the epigrammatic brilliancy and point of the poetry of Pope, but it possesses a richer sweetness, greater naturalness and a deeper human sympathy. Throughout there abound a freshness and love of nature that more than compensate for the unsoundness of its political theory, while the simplicity and neatness of its diction are equalled only by its charming descriptions and lovely images. The appearance of the *Traveller* was the great turning point in Goldsmith's career. It raised him in the estimation of the booksellers, opened his way into good society, and introduced him to the notice of the great. The Earl of Northumberland expressed a desire to serve him, but the generous-hearted poet recommended his brother Henry, saying of himself "that he looked to the booksellers for support, that they were his best friends, and that he was not inclined to forsake them for others."

He took advantage of his present popularity to collect and republish many of his essays which had appeared anonymously in various periodicals ; and, that he might have some permanent means of support, again resumed the medical profession, hoping that he might now secure a higher class of patients ; but meeting only disappointment, he soon abandoned it in disgust, to return to the service of his old "patrons."

The fourth edition of the *Traveller* had just been issued, and Goldsmith was enjoying the reputation of being the first poet of his age, when the *Vicar of Wakefield* was published. This charming novel of English domestic life, the earliest of its kind, was at first but coldly received by the Club, the leading journals of the day, and the higher classes of society. Yet, surely, if slowly, it grew in favour. Three editions were printed within four months, and the author lived to see it translated into several continental languages. Its plot is confused, and many of the incidents are highly improbable, but its quiet humor and lively wit amuse us at every turn and sparkle on every page. It overflows with a kindly sympathy for the failings of the race ; and the characters are drawn with such truth to nature, that they cannot fail to reach the heart. Its moral, too, is excellent—to show us how our lives may be made happy by "patience in suffering, persevering reliance on the providence of God, quiet labor, and an indulgent forgiveness of the faults of others." Little wonder that such a book has passed from country to country, and obtained a wider popularity than any other of its kind.

The celebrity which Goldsmith won by the publication of the *Traveller* and *Vicar* materially raised his social standing, but did not equally improve his circumstances. Debts and drudgery were still his portion. He was compelled to toil for the booksellers as before, with this difference, that his services now received a better remuneration. In the midst of this thankless labor, his leisure was devoted to work of another kind. He had won laurels as a poet, and as a novelist ; now he was emboldened to try his fortune as a writer of comedy. His first attempt, the *Good-Natured Man*, was acted at Covent Garden in 1768. It had been finished early in the preceding year, but, though recommended by Johnson, Burke, and Reynolds, he had much difficulty in inducing the managers to accept it. Its reception at a time when sentimentalism was the rage, could not be hearty ; yet the author received from his benefit nights and from the sale of the copyright upwards of £500, a sum many times larger than he had received for any of his previous writings. The plot of the *Good-Natured Man*, like all Goldsmith's plots, is very imperfect, but in character, repartee, and humor, this comedy has few superiors. Yet at the time when it was brought on the stage its very excellencies were its ruin. Anything that moved the audience to laughter was sure to be " hissed " from pit to boxes ; and accordingly the very scene which Goldsmith considered the best—and posterity has endorsed his opinion—was received with marked disapprobation, and had to be withdrawn after the first night.

With so great a sum as £500 in his possession, and with no small reputation as a poet, novelist, and dramatic author, Goldsmith thought proper to remove into more commodious and respectable lodgings. Leaving his shabby rooms at Jeffs', he leased apartments in Brick Court, Middle Temple, which he proceeded to furnish in elegant style, and then began a course of life which burdened him with debts and mental distress for the rest of his days. His pen was now more actively engaged than ever in writing for the booksellers, and his fame commanded a high return for his labor. For Tom Davies he compiled a *History of Rome* for which he received £300. Its rapid sale prompted Davies to offer £500 for a *History of England*, and at the same time Goldsmith was at work upon his *Animated Nature* for which Griffin agreed to give him 800 guineas.

These works are all written with the author's own easy, graceful flow of narrative, and never fail to please and interest the reader ; but the facts are taken at second-hand, without any elaborate inquiry into their correctness ; and consequently he has been led into making some ludicrous errors and absurd statements. Yet Johnson ranked him, as an historian, above Robertson, and declared that he would make his *Animated Nature* as "entertaining as a Persian tale." His histories, inaccurate as they are, have done much to make their subject interesting to young people, and they still rank amongst the most popular of abridged works.

While busy upon these toilsome tasks, he found a few spare moments left him to cultivate the muse, and added much to his poetical fame by publishing, in 1770, the *Deserted Village*. This poem leaped at once to the height of popularity, no fewer than five editions being required within the first three months. Nor was its popularity ephemeral, for the judgment of the time has been endorsed by tens of thousands of readers since, and seems likely never to be reversed.

But the " draggle-tailed muses," as Goldsmith was once heard to say, furnished but a scanty means of subsistence. Such at least did they in his case. His poetical fame brought him directly but small returns. Hence we find him, soon after the publication of the *Deserted Village*, again at work for his old " patrons," the booksellers. He made an abridgment of his Roman History, wrote an inferior *Life of Parnell*, and compiled a *Life of Lord Bolingbroke*. The biography of Bolingbroke, though written at a time of great political excitement, is entirely free from party prejudice, and gives a clear, entertaining account of this great statesman's life. In 1773, Goldsmith, with great difficulty, induced the managers to allow him to try his chances, a second time, with a comedy entitled *She Stoops to Conquer*. This play, like its predecessor, the *Good-Natured Man*, was based upon character and humor. The public taste still demanded the sentimental comedy of Cumberland and Kelly, and scouted everything that tended to produce boisterous mirth. The fun of Goldsmith's first comedy had driven it from the boards, and the fun of this one was uproarious when compared with it. It was brought out by Coleman, at Covent Garden. The actors, as well as the managers, are said to have had little hopes of its success. But all were disappointed, when pit, and galleries, and boxes, rang with peal upon peal of uncontrollable laughter. The play ran on every night for the remainder of the season, and is one of the very few comedies of the time which still retain possession of the stage. Nor was it fame alone that Goldsmith obtained by the success of the *Good-Natured Man*, for he reaped a rich pecuniary harvest. Yet all the money he received, and all he could manage to raise on works to be written, but not yet begun, were insufficient to satisfy the demands of his creditors, or to brighten his prospects for the future.

We find him trying to forget his troubles by a visit to the country, by attendance at the Club, and by frequenting gay society. But it was all in vain. His unfinished but prepaid engagements became doubly burdensome, as presenting no means of relief. Though his "knack at hoping" seemed to be failing him, yet he was full of plans, and at times was hard at work. He had almost completed his *Animated Nature* and *Grecian History*, was preparing a third edition of his *History of England*, revising his *Inquiry*, translating Scarron's *Comic Romance*, and arranging his papers for the most extensive work he had ever yet contemplated—*A Popular Dictionary of Arts and Sciences*. His plans for this *Dictionary*, though cheerfully entertained by his friends, did not secure the confidence of the booksellers, and the work was never completed.

In the midst of his disappointments and despondency, his poetical genius once more flashed forth in a little poem which he composed in reply to some gibing epitaphs written by his friends, while awaiting his usual late arrival at a dinner. Being unable to reply at the time he took to his pen, and with a few inimitable strokes sketched, in clear and vigorous language, the character of some nine or ten of his most intimate friends. He gave it the title of *Retaliation*, but, like his own generous nature, it had in it too much of the "milk of human kindness" to contain revenge. Short and unfinished as it is, its good sense and humorous raillery, its exquisite discrimination and graphic truth, will always mark it as a masterpiece.

But this facile pen must write no more. An illness, if

not induced, at least aggravated, by his pressing necessities and deranged circumstances, seized him while laboring under his present depression. He complained of pain in his head, and of fever. Contrary to the advice of his medical attendants, he persisted in taking some powders from which he had formerly obtained relief in other disorders. His malady fluctuated for some days, and hopes were even entertained of his recovery; but his sleep left him, his mind was ill at ease, and his appetite was gone. At length he fell into a deep sleep from which he awoke in strong convulsions, which continued till death brought release on the 4th of April, 1774. He was in his forty-sixth year. His death produced a deep sensation among his friends. On hearing he was dead, Burke burst into tears, and Reynolds laid up his pencil for the remainder of the day. A public funeral and a tomb in Westminster were at first proposed, but subsequently given up, and he was privately interred in the burying ground of the Temple Church. Shortly after his death, a cenotaph was erected to his memory in Westminster Abbey. Nollekens was the sculptor, and the inscription was written by Dr. Johnson.

Of all our English writers there is none over whose memory the reader lingers with more affectionate remembrance than over that of Goldsmith. Not that his character was faultless; far from it. There is much to admire, but also much to regret. He was a compound of weakness and strength, and his life was full of inconsistencies. His head was ever devising plans which he lacked resolution and energy to carry out. Indolence and procrastination were part of his very nature. At school his lessons were neglected for some idle sport. At college he feasted his city friends, and graduated last on the list of Sizars. Of these habits the booksellers had always to complain; and for this reason they rejected the scheme of his proposed *Dictionary.* Few men were more ambitious than he, and his ambition led him at times to put forth great, if spas· modic, efforts to win the praise which he heard bestowed upon others. He strove to outshine Johnson in conversa- tion, but his attempts brought upon him the derision of of the Club. His vanity led him into exhibitions of jealousy, and even of envy. His extreme sensibility made him writhe under the jests of which he was made the ob- ject, but his forgiving nature could never avenge the insults heaped upon him. It need not for a moment be supposed that Goldsmith had more of envy, jealousy, and vanity than many of his associates, but his blundering, outspoken, and transparent nature made his failings more conspicu- ous. He was frivolous, improvident, profuse and sensual. His benevolence often outran his judgment, for the soft- ness of his heart could hear no tale of distress without attempting whatever assistance lay in his power to relieve it.

Though he had graduated at Trinity College, and had professedly studied for the church and the medical pro- fession, yet there was not a single subject of which he could be said to be master. He knew nothing thoroughly. His prose writings exhibit no evidences of depth or close examination, but are superficial and inaccurate. But whatever he knew he could tell with clearness, and sur- round with charming interest. When he looks within his own heart and gives utterance to the feelings which fill his breast, he expresses himself with a naturalness, a grace, and a tenderness, which bespeak the true poet and the man of broad and deep human sympathy. But when he goes beyond his own experiences, he always blunders, al- ways fails. Happily, he has generally confined himself to subjects in which his acute and varied observation gave him a power that has largely compensated for his lack of imagination. His style is the perfection of ease. There is no straining after effect, no ponderous phrases, no heavily-turned periods. His words are aptly chosen, his diction select and terse, his language felicitous, and his taste excellent. Dealing chiefly with familiar topics, he always keeps above vulgarity, but he is at times justly chargeable with carelessness and want of precision in the construction of his sentences. In palliation of this, it may be said, that many of his productions were completed in great haste, under pressing necessities, and are not therefore fairly open to criticism. In everything he has written, there is an easy grace and elegance which have always made his writings popular, and which bid fair to perpetuate his fame as long as our language endures.

THE DESERTED VILLAGE.

INTRODUCTION.

GOLDSMITH seems to have conceived the idea of writing this poem while he was engaged upon the *Traveller*. Indeed, the main thoughts which are here illustrated—the increase of wealth and the consequent exile of the peasantry—had already been sympathetically touched upon in that poem. It is probable that after finishing the latter, he set to work upon this at his moments of leisure, in the midst of the multifarious labors that were now crowding upon him; for poetry was with him an amusement, not a business. After some four or five years of correction and improvement, this poem, which had been long promised, was at last given to the public on the 26th of May, 1770. It was published by W. Griffin, and the price was two shillings. What remuneration the author received is uncertain. It is said that Griffin paid him a hundred pounds for the copyright, and that Goldsmith returned a part of it, as some one told him that no poetry was worth five shillings a couplet. It at once became immensely popular. A second edition was issued on the 7th of June, a third on the 14th, a fourth on the 28th, and a fifth on the 16th of August. This sudden popularity was due, partly to the now famous name of the author, partly to the subject, but chiefly to the intrinsic beauty of the treatment, and to the deep and touching appeal to the great heart of humanity. It was now six years since the *Traveller* had begun to make the name of Goldsmith eminent, and four, since that charming story, the *Vicar of Wakefield*, had sharpened the public appetite for anything Dr. Goldsmith might write. Whatever came from his pen, especially as poetry, was sure to be eagerly devoured, for his reputation as the poet of his time, was thoroughly established. In the choice of his subject, he was, no doubt, influenced by his natural sympathy for the poor and the down-trodden, and his innate antagonism to tyrants and oppressors. It may be, too, though "he never paid much attention to interest," that he was swayed somewhat by policy ; and as he could scarcely look for patronage to the great and the fashionable who, if they admired poetry at all, admired it in such men as Whitehead and Beattie, he sought an audience amongst the people. Besides, reflective and didactic poetry was all the mode, and several prose writers had affected to mourn over the decreasing population of the country. But, though the poet chose to regard depopulation as a fact, and the increase of wealth as a lamentable evil, he seems to have had very serious misgivings of both. In fact, in the Dedication, he admits that he has little or no proof—certainly none from Ireland—nothing but his own conviction that what he writes is true, while he feels and acknowledges that the weight of intelligent opinion is against him. As a matter of fact, there was no depopulation going on at the time, but the number of inhabitants was increasing more rapidly than in any preceding century. It was probably true that in a few solitary instances, gentlemen desirous of extending their parks or pleasure grounds, had removed, perhaps evicted with seeming violence, some of their tenants. It is a matter of history that one General Napier did this near Lissoy during the poet's childhood ; and, doubtless, recollections of the hardships endured by some of these tenants, had grown big with the lapse of time, and, it may be, were strengthened by reports of one or two similar cases, so that he really believed that both in Ireland and in England such tyranny and suffering were general. Nor was he alone in thinking that the tenantry of his native country had their grievances nor yet the first whose muse has been inspired with this theme ; but he mistakes a few solitary cases for a general social tendency. He errs again in attributing this supposed depopulation to the growth of commerce. That wealth had long been rapidly increasing, particularly in .he large towns and cities, is one of the most patent facts of the history of the time ; but when the poet regards the increase of wealth and depopulation as cause and effect, he is once more entirely astray. It is now a recognised principle that the richer a country is the more labor it is able to employ and the greater number of people it can sustain. And it is somewhat remarkable that at the very time when Goldsmith was clothing this false theory in so pleasing a poetic garb, Adam Smith was engaged upon his great work, *The Wealth of Nations*, in which the relations between capital and labor were first correctly set

forth.   Again, the outburst of sympathy in which he
pictures the expatriated wanderers "taking a long farewell" of their native shore, leads him to so exaggerate the
trials and privations of their new home "beyond the
western main" as to cast an air of unreality over the clos-
ing scenes of the poem.

So much for the facts and the reasonings. Of the artistic structure, Lord Macaulay tells us that " More discerning judges, however, while they admire the beauty of
the details, are shocked by one unpardonable fault which
pervades the whole. A poet may easily be pardoned for
reasoning ill ; but he cannot be pardoned for describing
ill, for observing the world in which he lives so carelessly
that his portraits bear no resemblance to the originals, for
exhibiting as copies from real life monstrous combinations
of things which never were and never could be found together. What would be thought of a painter who should
mix August and January in one landscape, who should
introduce a frozen river into a harvest scene? Would it
be a sufficient defence of such a picture to say that
every part was exquisitely colored, that the green hedges,
the apple-trees loaded with fruit, the waggons reeling under the yellow sheaves, and the sun-burned reapers wip-
ing their foreheads, were very fine, and that the ice and
the boys sliding were also very fine ? To such a picture the
' Deserted Village' bears a great resemblance. It is
made up of incongruous parts. The Village in its happy
days is a true English village. The Village in its decay
is an Irish village. The felicity and the misery which
Goldsmith has brought close together belong to two dif-

ferent countries ; and to two different stages in the pro·
gress of society. He had assuredly never seen in his na·
tive island such a rural paradise, such a seat of plenty,
content and tranquillity, as his ' Auburn.' He had as·
suredly never seen in England all the inhabitants of such
a paradise turned out of their homes in one day and forced
to emigrate in a body to America. The hamlet he had
probably seen in Kent ; the ejectment he had probably
seen in Munster : but, by joining the two, he has produced
something which never was and never will be seen in
any part of the world." Of this censure, Mr. Black completely disposes. He says : " This criticism is ingenious
and plausible, but it is unsound, for it happens to over-
look one of the radical facts of human nature—the mag-
nifying delight of the mind in what is long remembered
and remote. What was it that the imagination of Goldsmith, in his life-long banishment, could not see when he
looked back to the home of his childhood, and his early
friends and the sports and occupations of his youth?
Lissoy was no doubt a poor enough Irish village ; and
perhaps the farms were not too well cultivated ; and perhaps the village preacher who was so dear to all the country round had to administer many a thrashing to a certain
graceless son of his ; and perhaps Paddy Byrne was something of a pedant ; and no doubt pigs ran over the ' nicely sanded floor' of the inn ; and no doubt the village
statesmen occasionally indulged in a free fight. But do
you think that was the Lissoy that Goldsmith thought of in
his dreary lodgings in Fleet-street Courts? No : It was
the Lissoy where the vagrant lad had first seen the ' prim-

rose peep beneath the thorn ;' where he had listened to the mysterious call of the bittern by the unfrequented river ; it was a Lissoy still ringing with the loud laughter of young people in the twilight hours ; it was a Lissoy forever beautiful, and tender, and far away. The grown-up Goldsmith had not to go to any Kentish village for a model ; the familiar scenes of his youth, regarded with all the wistfulness and longing of an exile, became glorified enough. 'If I go to the Opera where Signora Colomba pours out all the mazes of melody,' he writes to Mr. Hodson, ' I sit and sigh for Lissoy's fireside, and *Johnny Armstrong's Last Good Night* from Peggy Golden.'"

After all, it is neither the plan nor the theorizing of the poem that gives it such force and beauty. The reader is careless to enquire whether its facts are facts or its reasoning consequent, but he lingers with rapt delight over the inimitable description of the Village in its undimmed beauty and "humble happiness," warms with anger, as the poet rouses him against the ruthless destroyer of these scenes of peasant bliss, melts into tears at the distress of its exiled sons, curses that luxury which can be purchased only at the cost of so much woe, and turns with sadness from the desolate prospect whence poetry and the rural virtues have fled.

In these winning strains the poet has confined himself within narrow limits, but within these limits he is supreme. The tenderness, pathos and grace touch and charm the universal heart, as it listens with rapture to this "portion of the music of the great hymn of nature." No lofty flights of imagination, no strong appeals to the judgment dazzle or bewilder the reader, but a gentle voice speaks directly to his heart in tones that never fail to awaken his sympathy.

Then again, the skilful manner in which the whole is brought out claims the highest admiration. How language, so simple and unadorned, can appear so rich and mellow, how it can convey sentiments so tender, and set forth pictures so clear and full, how it can be rendered so graceful, flowing and harmonious, none but Goldsmith could enable us to realize. There is much of the neatness and exquisite polish of the Augustan poets both in diction and versification ; but there are, also, livelier touches of nature, tender feeling, greater earnestness and cordiality than these masters of artistic poetic excellence ever displayed. His poetical canon did not allow him to be "a rhymer who makes smooth verses and paints to our imagination when he should only speak to our hearts," and thus led him to touch a cord that shall vibrate forever.

DEDICATION

TO

SIR JOSHUA REYNOLDS.

DEAR SIR.

I can have no expectation in an address of this kind,
either to add to your reputation, or to establish my own.
You can gain nothing from my admiration, as I am ignorant of that art in which you are said to excel ; and I may
lose much by the severity of your judgment, as few have a
juster taste in poetry than you. Setting interest, therefore,
aside, to which I never paid much attention, I must be
indulged at present in following my affections.   The only
dedication I ever made was to my brother, because I loved
him better than most other men.   He is since dead.   Permit me to inscribe this poem to you.

How far you may be pleased with the versification and
mere mechanical parts of this attempt, I do not pretend
to inquire ; but I know you will object (and indeed several
of our best and wisest friends concur in the opinion), that
the depopulation it deplores is nowhere to be seen, and
the disorders it laments are only to be found in the poet's
own imagination.   To this I can scarcely make any other

answer, than that I sincerely believe what I have written ; that I have taken all possible pains, in my country excursions, for these four or five years past, to be certain of what I allege ; and that all my views and inquiries have led me to believe those miseries real, which I here attempt to display. But this is not the place to enter into an inquiry whether the country be depopulating or not : the discussion would take up much room, and I should prove myself, at best, an indifferent politician, to tire the reader with a long preface, when I want his unfatigued attention to a long poem.

In regretting the depopulation of the country, I inveigh against the increase of our luxuries ; and here, also, I expect the shout of modern politicians against me. For twenty or thirty years past, it has been the fashion to consider luxury as one of the greatest national advantages ; and all the wisdom of antiquity in that particular, as erroneous. Still, however, I must remain a professed ancient on that head, and continue to think those luxuries prejudicial to states by which so many vices are introduced, and so many kingdoms have been undone. Indeed, so much has been poured out of late on the other side of the question, that merely for the sake of novelty and variety, one would sometimes wish to be in the right.

I am, Dear Sir,

Your sincere friend and ardent admirer,

OLIVER GOLDSMITH.

THE DESERTED VILLAGE.

Sweet Auburn! loveliest village of the plain,
Where health and plenty cheered the labouring swain,
Where smiling spring its earliest visit paid,
And parting summer's lingering blooms delayed;
Dear lovely bowers of innocence and ease,   5
Seats of my youth, when every sport could please,
How often have I loitered o'er thy green,
Where humble happiness endeared each scene!
How often have I paused on every charm,
The sheltered cot, the cultivated farm,   10
The never-failing brook, the busy mill,
The decent church that topt the neighbouring hill,
The hawthorn bush, with seats beneath the shade,
For talking age and whispering lovers made!
How often have I blest the coming day,   15
When toil remitting lent its turn to play,
And all the village train, from labour free,
Led up their sports beneath the spreading tree;
While many a pastime circled in the shade,
The young contending as the old surveyed,   20
And many a gambol frolicked o'er the ground,

And sleights of art and feats of strength went round !
And still, as each repeated pleasure tired,
Succeeding sports the mirthful band inspired ;
The dancing pair that simply sought renown   25
By holding out to tire each other down,
The swain mistrustless of his smutted face,
While secret laughter tittered round the place ;
The bashful virgin's sidelong looks of love,
The matron's glance that would those looks reprove.   30
These were thy charms, sweet village ! sports like these,
With sweet succession, taught even toil to please ;
These round thy bowers their cheerful influence shed ;
These were thy charms—but all these charms are fled.

Sweet smiling village, loveliest of the lawn,   35
Thy sports are fled, and all thy charms withdrawn ;
Amidst thy bowers the tyrant's hand is seen,
And desolation saddens all thy green :
One only master grasps the whole domain,
And half a tillage stints thy smiling plain.   40
No more thy glassy brook reflects the day,
But choked with sedges works its weary way ;
Along thy glades, a solitary guest,
The hollow-sounding bittern guards its nest ;
Amidst thy desert walks the lapwing flies,   45
And tires their echoes with unvaried cries ;

Sunk are thy bowers in shapeless ruin all,
And the long grass o'ertops the mouldering wall;
And, trembling, shrinking from the spoiler's hand,
Far, far away thy children leave the land.   50

Ill fares the land, to hastening ills a prey,
Where wealth accumulates, and men decay :
Princes and lords may flourish, or may fade—
A breath can make them, as a breath has made—
But a bold peasantry, their country's pride,   55
When once destroyed, can never be supplied

A time there was, ere England's griefs began,
When every rood of ground maintained its man ;
For him light labour spread her wholesome store,
Just gave what life required, but gave no more :   60
His best companions, innocence and health,
And his best riches, ignorance of wealth.

But times are altered ; trade's unfeeling train
Usurp the land, and dispossess the swain ;
Along the lawn, where scattered hamlets rose,   65
Unwieldy wealth and cumbrous pomp repose ;
And every want to luxury allied,
And every pang that folly pays to pride.
Those gentle hours that plenty bade to bloom,
Those calm desires that asked but little room,   70

Those healthful sports that graced the peaceful scene,
Lived in each look, and brightened all the green,
These, far departing, seek a kinder shore,
And rural mirth and manners are no more.

Sweet Auburn ! parent of the blissful hour,   75
Thy glades forlorn confess the tyrant's power.
Here, as I take my solitary rounds,
Amidst thy tangling walks and ruined grounds,
And, many a year elapsed, return to view
Where once the cottage stood, the hawthorn grew,   80
Remembrance wakes with all her busy train,
Swells at my breast, and turns the past to pain.

In all my wanderings round this world of care,
In all my griefs—and God has given my share—
I still had hopes, my latest hours to crown,   8
Amidst these humble bowers to lay me down ;
To husband out life's taper at the close,
And keep the flame from wasting by repose.
I still had hopes, for pride attends us still,
Amidst the swains to show my book-learned skill,   90
Around my fire an evening group to draw,
And tell of all I felt, and all I saw ;
And, as a hare whom hounds and horns pursue,
Pants to the place from whence at first he flew,

I still had hopes, my long vexations past, 95
Here to return—and die at home at last.
　O blest retirement, friend to life's decline,
Retreats from care, that never must be mine!
How blest is he who crowns, in shades like these,
A youth of labour with an age of ease; 100
Who quits a world where strong temptations try,
And, since 'tis hard to combat, learns to fly!
For him no wretches, born to work and weep,
Explore the mine, or tempt the dangerous deep;
No surly porter stands, in guilty state, 105
To spurn imploring famine from the gate;
But on he moves to meet his latter end,
Angels around befriending virtue's friend;
Sinks to the grave with unperceived decay,
While resignation gently slopes the way; 110
And, all his prospects brightening to the last,
His heaven commences ere the world be past.

　Sweet was the sound, when oft at evening's close
Up yonder hill the village murmur rose;
There, as I passed with careless steps and slow, 115
The mingling notes came softened from below;
The swain responsive as the milk-maid sung,
The sober herd that lowed to meet their young,
The noisy geese that gabbled o'er the pool,

The playful children just let loose from school, 120
The watch-dog's voice that bayed the whispering wind,
And the loud laugh that spoke the vacant mind ;
These all in sweet confusion sought the shade,
And filled each pause the nightingale had made.

But now the sounds of population fail, 125
No cheerful murmurs fluctuate in the gale,
No busy steps the grass-grown footway tread,
For all the bloomy flush of life is fled—
All but yon widowed, solitary thing,
That feebly bends beside the plashy spring ; 130
She, wretched matron—forced in age, for bread,
To strip the brook with mantling cresses spread,
To pick her wintry fagot from the thorn,
To seek her nightly shed, and weep till morn—
She only left of all the harmless train, 135
The sad historian of the pensive plain !

Near yonder copse, where once the garden smiled,
And still where many a garden-flower grows wild ;
There, where a few torn shrubs the place disclose,
The village preacher's modest mansion rose. 140
A man he was to all the country dear,
And passing rich with forty pounds a year ;
Remote from towns he ran his godly race,
Nor e'er had changed, nor wished to change, his place :

Unpractised he to fawn, or seek for power   145
By doctrines fashioned to the varying hour ;
Far other aims his heart had learned to prize,
More skilled to raise the wretched than to rise.
His house was known to all the vagrant train,
He chid their wanderings, but relieved their pain ;   150
The long-remembered beggar was his guest,
Whose beard descending swept his aged breast ;
The ruined spendthrift, now no longer proud,
Claimed kindred there, and had his claims allowed ;
The broken soldier, kindly bade to stay,   155
Sat by his fire, and talked the night away,
Wept o'er his wounds, or, tales of sorrow done,
Shouldered his crutch and showed how fields were won.
Pleased with his guests, the good man learned to glow,
And quite forgot their vices in their woe ;   160
Careless their merits or their faults to scan,
His pity gave ere charity began.

Thus to relieve the wretched was his pride,
And even his failings leaned to virtue's side ;
But in his duty, prompt at every call,   165
He watched and wept, he prayed and felt for all ;
And, as a bird each fond endearment tries
To tempt its new-fledged offspring to the skies,
He tried each art, reproved each dull delay,

Allured to brighter worlds, and led the way.   170

Beside the bed where parting life was laid,
And sorrow, guilt, and pain, by turns dismayed,
The reverend champion stood.   At his control
Despair and anguish fled the struggling soul ;
Comfort came down the trembling wretch to raise,   175
And his last faltering accents whispered praise.

At church, with meek and unaffected grace,
His looks adorned the venerable place ;
Truth from his lips prevailed with double sway,
And fools, who came to scoff, remained to pray.   180
The service past, around the pious man,
With steady zeal, each honest rustic ran ;
Even children followed, with endearing wile,
And plucked his gown, to share the good man's smile :
His ready smile a parent's warmth expressed,   185
Their welfare pleased him, and their cares distressed ;
To them his heart, his love, his griefs were given,
But all his serious thoughts had rest in heaven ;
As some tall cliff that lifts its awful form,
Swells from the vale, and midway leaves the storm,   190
Though round its breast the rolling clouds are spread,
Eternal sunshine settles on its head.

Beside yon straggling fence that skirts the way,
With blossomed furze unprofitably gay,

There, in his noisy mansion, skilled to rule,   195
The village master taught his little school.
A man severe he was, and stern to view,
I knew him well, and every truant knew;
Well had the boding tremblers learned to trace
The day's disaster in his morning face;   200
Full well they laughed with counterfeited glee
At all his jokes, for many a joke had he;
Full well the busy whisper, circling round,
Conveyed the dismal tidings when he frowned:
Yet he was kind, or if severe in aught,   205
The love he bore to learning was in fault.
The village all declared how much he knew;
'Twas certain he could write and cipher too:
Lands he could measure, terms and tides presage,
And even the story ran that he could gauge.   210
In arguing, too, the parson owned his skill,
For even though vanquished, he could argue still;
While words of learned length and thundering sound,
Amazed the gazing rustics ranged around,
And still they gazed, and still the wonder grew   215
That one small head could carry all he knew.

But past is all his fame.   The very spot,
Where many a time he triumphed, is forgot.
Near yonder thorn that lifts its head on high,

Where once the sign-post caught the passing eye,   220
Low lies that house where nut-brown draughts inspired,
Where gray-beard mirth and smiling toil retired,
Where village statesmen talked with looks profound,
And news much older than their ale went round.
Imagination fondly stoops to trace   225
The parlour splendours of that festive place :
The white-washed wall, the nicely sanded floor,
The varnished clock that clicked behind the door ;
The chest contrived a double debt to pay,
A bed by night, a chest of drawers by day ;   230
The pictures placed for ornament and use,
The twelve good rules, the royal game of goose ;
The hearth, except when winter chilled the day,
With aspen boughs, and flowers and fennel gay ;
While broken tea-cups, wisely kept for show,   235
Ranged o'er the chimney, glistened in a row.

Vain transitory splendours ! could not all
Reprieve the tottering mansion from its fall ?
Obscure it sinks, nor shall it more impart
An hour's importance to the poor man's heart ;   240
Thither no more the peasant shall repair
To sweet oblivion of his daily care ;
No more the farmer's news, the barber's tale,
No more the woodman's ballad shall prevail ;

No more the smith his dusky brow shall clear, 245
Relax his ponderous strength and lean to hear ;
The host himself no longer shall be found
Careful to see the mantling bliss go round ;
Nor the coy maid, half willing to be pressed,
Shall kiss the cup to pass it to the rest. 250

Yes ! let the rich deride, the proud disdain,
These simple blessings of the lowly train ;
To me more dear, congenial to my heart,
One native charm, than all the gloss of art ;
Spontaneous joys, where nature has its play, 255
The soul adopts, and owns their first-born sway ;
Lightly they frolic o'er the vacant mind,
Unenvied, unmolested, unconfined.
But the long pomp, the midnight masquerade,
With all the freaks of wanton wealth arrayed, 260
In these, ere triflers half their wish obtain,
The toiling pleasure sickens into pain ;
And, even while fashion's brightest arts decay,
The heart distrusting asks, if this be joy.

Ye friends to truth, ye statesmen who survey 265
The rich man's power increase, the poor's decay,
'Tis yours to judge how wide the limits stand
Between a splendid and a happy land.
Proud swells the tide with loads of freighted ore,

And shouting Folly hails them from her shore ; 270
Hoards even beyond the miser's wish abound,
And rich men flock from all the world around ;
Yet count our gains : this wealth is but a name
That leaves our useful products still the same.
Not so the loss.   The man of wealth and pride 275
Takes up a place that many poor supplied ;
Space for his lake, his park's extended bounds,
Space for his horses, equipage, and hounds :
The robe that wraps his limbs in silken sloth
Has robbed the neighbouring fields of half their growth :
His seat where solitary sports are seen, 281
Indignant spurns the cottage from the green ;
Around the world each needful product flies
For all the luxuries the world supplies :
While thus the land, adorned for pleasure, all 285
In barren splendour feebly waits the fall.

As some fair female, unadorned and plain,
Secure to please while youth confirms her reign,
Slights every borrowed charm that dress supplies,
Nor shares with art the triumph of her eyes ; 290
But when those charms are past, for charms are frail,
When time advances, and when lovers fail,
She then shines forth, solicitous to bless,
In all the glaring impotence of dress :

Thus fares the land, by luxury betrayed ;   295
In nature's simplest charms at first arrayed,
But verging to decline, its splendours rise,
Its vistas strike, its palaces surprise ;
While, scourged by famine, from the smiling land,
The mournful peasant leads his humble band ;   300
And while he sinks, without one arm to save,
The country blooms—a garden and a grave.

Where then, ah ! where shall poverty reside,
To 'scape the pressure of contiguous pride ?
If to some common's fenceless limits strayed   305
He drives his flocks to pick the scanty blade,
Those fenceless fields the sons of wealth divide,
And even the bare-worn common is denied.

If to the city sped—what waits him there ?
To see profusion that he must not share ;   310
To see ten thousand baneful arts combined
To pamper luxury, and thin mankind ;
To see each joy the sons of pleasure know,
Extorted from his fellow-creatures' woe ;
Here, while the courtier glitters in brocade,   315
There, the pale artist plies the sickly trade ;
Here, while the proud their long-drawn pomps display,
There, the black gibbet glooms beside the way.
The dome where pleasure holds her midnight reign,

Here, richly decked, admits the gorgeous train ; 320
Tumultuous grandeur crowds the blazing square,
The rattling chariots clash, the torches glare.
Sure scenes like these no troubles e'er annoy !
Sure these denote one universal joy !
Are these thy serious thoughts ? Ah ! turn thine eyes
Where the poor houseless shivering female lies. 326
She once, perhaps, in village plenty blessed,
Has wept at tales of innocence distressed ;
Her modest looks the cottage might adorn,
Sweet as the primrose peeps beneath the thorn ; 330
Now lost to all ; her friends, her virtue fled,
Near her betrayer's door she lays her head ;
And, pinched with cold, and shrinking from the shower,
With heavy heart deplores that luckless hour,
When idly first, ambitious of the town, 335
She left her wheel and robes of country brown.

Do thine, sweet Auburn, thine, the loveliest train,
Do thy fair tribes participate her pain ?
Even now, perhaps, by cold and hunger led,
At proud men's doors they ask a little bread. 340

Ah, no ! To distant climes, a dreary scene,
Where half the convex world intrudes between,
Through torrid tracks with fainting steps they go,

Where wild Altama murmurs to their woe.
Far different there from all that charmed before,   345
The various terrors of that horrid shore ;
Those blazing suns that dart a downward ray,
And fiercely shed intolerable day ;
Those matted woods where birds forget to sing,
But silent bats in drowsy clusters cling ;   350
Those poisonous fields, with rank luxuriance crowned,
Where the dark scorpion gathers death around ;
Where at each step the stranger fears to wake
The rattling terrors of the vengeful snake ;
Where crouching tigers wait their hapless prey,   355
And savage men more murderous still than they ;
While oft in whirls the mad tornado flies,
Mingling the ravaged landscape with the skies.
Far different these from every former scene,
The cooling brook, the grassy-vested green,   360
The breezy covert of the warbling grove,
That only sheltered thefts of harmless love.

Good Heaven ! what sorrows gloomed that parting day,
That called them from their native walks away ;
When the poor exiles, every pleasure past,   365
Hung round the bowers, and fondly looked their last,
And took a long farewell, and wished in vain
For seats like these beyond the western main ;

And, shuddering still to face the distant deep,
Returned and wept, and still returned to weep.   370
The good old sire the first prepared to go
To new-found worlds, and wept for others' woe ;
But for himself, in conscious virtue brave,
He only wished for worlds beyond the grave.
His lovely daughter, lovelier in her tears,   375
The fond companion of his helpless years,
Silent went next, neglectful of her charms,
And left a lover's for a father's arms.
With louder plaints the mother spoke her woes,
And blessed the cot where every pleasure rose,   380
And kissed her thoughtless babes with many a tear,
And clasped them close, in sorrow doubly dear ;
Whilst her fond husband strove to lend relief
In all the silent manliness of grief.

O Luxury ! thou curst by Heaven's decree,   385
How ill exchanged are things like these for thee !
How do thy potions, with insidious joy,
Diffuse their pleasures only to destroy !
Kingdoms, by thee to sickly greatness grown,
Boast of a florid vigour not their own :   390
At every draught more large and large they grow,
A bloated mass of rank unwieldy woe ;
Till, sapped their strength, and every part unsound,
Down, down they sink, and spread a ruin round.

Even now the devastation is begun, 395
And half the business of destruction done ;
Even now, methinks, as pondering here I stand,
I see the rural virtues leave the land.
Down where yon anchoring vessel spreads the sail
That idly waiting flaps with every gale, 400
Downward they move, a melancholy band,
Pass from the shore, and darken all the strand.
Contented toil, and hospitable care,
And kind connubial tenderness are there ;
And piety with wishes placed above, 405
And steady loyalty, and faithful love.
And thou, sweet Poetry, thou loveliest maid,
Still first to fly where sensual joys invade ;
Unfit, in these degenerate times of shame,
To catch the heart, or strike for honest fame ; 410
Dear charming nymph, neglected and decried,
My shame in crowds, my solitary pride ;
Thou source of all my bliss, and all my woe,
That found'st me poor at first, and keep'st me so ;
Thou guide by which the nobler arts excel, 415
Thou nurse of every virtue, fare thee well !
Farewell ! and, oh ! where'er thy voice be tried,
On Torno's cliffs, or Pambamarca's side,
Whether where equinoctial fervours glow,
Or winter wraps the polar world in snow, 420

C

Still let thy voice, prevailing over time,
Redress the rigours of the inclement clime ;
Aid slighted truth with thy persuasive strain ;
Teach erring man to spurn the rage of gain ;
Teach him, that states, of native strength possessed,   425
Though very poor, may still be very blest ;
That trade's proud empire hastes to swift decay,
As ocean sweeps the laboured mole away ;
While self-dependent power can time defy,
As rocks resist the billows and the sky.   430

NOTES.

THE DESERTED VILLAGE.

EPITOME.

The poem opens with a description of the village and village life as they loom up in the recollection of the poet. Then follows a picture of the village in its desolation and decay. This change has been produced by "trade's unfeeling train" that has invaded the land and driven out the happy peasant life. Auburn, too, has fallen. All his life long, the poet had cherished the idea of spending his old age in the home of his childhood ; but all that inclined him to return is gone. Yet he lingers over the "saddened green" to review in fancy its departed attractions, "the village murmur," the preacher and his flock, the master and his school, the inn and its forgotten statesmen ; but all are gone; their very "mansions" are no more. Still this rural happiness was far superior to the "toiling pleasure" of the great. Moreover, splendor is not happiness, nay, the outward "pomp" of a country is an indication of its approaching ruin. But "grandeur" has not only occupied the country, it has monopolized the city, too, so that the poor are entirely expatriated ; the inhabitants of "Sweet Auburn," with the rest, are forced into exile in the swamps and forests of America. The departure of the exiles from their home and friends is then pathetically described, and Luxury cursed as the insidious cause of national ruin. These elegiac strains draw to a close, bewailing the fate of the devastated land which poetry also has forsaken for some distant clime, where she is to teach that riches are not happiness, and that a bold peasantry, not commercial prosperity, is the safe foundation of a nation's security.

1 Auburn. This soft and harmonious name (suggested by Langton), composed almost entirely of vowels and liquids, was probably chosen by the poet for the sake of its agreeable sound. There can be no doubt that, in the mind of Goldsmith, it represented some scene which was endeared to him by early associations, and by family reminiscences. Various attempts have been made to identify Auburn with Lissoy, near Ballymahon, in the county of Longford. Here Goldsmith's early years were spent. In the adjoining parish, where he himself was born, his brother Henry was for many years the humble and much-loved curate of a rustic but appreciative flock, and in this neighborhood lived Mr. Hodson, his brother-in-law, with whom he spent some two years after finishing his college course.

Doctor Strean, Henry Goldsmith's successor, by whom the earliest attempt to identify Auburn with Lissoy was made, in 1807, tells us: "The poem of the *Deserted Village* took its origin from the circumstance of General Robert Napier (the grandfather of the gentleman who now lives in the house, within half a mile of Lissoy, and built by the General) having purchased an extensive tract of country surrounding Lissoy, or *Auburn;* in consequence of which many families, here called cottiers, were removed, to make room for the intended improvements of what was now to become the wide domain of a rich man, warm with the idea of changing the face of his new acquisition ; and were forced, 'with fainting steps,' to go in search of 'torrid tracts' and distant climes. This fact alone might be sufficient to establish the seat of the poem ; but there cannot remain a doubt in any unprejudiced mind, when the following are added, viz. : that the character of the village preacher, the above named Henry, is copied from nature. He is described exactly as he lived, and his 'modest mansion' as it existed. Burn, the name of the village master, and the site of his school-house ; and Catherine Giraghty, a lonely widow—

> 'The wretched matron, forced in age for bread,
> To strip the brook with mantling cresses spread,—'

(and to this day the brook and ditches near the spot where her cabin stood abound with cresses), still remain in the memory of the inhabitants, and Catherine's children live in the neighborhood. The pool, 'the busy mill,' the house where 'nut-brown draughts inspired,' are still visited as the poetic scene ; and the 'hawthorn-bush,' growing in an open space in front of the house, which I knew to have three trunks, is now reduced to one ; the other two having been cut, from time to time, by persons carrying pieces of it away to be made into toys, &c., in honour of the bard, and of the celebrity of his poem. All these contribute to the same proof ; and the 'decent church,' which I attended for upwards of eighteen years, and which 'tops the neighbouring hill,' is exactly described as seen from Lissoy, the residence of the preacher." Quoted by Rolfe.

By the etherealizing process to which poetry subjects its theme these circumstances became idealized as the poet affectionately viewed them through the "dim distance" of long years of exile. As Mr. Forster remarks : "Scenes of the poet's youth had, doubtless, risen in his memory as he wrote, mingling with, and taking altered hue from, later experiences ; thoughts of those early days could scarcely have been absent from the wish for a quiet close to the struggle and toil of his mature life, and very possibly, nay, almost certainly, when the dream of such a retirement haunted him, Lissoy formed part of the vision ; it is even possible he may have caught the first hint of his design from a local Westmeath poet and schoolmaster, who, in his youth, had given rhymed utterance to the old tenant grievances of the Irish rural population; nor could complaints that were also loudest in those boyish days at Lissoy, of certain reckless and unsparing evictions by which one General Naper (Napper or Napier) had persisted in improving his estate, have passed altogether from Goldsmith's memory."

Village. Lat. *Villa*, a country-house. Hence originally the residence and other buildings of the farmer, as well as the houses of his work-people.

It is the general condition of the country that the poet intends to depict, but as particular instances strike us much more forcibly than general statements, poetry prefers a single object as its theme. For this reason one village is here selected, and its fate dwelt upon.

2 Cheered. Note the force of the past tense. This use of it is called *Metalepsis*. Cf. Virgil, *Æn.*, ii. 38. "Fuimus Troes, fuit Ilium."

Swain. This word belongs chiefly to poetic diction.

3-4 Smiling, parting, lingering. Epithets in poetry are either *essential* or *ornamental*, and a correct taste and nice discrimination in their choice add greatly to the pleasing effect which it is the object of poetry to produce. The delicacy displayed by Goldsmith in this particular, is one of the charms of his style.

Parting = departing. Cf. ll. 171 and 363, also Gray's *Elegy* l. 1 : "parting day."

5 Bowers. A. S. *bur*, a cottage. Contrary to the usual course, the meaning of this word has been raised. It has also become specialized, as lady's bower.

6 Seats, &c., the places in which he used to spend his time when young.

8 Each. Observe how frequently *each* takes the place of every. This is common in poetry. Account for it.

9 How often, &c. This figure of speech, which, by a

D

repetition of the same word or phrase, carries the mind back to the same idea, is called *Anaphora*.

10 Cot, farm, &c. An example of *Accumulation*. See note on ll. 3 4, regarding Goldsmith's epithets.

12 Decent, presenting a neat and respectable appearance. Lat. *decens*, comely. Cf. Milton *Il Pens.* "Thy decent shoulders."

Topt = crowned.

13 With. For parsing, some such word as *furnished* may be supplied. The preposition in such cases might be replaced by the participle *having*.

14 This line forms a complement of *seats*.

Talking and whispering. Note these well-chosen epithets.

Age is an example of *Metonymy*, the abstract for the concrete. The abstract *age* and concrete *lover*, in the same line, give a pleasing variety.

16 When —play. This clause is adjectival to *day*.

Remitting = ceasing for a time.

Its, evidently refers to *play*, but from its position seems at first sight to refer to *toil*.

17 Train. Goldsmith has a great fondness for certain words, as *train*, *mansion* and *smiling*.

18 Led up = marshalled or arranged.

Spreading tree. " An inseparable accompaniment of the ideal village green." Sankey.

19 Many a. This is a more than ordinarily difficult construction. Archbishop Trench in the first editions of his *English Past and Present*, explained " many a man" as a corruption of " many of men." In later editions he quietly withdrew this statement. Many excellent grammarians, such as Fleming, Dr. Adams, Rushton, adopted his solution without due examination. In early English, it was a frequent practice to emphasize the adjective by a change of position, as *long a time*, for *a long time*. In Layamon, I. 24 : " *on moni* are wiser (*later text* mani ane) ; *monianes* cunnes," *ib.* 39 ; *of many a kind*. Dr. Abbott in his *How to Parse*, par. 218, says the regular construction for *many a man has tried*, would be *many men have tried* ; but this appears to have been confused with " many times a man has tried." Hence he parses *many* as an adverb, modifying *a* or as part of the compound adjective *many-a* = many-one = *A. S.*, mani-an.

Other authorities regard *many* as an adjective, and the construction as inverted. See Mason, par. 93 ; Dr. Adams, par. 571 ; Angus, sec. 480 ; Rushton, pars. 281, 299-302.

Pastime. See Trench's interesting remarks on this word in *Study of Words*, page 14.

20 The young contending is in the nominative absolute, forming an adverbial extension of *circled*.

As brevity and terseness give strength to style, and force to description, poetry aims at the attainment of these objects by employing the absolute construction, appositives and adjectives, instead of dependent adverbial and adjectival sentences.

In this line, the contrast between the young and the old, and the part acted by each, is very pleasing. The athletic activity of the one, and the contemplative pride of the other, are agreeable manifestations of *power* and *repose*.

21 Gambol. Ital. *gamba;* Fr. *jambe*, the leg. Fr. *gambiller*, to kick about. *Gambol* is used by *Metonymy* for the persons who were indulging in these gambols.

22 Sleights=‘‘dexterous feats.’’

23 Tired = grew tiresome.

24 Succeeding sports=a varied succession of sports.

25 Simply=‘‘in a simple manner, artlessly.’’

Pair, swain, looks and **glance**, are in apposition to *sports*.

26 Holding out=continuing to dance on. Whatever may have been the origin of such words as *holding*, it would save some of our grammarians a great amount of unnecessary trouble, candidly to admit that when used as in this instance, they are nouns. As they are names of actions, it seems quite gratuitous to invent some new term obscurely to indicate the fact. Of course, *out* is a part of the noun, as *holding* stands for one idea, and *holding out* for quite a different one.

Each other. Grammarians tell us that the construction is, *each* holding out *to tire* the *other down*. But in poetry, at least, ‘‘each other’’ is often regarded as a compound pronoun, as here. See *How to Parse*, pars. 223, 385, 531 ; Dr. Adams, par. 258.

27 Mistrustless of = unconscious of, not suspecting.

28 Secret, as hidden from the *swain*.

Laughter tittered. Note the frequent recurrence of this figure, as *pastime circled, gambol frolicked. &c.*

29 Sidelong. Mr. Hales thinks that *long* is probably a corruption of *ling*, which yet survives in *grovelling* and *darkling*, and which in oldest English occurs in the form of *linga* or *lunga*, as baeclinga=backwards.

30 Would = ostensibly desires to. Here a principal verb.

32 With sweet, &c. ‘‘Following one another merrily shewed how even a life of labor might be enjoyable.’’—Sankey.

Toil to please. Whether it is best to regard both these words as accusatives after *taught* (with Angus), or to consider *to please* the object of some preposition understood (with Fleming) as *taught to* concerning *pleasing* (*to please*), or finally to regard *toil* as the indirect object, and *to please* the direct, appears to be still an open question. The last is probably the best.

33 Influence. "This word is an example of the way in which old errors, themselves dismissed long ago, may yet survive in language, being bound up in words that grew into use when those errors found credit, and which, now that those errors are dismissed, maintain still their currency among us." Other examples are dwarf, wight, urchin, hag, from Gothic mythology ; mercurial, jovial, saturnine, disastrous, ascendency, from English astrology. See Trench, *Study of Words.*

34 In this beautiful and pathetic line, notice the force of the past tense, the effect of the arrestive conjunction, *but*, and of repeating *charms* in the second clause.

35-50 These lines contain the companion picture to that presented in ll. 1-34. All that pleases us in the one, saddens us in the other. The first is an earthly paradise, full of life and pure enjoyment, the second, a scene of desolation and ruin ; in the former we revel in the fulness of simple human bliss, in the latter, one man's selfishness has laid waste the Eden of others without improving his own. The home of peasant joy has become the abode of lonely birds, a waste of "shapeless ruin."

Painful effects should not be introduced into poetry unless they are fully redeemed. The exercise of sympathy they call forth, the opportunity afforded the poet, by tenderness and the charm of imagery, to cast a spell over suffering, and the belief that such scenes occur in real life, serve to justify their admission here.

35 Smiling. Mr. Sankey tells us that this is "an instance of what Mr. Ruskin calls the pathetic fallacy, which consists in the attribution of the personal feelings of the observer to the inanimate object observed." In this Mr. Sankey is quite mistaken. The feelings of the poet are here pensive, not joyous. It is simply an example of *personal metaphor*, introduced to describe the "village" before "its charms were fled."

37 The tyrant's hand. "An English gentleman, General Robert Napier, purchased the estates of Lord Dillon, which included Lissoy, and ejected some of his tenants. The land which they had occupied was thrown into the park. The Napier estate was the subject of a protracted lawsuit, and was sold in 1838."-- Mason.

Hand = results of the acts done by the tyrant's hand.-- *Metonymy.*

38 Green = the *plain* which is covered with verdure. One of the distinctive features of poetical diction in the use of the epithet instead of the object, as *green* for the *green lawn.*

39 One only master = a single master, the *tyrant* of l. 37. Cf. Shakes. *J. C.*, i. 2, "One only man."

40 Half a tillage. In a few phrases, as half a, many a, what a, such a, as well as when the adjective is preceded by the adverbs too, so, "a" is placed after the adjective. This mere change of position, however, does not appear sufficient to justify the view taken by Dr. Abbott, that the adjective is semi-adverbial. See *How to Parse*, 213–218 ; also, note on l. 19.

Stints is a diminutive from stunts.

The meaning is that the limited cultivation which the *plain* receives from its present occupant (General Napier), who of course, is intended to represent a class (as the particular stands for the general), fails to call forth that luxuriant production which was the result of the labors of the former peasant population .

41 Glassy and **day**—examples of *Metonymy*.
Cf. *Threnodia Augustalis :*—

"There sorrowing by the river's glassy bed."

42 "This is a well constructed line. The description is vivid and terse. Every word tells ; and the alliteration at the end gives a heaviness and monotony to the close of the description that accords admirably with the idea that has to be expressed."
—Mason.

44 Hollow sounding bittern. "The Common Bittern (*Botaurus Stellaris*) is nearly as large as the heron. Formerly it was common in Britain, but the extensive drainage of late years has greatly diminished its numbers, and it is now a permanent resident only in the fen districts of England. During the breeding season it utters a booming noise, from which it probably derives its general name, *Botaurus*, and which has made it in various places an object of superstitious dread."—Enc. Brit.

Cf. Scott, *Lady of the Lake*, I. 31 :—

And the bittern sound his drum
Booming from the sedgy shallow.'

45 Desert = deserted.
Lapwing. "The common Lapwing or Peewit (*Vanellus Cristatus*), is a well-known British bird. It is not quite so large as a pigeon, and has a head surmounted with a beautiful crest. The name, Lapwing, is derived from the sound which the wings make in flight ; the name Peewit from the plaintive note. The Lapwing is very plentiful in moors, open commons and marshy districts."—Chambers' Enc.

46 Their refers to *cries*.
47 Note the arrangement. *Sunk* and *all*, the most important

words, occupy the two places of greatest emphasis—the first and last.

All agrees with *bowers*.

43 Spoiler.   See note on l. 37.

50 Far, far.   An example of *Epizeuxis*--a repetition of the same word to give emphasis.

51 Ills.   Goldsmith frequently repeats the same words, close together, in a different sense.   Point out other examples of this fault.

51-6 These lines owe much of their force to the *Antitheses* they contain.

52 This line contains, in brief, the burden of the poem. With Goldsmith the second idea—the decrease in the number of the inhabitants of the country—results from the first, the accumulation of wealth, and, therefore he indulges in depreciating trade as the cause of the country's ruin.   In this, consists from the economist's point of view, the grand mistake of the poem ; but the world has reason to rejoice that he was a bad economist if thereby he has produced so excellent an elegy. See Introduction.

53 Fill up the hiatus between this line and the next by adding after *fade*, without affecting the happiness and prosperity of the country, *since a breath, &c.*

54 Breath = "the mere word of a King."   The King is the fountain of honor, and can create titled nobility at his will.   Cf. Burns' *Cotter's Sat. Night*, l. 165 :

"Princes and lords are but the breath of Kings."

56 Destroyed = driven away from the land.

57 Griefs = present griefs, those arising from the increase of wealth.

58 When away, &c.   An *Hyperbole*, meaning when the country was fully populated by the "bold peasantry."   It is not a question in the poet's mind, as some have supposed, whether small farms or large farms are best adapted to make a country productive, but his decided opinion is that the peasants should not be expelled to make room for the parks and mansions of the wealthy.

60 To express the meaning intended *just* should be placed before *what*.

Required.   Why not the present tense ?

63 Trade's unfeeling train.   Explain this, fully expressing all that is conveyed in the term *unfeeling*.

64 Usurp. &c., i.e., buy up and take possession of the land, which, in the poet's estimation, they cannot rightfully acquire, since rearing "solitary mansions," with their appertaining parks and other domains, necessitates an eviction of the tenant families that for centuries have tilled the soil.

Usurp. On the agreement of verbs with collectives, see Bain's *Companion to the Higher Grammar*.

Hamlet. A. S. *hame*, home, and *let*, little, properly a little home ; now chiefly used in poetry and the more elevated prose, to indicate a small village ; here, small tenant houses.

66 For the meaning of this line, see note on l. 64.

Observe how frequently the poet uses the figure *Metonymy*, as *wealth, pomp, want, pang, hours, desires*.

Pomp. Gr. πομπή, from πέμπω, to send : Lat. It. and Sp. *pompa*. From meaning a procession with all its attendant display, this word has come to mean any great display. Here it means a magnificent mansion.

67 Allied. Account for the use of this word, and suggest the one required by the sense.

68 The troubles and vexations that people frequently have to endure for naving foolishly gratified their pride.

Grammatically, the verb *reposes* is understood after *want* and also after *pang*, but to make good sense *is found* or *exists* would be the proper word. When a word is thus to be supplied in a sense different from that in which it is expressed, we have the figure called *Zeugma*.

70 Those persons of moderate desires, who were contented with their sphere in life—*Metonymy*.

73 These far departing, &c. Cf. *Traveller*, ll. 237-8.

> " These, far dispersed, on timorous pinions fly,
>   To sport and flutter in a kinder sky."

Kinder. Compare this with the picture of the emigrant's situation in America.

74 Observe the alliteration. *Manners*, the style of life formerly customary among the peasantry.

75-96 The poet becomes deeply affected when he finds that the sad fate of the country in general is also that of his "*Sweet Auburn*," and in tender, melting strains pours out the bitterness of his disappointment. Every line of this beautiful passage is steeped in pathos, and we seem to share his distress when we see his hopes, so long and fondly indulged, blasted forever, and the chains of his exile rendered perpetual.

78 Tangling. Overgrown with vines and briers.

79 Many a year elapsed=after the lapse of many years See note on l. 19.

Where—stood. This is a noun clause, the object of *to view*, which is adverbial to *return*.

80 Cottage, the " preacher's modest mansion." **Hawthorn.** See note on l. 1.

81 Remembrance—train. This *Metaphor*, though pleasing, is somewhat objectionable, as *its train* does not properly consist of attendants, as is implied, but of the succession of thoughts which follow each other. The epithet *busy* serves to still further confuse the figure.

82 Turns—pain. The recollections of the past become painful to me on account of the sad change that the " tyrant's power " has produced.

83 Wanderings. A most appropriate word to express the poet's moves in life, which, though apparently aimless, yet largely assisted in making him what he was.

83-96 " We shall not dwell upon the peculiar merits of this poem ; we cannot help noticing, however, how truly it is a mirror of the author's heart, and of all the fond pictures of early life forever present there. It seems to us as if the very last accounts received from home, of his 'shattered family,' and the desolation that seemed to have settled upon the haunts of his childhood, had cut to the roots one fondly cherished hope and produced those exquisitely tender and mournful lines."—Irving.

84 So the poet consoles himself by throwing the blame on Providence ; but he might, perhaps, have profitably enquired whether such consolation was founded on fact. " If one's sword is too short," said the wise Roman, "he may make it long enough by taking a step forward."

85 To lay, to husband, to keep=of laying, &c. These infinitives are used adjectively to qualify *hopes*.

90-2 No doubt the thought of occupying among the "swains " such a position as Dr. Johnson held in the conversations of the club, was in the poet's mind as he penned these lines.

Felt, saw. The sequence of tenses requires *had felt*, *had seen*.

93 Note the effect of alliteration.

Whom is here used with excellent effect, and makes the figure more striking by representing the hare as possessing human feelings.

94 Pants. An attendant and resulting action put for the main one, rapid motion—*Synecdoche*.

95 I still had hopes. This passage owes not a little of its beauty to the well-timed use of the figure, *Anaphora*.

Vexations. Nominative absolute. See note on l. 20.

95·6 Such an expression of feelings that are common to men shews that all the buffetings of life had not been able to render him entirely worldly or heartless.

100 Age = old age.

102 To combat.   A noun infinitive, in opposition to *it*, the grammatical subject.

To fly = to avoid temptation.

104 Tempt.   Lat. *tentare*, to make trial of.

Cf. Milton, *P. L.* ii. 404 :—

> "Who shall tempt with wandering feet
> The dark, unbottomed, infinite abyss."

105 Guilty state.   "Gay livery," splendor, acquired at the expense of the homes and happiness of the peasants.

106 Famine = a famished person, a beggar —*Metonymy*.

107 Latter end.   *Latter* is pleonastic, but the expression is common.   See Prov. xix. 20.

108 On the construction.   See note on l. 20.

110 Resignation.   Sir Joshua Reynolds, in order to show how gratefully he received the dedication of this poem, painted his picture, *Resignation*, had it engraved by Thomas Watson, and inscribed upon it these words : "This attempt to describe a character in the *Deserted Village* is dedicated to Dr. Goldsmith by his sincere friend and admirer, Joshua Reynolds."

108-13 These exquisite lines, which are doubtless a description of the way in which the poet hoped to close his life, afford a pleasing testimony of the goodness of his heart and the sincerity of his faith.

114-136 The contrast here presented is similar to that with which the poem opens, yet so varied as to be as interesting as the first.   The variation consists in contrasting different features in village life and scenery.

115 Careless.   Unburdened with care, as in youth.

116 Cf. Arnold's *Light of Asia*, Bk. ii :

> "Save if the city's hum
> Came on the wind no harsher than when bees
> Hum out of sight in thickets."

116-122 These lines shew how much the sound of the words may assist the sense.

117 Responsive, i.e., replying by another song.

119 Gabbled.   *Onomatopœia*, i.e., the sound of the word resembles the sound for which it stands.   Cf. *lowed*, l. 118; *plashy*, l. 130.

121 Bayed = bayed at.   Cf. Shakes. *J. C.* iv. 3 : "I had rather be a dog and bay the moon."

Whispering, ominously foreboding ill in a language that dogs can understand.   A superstition now nearly passed away.

122 Vacant mind. As these people had no worrying cares, the poet means by the *vacant mind*, the mind that is not depressed by the anxieties of the "tyrant who has ruined their homes," or even by the "toiling pleasures of the great,"—free from all trouble. It bears the same meaning in l. 257.

123 Each pause. The nightingale often comes to an abrupt pause in its singing.

Had made. The sequence of tenses requires *made*.

124 Nightingale. A. S. *niht*, and *galan*, to sing. *In* is merely a connective participle. "As the nightingale is not found in Ireland, the introduction of the bird here is either a Hibernicism or a poetic license."—Rolfe.

126 Fluctuate=float upon. Note the scansion.

128 Bloomy, &c. People full of health and spirits. Perhaps there is an allusion to the complexion of English and Irish farm laborers. Cf. *Traveller*, l. 18: "all the ruddy family."

129 Solitary thing. *Thing* is here used very effectively. This lonely widow, so sunken in decrepitude and misery as to be scarcely recognizable as a human being, is a fitting climax to the desolation of the "village." *Thing* in this line approaches as nearly as possible to a pronominal use. See Earle's *Philology*, par. 234, also note on l. 1.

130 Plashy. Another form of *splashy*. Cf. hoot, shout; hoop, whoop.

132 Mantling. See note on l. 248.

135 Pensive, i.e., causing gloomy thoughts in the beholder —*Transferred Epithet*.

136 Historian. Not literally, but in the picture of utter desolation which she presents, may be read the sad story of the "plain." Poetry seeks to combine in a single picture as many pleasing features as possible. It is scarcely to be supposed that all the agreeable sounds and sights just enumerated were ever found in *sweet confusion* on the same evening. Again, when thus clustering together what is attractive and delightful, it is careful to omit what in nature is painful or offensive. There was another side to the life of this happy "village" even in its brightest days, and there were other scenes, but these are hidden from our view. Observe, further, how the poet gains our attention by placing side by side in vivid contrast the most delightful views of the village in its prosperity, and the saddest pictures of its loneliness and ruin. The chief object he keeps in view is to awaken the fine art emotions in the breast of the reader, and thereby give pleasure. For this purpose, no means is more potent than thus to pass from one extreme to the other. To produce such an effect, the painful scene of the lonely widow may be considered admissible in poetry, since, on the whole, the effect is one of pleasure. It also awakens sympathy and compassion, which is agreeable within certain limits.

137 Copse, Gr. κόπτω, I cut ; Fr. *couper*, contracted from coppice. A growth of shrubs and bushes. Observe the description is made *real* by being localized and individualized.

138 Still. Account for the position of *still*.

139 Disclose, i.e., point out.

140 Preacher. For this gallery of exquisite portraits, we are indebted to some of the choicest experiences of Goldsmith's own life, idealized to be sure, but still drawn from the scenes of by-gone days. Not long before this poem was written, he had received tidings of the death of his brother Henry, the much-loved pastor of Lissoy. And it seems more than probable that the tender emotion thereby awakened, had led him to recall the noble traits of this brother whom he fondly loved, and intermingle them with similar recollections of his father, in this inimitable description of the "village preacher." Henry was the eldest of the family. In his college course, he was successful in winning a scholarship ; but an early marriage compelled him to leave his studies unfinished and begin to teach school. After a short time, he obtained a curacy at Lissoy, worth forty pounds a year, where he spent the remainder of his life in domestic happiness, and in the enjoyment of the love and affection of his people.

The parson has been a favorite subject with English poets. Cf. Chaucer, *Prologue to Canterbury Tales*, ll. 477–528 ; Dryden's *Character of a Good Parson ;* Crabbe's *Village*, Bk. I. ; Wordsworth's *Excursion*, Bk. V. ; also, Cowper's *Task*, Bk. II. ll. 326–480, especially ll. 395–413 :—

> " Would I describe a preacher, such as Paul,
> Were he on earth, would hear, approve, and own,
> Paul should himself direct me. I would trace
> His master-strokes, and draw from his design.
> I would express him simple, grave, sincere ;
> In doctrine uncorrupt ; in language plain ;
> And plain in manner ; decent, solemn, chaste
> And natural in gesture ; much impress'd
> Himself, as conscious of his awful charge,
> And anxious mainly that the flock he feeds
> May feel it too; affectionate in look
> And tender in address, as well becomes
> ‘A messenger of grace to guilty men.
> Behold the picture !—Is it like ?—Like whom ?

> The things that mount the rostrum with a skip,
> And then skip down again ; pronounce a text,
> Cry hem ! and reading what they never wrote,
> Just fifteen minutes, huddle up their work,
> And with a well-bred whisper close the scene."

See further, *Traveller*, ll. 11-22. These lines refer directly to his brother, and the resemblance to the picture before us cannot be mistaken.

Mansion is in this poem used in a general sense, as was usual in the last century. The preacher has his *modest mansion ;* the village master, his *noisy mansion :* and the host, his *tottering mansion.* From Lat. *manco*, to remain, it originally meant any place of abode. In England the *mansio* was the dwelling of the lord of the manor. Hence its modern application.

142 Passing is usually said to mean exceedingly, as if it was by *Aphaeresis*, and *Apocope* for *surpassingly ;* and in this sense it is frequently used in Shakespeare, as passing fair, passing strange. Might it not here mean *passing for ?*

Forty pounds. The income of his father while at Pallas, and also of his brother Henry. It seems to have been a common salary for a curate even in England at this time.

145 Cf. Heb. xii. 1.; also, the *Elegy* in the *V. of IV.* chap. xvii :—

> " In Islington there was a man
>   Of whom the world might say,
> That still a godly race he ran,
>   Whene'er he went to pray."

144 Nor e'er had changed. True of his brother, but not of his father. See *Life.* Cf. *Traveller*, l. 184 :—

> " Each wish contracting, fits him to the soil."

146 Unlike the famous vicar of Bray, who used to say :—

" For in my faith and loyalty, I never more will falter,
  And George my lawful king shall be until the times do alter."
 —*From an old Ballad.*

149 Vagrant. Lat. *vagor*, I wander. It is now used in a bad sense. An idle, vicious wanderer.

150 Long remembered, i.e., known a long time, as he had for years tramped the same beat.

153 Spendthrift. "There is a whole family of words,—many of them are now under ban,—which were at one time formed almost at pleasure, the only condition being that the combination should be a happy one. I refer to those singularly expressive words formed by a combination of a verb and substantive, the former governing the latter ; as telltale, turncoat, turntail." Many are obsolete, as spendall, pickquarrel, killman, carrytale. See Trench's *English Past and Present*, pp. 201-204.

155 Broken=broken down. Cf. Campbell's *Soldier's Dream :* —"their war-broken soldier," also Virgil, *Aen.* ii. 13 : "fracti bello."

157 Sorrow is in the nominative absolute. *Done*=finished.

158 Were won, i.e., used to be won when he was there to help.

159 Glow, i.e., with interest and attention.

161-2 As he did not care to inquire particularly into their case, he allowed his pity to prompt him to relieve their necessities without satisfying himself whether they were deserving objects of charity. Like Goldsmith himself, he was moved to relieve distress by his heart, not his head. See *Life*.

164 This line is quoted by *Burns*, in the *Character of my Father*.

168 To the skies. To try to fly upward from the nest.

172 Dismayed the dying man. A.S. *dis*, not, and *maht*, strength.

173 Reverend. "This word is not here used as a formal title of honour or courtesy, but as a mere adjective, indicating that the 'preacher' was worthy of reverence on account of his high character. The title 'Reverend' now applied exclusively to ministers of religion, was formerly applied to other persons as well.

> ' Most potent, grave, and reverend seigniors.'
> —Shakes. *Othello*, i. 3.

In the ' Paston Letters,' written in the 15th and 16th conturies, ladies and gentlemen address one another as Rev. and Right Rev. In the 16th and 17th centuries, the term Reverend was applied to judges."—Stevens and Morris.

Champion. A. S. *campian*, to fight ; Lat. *campus*, a field, especially a field of battle ; Fr. *champ*. One who fights for another and comes off master of the field. It is very applicable to the minister of religion, by whose presence the deepest human grief is assuaged, and through whose assistance a complete victory is won.

175 Wretch. A. S. *wraecca*, an exile. A person in the deepest distress.

176 Accents=words, well applied here to the almost inaudible words of the dying person. They are so low and hesitating (*faltering*), that though a sound (*accent*) is heard yet it is barely intelligible.

177 Before *at church* supply *as he conducted himself*.

184 Plucked his gown. " The practice of preaching in a black gown was very general in Goldsmith's day ; and the clergy usually wore these gowns on Sundays, as is their custom even now in many places, when going to and from church."—Stevens and Morris.

187-8 He sympathized with them in their sorrows, and rejoiced in their prosperity, but all was done that he might lead them to heaven—this was to him the one thought of serious moment.

189-192 Few poets are happier in their imagery than Goldsmith. Nothing could more beautifully portray the true Christian minister, whose constancy amid the storms of life is like the immoveable rock, whose lofty character inspires confidence and respect, and so raises him beyond the turmoil of this life, that above its storms he finds an unbroken calm of peace and joy.

" Lord Lytton (*Miscellaneous Works*, vol. i. p. 65), has traced this simile to a poem by the Abbé de Chaulieu, who lived 1639-1720, and whose verses were popular at the time when Goldsmith was travelling on the Continent :

> ' Tel qu'un rocher dont la tête
> Egalant le Mont Athos,
> Voit à ses pieds la tempête
> Troublant le calme des flots,
> La mer autour bruit et gronde ;
> Malgré ses émotions,
> Sur son front élevé règne une paix profonde.'

Every one," adds Lord Lytton, " must own that, in copying, Goldsmith wonderfully improved the original, and his application of the image to the Christian preacher gives it a moral sublimity to which it has no pretensions in Chaulieu, who applies it to his own philosophical patience under his physical maladies."—Rolfe.

Goldsmith's similies usually set all rules of grammar at defiance. This one may be subjected to modern notions of analysis, by supplying *He was* before *as*, and *is* after it, changing *on its head* into *on the head of which*, and placing these words before *though round, &c.*

189 Cliff, A. S. *clif*, from *cleafan*, to split, usually means an overhanging rock on the shore. Here it is a lofty crag standing alone.

190 Cf. *Traveller*, l. 33 :—

"And placed on high above the storm's career."

193 **Straggling.** Untrimmed, grown irregular.

194 **Furze** is a beautiful flowering evergreen. The blossom is of a bright yellow color. "The green young species give food to horse and cow, or donkey may be, and its old branches make a first-rate fence." It is said here to grow *unprofitably*, as there are now no inhabitants to make use of it.

196 **The village master.** It is thought that Goldsmith has drawn the portrait of his old master, Byrne, in this sketch. It is quite reasonable to suppose that some of the peculiarities of the old soldier are embodied in the description ; but as no work of art, even when coming from the hands of a Goldsmith, is an exact copy of nature, there can be no good grounds for forcing the resemblance too closely, and excluding the effect of other experiences or even the poet's imagination. The naturalness, ease and sly humor of this picture cannot fail to strike the most careless reader. The effect is still further increased by the activities that are introduced and ascribed to definite persons.

198 **Truant.** *Truand*, a wanderer, a vagrant. It is now applied to the class of wanderers who miss their way to school.

199 **Boding**=who had suspicions that the master's ill-temper might vent itself upon them.

200 **Day's disaster.** A whipping inflicted on account of the master's humor rather than of desert.

Disaster. Gr. $\delta v\varsigma$, ill, and $\dot{a}\sigma\tau\acute{\eta}\rho$, a star. Misfortune caused by the baleful influence of the stars. See note on l. 33.

201 **Counterfeited glee.** The little rogues. Just like Goldsmith when he was a boy.

205-6 **Fault** is by some authorities pronounced *fawt*. Pope has the same rhyme. Cf. *Essay on Man.* I, 69-70 :—

"Then say not man's imperfect, Heav'n in fault ;
Say rather, man's as perfect as he ought."

207 **Village**=villagers—*Metonymy*.

208 **Cypher** and zero are different adoptions of the same Arabic word.

Too. The rhyme should bring important words into prominence.

209 **Terms.** "The days of session and vacation observed in universities and law courts."—Sankey.

Tides, A. S. *tid*, time, here seems to mean the moveable fasts and **other** holidays.   In this sense it is used in Shakes. *King John,* iii. 1, 85 :—

> " Among the high tides in the Calendar."

It may, however, be used in its ordinary application, the periods of high and low water.

210 Gauge.   To measure the contents of casks with a gauge or rule.

211 Parson, the "village preacher." *Parson* is the same word as person—Lat. *persona.*

215 Still is properly repeated here as it gives more vigor to the expression than any of its synonyms could.

217. Observe the effect of placing *past* first in the sentence.

218 Triumphed, not by argument, but by *talking* the parson down.

221 Draughts, for the ale, what figure ?

222 Gray-beard mirth.   Cf. *Traveller* ll. 253-4 :—

> " And the gay grandsire, skilled in gestic lore,
>   Has frisked beneath the burden of three score."

Mirth and **toil**=mirthful men and toilers—*Metonymy.*

224 News, to be interesting, must be fresh, ale, to be good, needs to be old.   Hence the greater innocence of the people who could so easily be pleased.

What would be the news of the day at this time ?

226 Parlour.   Gr. $\pi\alpha\rho\alpha\beta o\lambda\acute{\eta}$, parable ; Fr. *parler,* to speak. Originally, a parlor was a room in a monastery for conversation, then any room for that purpose.

Probably it here supplied the place of the modern bar-room and sitting-room.   As the preceding picture is drawn from Gold-smith's school experience, so he here describes scenes he had often taken part in along with cousin Bryanton, at Conway's inn in Ballymahon.   See also *She Stoops to Conquer.*

Festive=used for merry-making.

227 Wall, floor, &c., are in the objective case in apposition to *splendours.*

232 The twelve good rules.   These were : 1, Urge no healths ; 2, Profane no divine ordinances ; 3, Touch no State matters ; 4, Reveal no secrets ; 5, Pick no quarrels ; 6, Make no companions ; 7, Maintain no ill opinions ; 8, Keep no bad company ; 9, Encourage no vice; 10, Make no long meals ; 11, Repeat no grievances ; 12, Lay no wagers.—Hales.

The royal game of goose.   Strutt, in his *Sports and Pastimes,* describes this game at considerable length.   He tells us that it is a childish diversion usually introduced at Christmas time. The table on which it is played is usually an impression from a copper-plate about the size of a sheet almanac, divided into sixty-two small compartments arranged in a spiral form, having an open space in the middle marked with the number sixty-three. The game is played with two dice, and the players throw in turn. It is called the Game of Goose because at every fourth and fifth compartment in succession a goose is depicted.

233 Except, though once a participle, has now the force of a preposition. It here shews the relation between *gay* and the noun clause following. For former use, cf. Milton *P. L.* Bk. ii. 299, 300 :—

> " Which when Beelzebub perceived, than whom
> Satan except, none higher sat."

234 Aspen. " Aspen tree, called also the trembling-leaved poplar (*populus tremula*), is a native of Britain, and is found generally in moist places. The name 'trembling' is applied to it on account of the constant movement of the leaves even with a gentle breeze. This mobility depends on the leaves being suspended by leaf-stalks flattened laterally, and when subjected to a slight wind, by their friction on each other they give rise to a rustling sound."—Enc. Brit.

Fennel. " Common fennel (*foeniculum vulgare*), is a perennial from 2 or 3, or when cultivated, 4 feet in height ; the plant appears to be of South European origin, but now is met with in various parts of Britain and the rest of temperate Europe, and in the West of Asia."—Idem.

Gay. Qualifies *hearth*.

235 Wisely = cunningly or prudently.

236 Ranged over the chimney = arranged on the chimney-piece.

" It was a very graceful and pretty amusement for Mr. Hogan, when he settled in the neighborhood, to rebuild the village inn, and, for security against the enthusiasm of predatory pilgrims, to fix in the wall 'the broken tea-cups wisely kept for show ;' to fence round with masonry what still remained of the hawthorn, to keep up the tottering walls of what was once the parish school, and to christen his furbished-up village and adjoining mansion by the name of Auburn. All this, as Walter Scott has said, 'is a pleasing tribute to the poet in the land of his fathers,' but it certainly is no more."—Forster.

227-336 In a letter to his brother, Henry, in **1759**, Goldsmith

E

gives the following as a specimen of a heroi-comical poem he proposed to write :

> " The window, patched with paper, lent a ray
> That feebly showed the state in which he lay.
> The sanded floor that grits beneath the tread,
> The humid wall with paltry pictures spread ;
> The game of goose was there exposed to view,
> And the twelve rules the royal martyr drew ;
> The Seasons, framed with listing, found a place,
> And Prussia's monarch showed his lamp-black face.
> The morn was cold ; he views with keen desire
> The rusty grate unconscious of a fire ;
> An unpaid reckoning on the frieze was scored,
> And five cracked tea-cups dressed the chimney-board."

*   *   *   *   *   *

237 Splendours, i.e., in the estimation of the villagers.

238 Reprieve. Lat. *reprehendere*, Fr. *reprendre*. p. p. *repris*. To delay the execution of a sentence. Observe the animation imparted by the *Interrogation*, a figure by which a question is substituted for an assertion.

Obscure = into obscurity. See note under l. 358.

240 Poor man. Is the proprietor or the peasant meant ?

241 Peasant = one of the village train. Fr. *paysan*, one living in the country, from *pays*, country ; Lat. *pagus*, a district.

242 To = in order to find.

243 The farmer's news. As the farmer would be frequently at the nearest market town, he would have opportunities for learning the news of the day.

Barber's tale. "The barber in country places commonly visits the villages in the neighborhood of his home, and calls upon those who require his services. He thus picks up all the gossip of the place."—Stevens and Morris.

244 Woodman's ballad. *Woodman* formerly meant a hunter, now it means a wood-cutter. *Ballad*, Gr. βαλλίζω, to throw the leg about, once meant a dancing song, now it means a short narrative poem.

Prevail, be the chief song, be often heard.

245 No more. Note the effect of the *Anaphora*.

247 Host, in this sense is from Lat. *hospes*, a guest ; host, an army, is from *hostis*, an enemy ; and "the host," from *hostia*, a victim.

248 Mantling bliss. The bliss or merriment which the ale produces is put for the ale by *Metonymy*. It is termed *mantling* because the foam covers the top of a tankard like a mantle. Cf. Pope :—

> " And the brain dances in the mantling bowl."

249 Coy. Lat. *quietus*, quiet ; Ital. *cheto* ; O. Fr. *quoy*, or *coy*.

To be pressed, i.e., to taste the cup.

250 Shall. What would be the meaning if *will* were used here ?

240-250 The characters here enumerated, along with those previously described, form a directory of the " Village."

256 Deride. The infinitive when thus used is called the Complementary Infinitive because it forms part of the object. See *How to Parse*, pars. 97, 98.

254 Native=natural, not of art.

Gloss of art=artificial splendor, mere outside grandeur.

255 This line is an amplification of *native charm*.

256 First-born sway. As this power existed before that arising from the "gloss of art."

257 Vacant. See note on l. 122.

258 Cf. Shakes. *M. of V.* III. 2 :—" Is an unlesson'd girl, unschool'd, unpractis'd."

Milton, *P. L.* II. 185 ;—" Unrespited, unpitied, unreprieved."

Byron. *Childe Harold:*—" Unknelled, uncoffined and unknown."

Sir W. Scott. *Lay*, VI. 1 :—

> " Unwept, unhonored, and unsung."

Pomp=procession.

Masquerade. Germ. *maske*. Or, perhaps, from Sp. *mas*, more, and *cara*, a face, a second face. A ball in which the company is masked.

260 Wanton. An example of degradation in meaning, to be met with in many words. It formerly meant sportive.

Cf. Shakes. *H. VIII.*

> " Like little wanton boys that swim on bladders."

261 These=*pomp* and *masquerade*, which stand for the artificial pleasures of the *rich* and *proud*.

262 The toiling pleasure, i.e., the pleasure of those who toil in vain to be happy. *Toiling* is an example of *Transferred Epithet*.

263 Even, an adverb qualifying the phrase *while*, *&c.*

Fashion's brightest arts. Explain. See note on l. 261.

264 If—joy, a noun clause, the object of *asks*.

265 Survey = see. Required by the measure and rhyme.

266 See, in *How to Parse*, pars. 387, 388, the very interest ing remarks of Dr. Abbott, on the confusion of the infinitive and participle, and on the omission of "to."

How wide, &c. = how great the difference, &c.

268 Splendid = which has the grandeur and pomp of wealth.

269-70 The very ocean takes a pride in assisting in the commerce by which the land is filled with wealth, and the people in their folly grow jubilant over their pernicious prosperity.

Tide = ocean, *Synecdoche*.

Freighted ore = gold or merchandise with which the vessel is freighted.

See note on l. 262. **Cf.** *Traveller*, l. 397-8 :—

> " Have we not seen, round Britain's peopled shore,
> Her useful sons exchanged for useless ore ? "

272 And rich, &c. England becomes the emporium of the commerce of the world.

273-5 The wealth which is acquired by these merchant princes, who have secured large fortunes in commerce is no real benefit to the country ; it does not assist in developing the agricultural (useful) resources of the land, but, on the other hand, ultimately forces the peasant laborer to leave the country, as the land which he formerly tilled is now bought up to be turned into parks, lakes and grounds, for "trade's unfeeling train ! "—Cf. Horace, *Odes*, ii. 15.

275 Loss, i.e., of the peasantry.

277 Space. Recalling a term to make some further explanation or addition is called *Epanorthosis*.

279 Silken sloth. See note on l. 262.

280 Cost a sum equal to the value of half the produce of the "neighbouring fields." Such a statement, in which anything is represented as greater than it really is, is called *Hyperbole*.

281 Solitary sports. There may have been a large number of persons—the family and visitors—enjoying the sports, but they are termed *solitary*, as this was the only place for miles around where any person lived.

283-4 Our natural products necessary for the support of the peasantry are exported to the various seaports of the world, to be exchanged for luxuries to regale the rich.

285 All qualifies *land*.

286 The is emphatic. *The* fall that must be the fate of a nation which is thus violated.

287-95 This *Simile* is well conceived. It is easily understood, impressive, pleasing, and clearly illustrates the subject in hand.

The grammatical construction will be made plain by arranging thus :—The land fares (acts) as some fair female acts (i.e., slights and shares not, but shines forth).

287 Plain, i.e., in dress and demeanor.

288 Secure to please = confident of pleasing.

290 The triumph of her eyes, i.e., which the charm of her eyes can win of itself.

Frail. Lat. *fragilis*, frail, from *frango*, I break.

The loss of the consonant between two vowels is of a frequent occurrence. Cf. fair, A. S. *faeger*; nail, A. S. *naegel*.

293 Time = age.

293 Shines is co-ordinate with *slights* and *shares*.

Solicitous to bless, i.e., anxiously desirous of conferring her favors.

295 Fares. A. S. *faran*, to go. Literally, goes on.

296 For analysis, supply *it is* after *charms*.

297 Verging to = approaching. See note on l. 20.

Decline is a noun, not a verb.

Verging to decline forms an adverbial extension of *rise*. Cf *Dedication of the Traveller.* "A country verging to the extremities of refinement."

298 Vistas. Ital. *vista*, a view. It usually means a "prospect through an avenue, as of trees."

301 Without—to save. An absolute clause. The noun with the preposition is used instead of the nominative absolute.

302 A garden and a grave. A garden for the pleasure of the rich man and a grave where the poor man's hopes if, indeed, not himself, are buried.

Garden and **grave** are in the predicate nominative after *blooms*. This is a species of *Antithesis*. The effect is increased by placing side by side things of an opposite nature. The alliteration also assists.

304 Cf. *Traveller* ll. 179-80 ;—

> "Sees no contiguous palace rear its head
> To shame the meanness of his humble shed "

Also *Vicar of Wakefield*:—"The mortification of contiguous tyranny."

305 To some—strayed. This clause forms a complement of *he* in l. 806. *Commons' fenceless limits*—lands which the peasant supposed were a free common, but which he finds are closed up against him.

"The enclosure of Commons, a measure by no means always dictated by mere greed, but sometimes in the highest degree prudential and considerate, has always been an extreme popular grievance. See Latimer's *Last sermon preached before King Edward VI., Ballads on the Condition of Eng. in Hen. VIII. reign, &c.*, Part I. ed. Furnivall p. 54, &c. &c. Some 1600 or 1700 Inclosure Acts are said to have been passed before the beginning of the present century. Goldsmith ignores the fact that 'half a tillage stinted the plains,' where the old Commons lay extended. If the enclosure were made without proper compensation to the Commoners, then assuredly nothing can be more shameful."—Hales.

306 Blade for grass—*Synecdoche*.

305-8. To analyze this sentence, supply some such expression as *he finds*. Then the clause *If—blade* is adverbial to *finds*, and the clauses *Those—divide* and *even—denied* are noun propositions, the object of *finds*. The sense is destroyed by making the clause *If—blade* adverbial to *divide*.

307 Fenceless=once fenceless.

Divide, i.e., have divided among themselves, and hedged in.

Sons of wealth. Cf. sons of pleasure in l. 313. *Personification*.

308. Bare-worn, i.e., even the scanty pasturage of the common, grazed to the ground by the flocks of the peasants is now denied the poor man.

265—308 The student should make himself acquainted with the condition of England at this time (1770), and examine into the correctness of the poet's views. He will find the subject fully discussed in Knight's *Popular History of England*, chaps. clxxvii—clxxxii.

309 Sped = gone. Before *sped*, supply *is* or *has*. *Waits* is here transitive. *Awaits* is the usual transitive form.

Must = can.

310-18. These lines show well the pleasing effect of an accumulation of *Antitheses*.

311 Thin mankind. i.e., injure the common people.

313 Know = enjoy, or participate in.

314 Extorted. How? See ll. 265-286.

316 Pale. This word contains an *Allusion* to the effect produced upon the complexion by being employed in the close air of factories.

Artist = artisan. The distinction between these words is of quite recent introduction. The former meanings have been nearly reversed.

Plies = works at. Cf. Sir W. Scott, *Lady of the Lake*, vi. 17 :—

" Their plight they ply."

317 Long-drawn = long. Cf. Gray's *Elegy*, l. 39 :—

" Long-drawn aisle and fretted vault."

Pomps. See note on l. 259.

318 There the black, &c. Hanging was a common punishment at this time.

Glooms. Strikes the passers-by with horror and dismay.

315-18. These two couplets place before the reader in vivid contrast, the poet's idea of the relative conditions of the rich and the poor.

319 Dome. Spacious hall. Cf. *Traveller*, l. 159 ;

" As in those domes where Cæsars once bore sway."

Pleasure is here personified.

Midnight. Explain the *Allusion*.

320 Decked. The *e* of the weak unaccented syllable *ed* is dropped in conversation, so that the word loses its additional syllable, and we are forced to pronounce a *t* instead of a *d*. In attempting to pronounce, in one syllable a *surd* and a *sonant*, either the surd will become a sonant, or the sonant will become a surd. Thus *sofd* will become either *sovd* or *soft*. So *d* will pass into *t* after *p*, *sh*, *s* sharp, *x*, *ch* and *ck*.

321 Blazing, i. e., filled with a grand display of people with richly ornamented equipage and apparel. *Metaphor*.

322 Torches. " Before the introduction of street-lights, people who could afford it were preceded by torch-bearers when going abroad at night." Rolfe.

Huge extinguishers still remain at the gates of some old mansions in London.

323 Sure = surely. *Like* is here an adjective qualifying *scenes*.

23-4 These two lines are supposed to be uttered by the reader, to whom the poet has shewn the outside life of *grandeur*. In the subsequent lines he is made acquainted with the ruin which is hidden from public gaze.

326 Poor houseless shivering. It will be observed that the adjectives *houseless* and *shivering* are each applicable to the noun female, that the word *poor* is used rather as an epithet of commiseration than to express the idea of poverty, and that it is applied, to the expression *houseless shivering female* as a whole, not to the term *female* alone. This accumulation of adjectives is purposely made to give the line a heavy and distressing effect.

327 **Blest** = happy.

328 **Has wept.** By poetic licence for wept.

329 **Might adorn,** for might have adorned. See note on l. 328.

330 For analysis, arrange thus :—*Her modest looks (which were) sweet as the primrose (is sweet, that) peeps beneath the thorn.* This beautiful *Simile* is the sweetest line in the poem. The alternation of consonants with vowels, the variety of the vowel sounds, and the preponderance of vowels, add richness and softness to the melody.

To all, i.e., to all that is good and happy.

Friends and **virtue** are in the nominative absolute.

334 **With,** in such a case is not instrumental. See note on l. 301.

That is more emphatic than *the*.

335 **Idly,** i. e., as she was tired of country life.

336 "**Wheel.** Almost every cottage in Goldsmith's time had a spinning-wheel upon which wool and flax were spun for domestic use. This was mostly done by the single women of the family. Hence an unmarried woman was, and is still, called a *spinster*."—Stevens and Morris.

338 **Tribes.** Lat. *tres*, three ; as the Roman people were anciently divided into three divisions. Hence, generally, a part of any nation. Here it is used for inhabitants and is simply a variation for *train*, which has already been repeated too frequently.

Participate is usually followed by " in."

341 Ah, no ! exclaims the poet, they are not permitted even the wretched consolation of begging from those whose prosperity has caused their ruin, but are

> " Forced from their homes, a melancholy train,
> To traverse climes beyond the western main."

For analysis, some such expression as *they are compelled to go* must be supplied before *to distant climes.* It would, of course, be rank nonsense to read *they go through torrid tracts to distant climes, &c.*

342 **Where—between.** It is somewhat difficult to extract a rational meaning from this line as it stands. *Where* may be taken as used for which, and the line made to read *between which and the mother land half the convex world intrudes,* i.e., half the world intervenes between England and America.

Convex. An ornamental epithet used merely to fill up the line.

343 Fainting. Cf. *Traveller*, l. 420 :

"To stop too fearful, and too faint to go."

344 Wild refers to the uninhabited districts along the river.

Altama. Probably Alatahama, a river of Georgia, is meant ; but, of course, it is a particular river used for any one in that part of the New World, to which the emigrants have gone.

Altama Murmurs. Making this lonely river sympathize with the distress of the exiles has a very fine effect.

347 Blazing, producing great heat. *Blazing* probably contains an *Allusion* to the belief that the sun is a mass of fire.

Suns, woods, fields are in apposition to *terrors*.

Suns. The plural for the singular, *Enallage*.

Downward = perpendicular, as being more nearly under the equator.

348 Day is used for heat of daytime, *Metonymy*.

349 Matted. A rich growth of all kinds of trees, shrubs and vines twined closely together. Cf. Scott, *Lady of the Lake*, i. 25 :—

"That winded through the tangled screen."

Forget to sing. A very striking contrast to England, where, according to our poet,

"Gentlest music melts on every spray."—*Traveller*, l. 322.

In this particular, as indeed in the whole of this description, he is as completely astray as he is when he tells us that the North American Indians go up and down the Niagara Falls in their canoes with ease.

350 Bats. Bats sleep in the daytime. Their position of repose is hanging from the limb of a tree with their heads downward.

352 Dark Scorpion. Scorpions belong to the genus *Arachnida*. They abound in warm countries, and are greatly dreaded on account of their stinging, which seldom proves fatal, but causes great pain.

Gathers death, i.e., collects the poison which produces death.

354 Rattling terrors. *Terrors* is by *Metonymy* for what inspires them. The rattlesnake (*Crotalus horridus*) is common in many parts of North and South America. Its bite generally produces death in man and most animals except pigs.

355 Tigers. Tigers are found only in Asia ; but the " Jaguar (*felis onca*), one of the largest of the cat-tribe, is by far the most powerful and dangerous of the American beasts of prey. It is sometimes called the American Tiger." Chambers' *Encyclo. pædia.*

Cf. Campbell, *Pleasures of Hope:*

" On Erie's banks where tigers steal along."

Wait. See note on l. 309.

356 Savage. Lat. *silva,* a wood ; *silvaticus,* an inhabitant of the woods ; It. *schiaggio ;* Fr. *sauvage.* Here it means barbarous, uncivilized.

357 Mad tornado. Gr. $\tau\acute{o}\rho\nu o\varsigma$, a lathe, Lat. *tornus,* from *tornare,* to turn, past participle, *tornatus,* in Spanish *tornado.*

358 Mingling is a supplement of the verb *flies.* It will be observed that when an adjective or participle is used as the supplement of a verb the expression is equal to a compound predicate, thus *flies mingling*=flies and mingles.

360-2 Mr. Sankey has pointed out the care that has been taken to heighten, by a judicious selection of epithets, the contrast between these home scenes and those of Georgia.

361 Warbling, *Transferred Epithet.*

361-2 Grove, love, an imperfect rhyme. They are very rare in Goldsmith. Cf. *Traveller,* ll. 151-2.

Thefts. Cf. Thomson's *Winter.*

" Snatched hasty from the side-long maid,
On purpose guardless, or pretending sleep."

363 Gloomed = cast a gloom over.

Parting day = day of separation.

363-64 Observe that in these deeply touching lines, the poet begins with general statements about the bitterness of the grief experienced by these homeless exiles when they come to the stern realities of separation from their friends and their homes, and then places before us a single family overwhelmed with distress at their departure. The reason why this course is adopted in poetry has already been pointed out. See note on l. 1.

365 When—bowers. This clause is adjectival to *day.*

366 Bowers—a part for the whole, as frequently.

A line of great pathos and richness.

367 Long Farewell = a farewell for a long time, i.e., for ever. Cf. *Shakes. II. VIII.* "A long farewell to all my greatness."

368 Seats, poetically for abode, homes. The word is often used of a gentleman's estate, as a country-seat.

Main. Lat. *magnus,* great ; A. S. *maegen,* strength. It is applied to the ocean when the idea of its greatness or majesty is to be made prominent.   Cf. *Traveller*, l. 410.

"To traverse climes beyond the western main."

Also, Shakes. *M. of V.*

"Bid the main flood bate his usual height."

369 The distant deep.   Not in the sense of remote or far away, but of great distance across.   Cf. *Traveller*, l. 284 :— "The broad ocean."

371 The good old, &c.   Perhaps the easiest way of disposing of this idiom, is to read *The good old sire (was) the first (that) prepared to go.*

373 For himself.   On this use of *for*, See *How to Parse*, par. 364,   *In conscious virtue brave* = brave from a consciousness of his own virtue.

Cf. Virgil, *Æneid.* i. 604 : "Mens sibi conscia recti."

378 Mr. Hales asks, "Was the lover never able to go too?"

379 Plaints, by *Aphaeresis* for complaints, a form common with the poets.

380 Cot, poetic, and by *Apocope* for cottage = home.
Every pleasure, *Hyperbole.*

381 Thoughtless.   Too young to comprehend the sadness of the situation.

In—dear.   This clause is a complement of *them.*

383 Strove to lend.   In such a construction, as Dr. Angus remarks (See *Handbook*, par. 534), "the objective infinitive is allied to the infinitive of purpose," and it is difficult to determine whether it is used as a noun or an adverb.

385 In this *Apostrophe* to Luxury which is regarded by the poet as the natural outcome of commercial wealth, the reader is forcibly reminded of some passages in the *Traveller*, which have a similar forecast.

386 This line contains one of the many examples of Goldsmith's faculty for making his meaning clear, while violating all ordinary rules of grammatical construction.

Things like these, i. e., the happy condition of the "bold peasantry" before the destroying arm of wealth had sown desolation over the once "smiling village."

387 Potions.   Luxury is represented as mixing for its votaries, cups which, though creating great pleasure, bring, in the end, only certain destruction.

389 Cf. *Traveller* l. 143 4 :—

> " And late the nation found, with fruitless skill,
>   Its former strength was but plethoric ill."

390 Florid, i. e., having the appearance of blooming health.
391 Draught, i. e., of the potions of wealth.
397 Methinks. A. S. *thincan*, to seem. *I see, &c.*, is a noun clause, the subject of *thinks*, and *me*, an old dative is the indirect object.

The student will observe how the poet, in this scene, presents a picture to the eye. The sight is the keenest of our senses. Poetry takes advantage of this fact, and, when possible, chooses to describe scenes of which the reader is rather a spectator than a listener. This description is further enlivened by the circumstances of motion that are introduced.

399 Where—sail. This clause qualifies some words understood as *to the shore.*
Anchoring=lying at anchor.
407 Maid. So called in allusion to the nine muses of ancient mythology. Cf. *Nymph* of l. 411.
Where—invade. This is an adjectival clause, used substantively after *to fly*, which, by poetic license, is used transitively to render the expression more terse. See *How to Parse*, par. 532.

Cf. *Traveller*, l. 124 :—

> " And sensual bliss is all the nation knows.'

409 Degenerate times. This has been a favorite idea with poets from Homer down. All deplore the lost " golden age."
410 Honest fame=fame honestly acquired.
412 My shame in crowds. Because people are too intent on other pursuits to take an interest in poetry. Note the *Antithesis* in this line.
413 Cf. Wither's address to the muse in *The Shepherd's Hunting.* Also Scott, *L. of L.* vi. 28 :—

> " Much have I owed thy strains on life's long way,
>   Through secret woes the world has never known,
>   When on the weary night dawned wearier day,
>   And bitterer was the grief devoured alone.
>   That I o'erlive such woes, Enchantress ! is thine **own**."

414 The former part of this line is literally true, and so far as deriving pecuniary assistance directly from poetry is concerned, the latter is, if we credit the poet's own story, equally so. He

said to Lord Lisburn, at one of the Academy's dinners : "I cannot afford to court the draggle-tail muses, my lord ; they would
let me starve ; but by my other labors I can make shift to eat,
and drink, and have good clothes." It must not, however, be
forgotten that Goldsmith owed his social position, and with it
his money-earning power, in no small degree, to the muse that
inspired the *Traveller*.

415 Nobler. This comparative has merely the force of a
positive. The same idea would be expressed by "noble arts,"
i.e., painting, sculpture, music, &c., which are called noble in
comparison with mechanical arts.

The poet means that the condition of poetry in a country is a
gauge by which we may determine the state of the other fine
arts. When it flourishes, they flourish ; when it fails, they fail.

416 If poetry is the "muse of every virtue," how is it that
only the "rural virtues leave the land" with it? Does the
poet wish us to understand that the "bold peasantry" was the
only virtuous class in England?

Fare thee well. An example of *Tmesis*.

Thee is here archaic. In early English, many verbs were
used with a reflexive pronoun, which do not admit it in modern
usage, as :—It repents me. Consequently *thee* in *fare thee well*
is not the subject, but the reflexive pronoun, the subject *thou*
being understood.

417 Farewell. When one sentence or clause begins with
the same word as that with which the preceding ends, we
have the figure, *Anadiplosis*.

Be tried i. e., wherever the exiled poet may settle and attempt to sing. This clause is concessive adverbial to *Let thy
voice, &c.,* in l. 421.

418 Torno. Probably around Lake Tornea in the extreme
North of Sweden.

Pambamarca is said to be one of the peaks of the Andes,
near Quito.

These two names were, no doubt, chosen simply because of
their sound and of their suitability for filling up the line, and stand
for any desolate and unpeopled countries, one lying in the frozen
North and the other beneath the burning heat of the equator.

419-20 This couplet is a repetition in a different form of the
meaning of the preceding line.

Equinoctial for equatorial, by *Metonymy*.

421 Prevailing over time, i.e., enabling the exiled wanderer
to rise superior to the hardships of his lot.

424 Rage of=rage for.

425 Native—that which naturally belongs to them, i.e., in England a "bold peasantry," to till the soil and live in innocent happiness.

426 Poverty and happiness seem to the poet to have a connection as inseparable as wealth and misery. Perhaps in his own poverty he felt happy in imagining that the great were not so.

Cf. *Traveller*, ll. 185-208.

427-30 These four lines were written by Dr. Johnson. To the *Traveller*, Dr. Johnson likewise added a few lines, and had the temerity to engraft upon Goldsmith's poem an inference which the arguments were never intended to bear, and which strikes the reader as a forced and unwarranted conclusion towards which he has not been led, and which, so far as the poem is concerned, rests upon the mere assertion of the poet. In this poem, the added lines are in harmony with the general train of thought, and form a very fitting conclusion to the main topic. But whatever credit 'they may be to Johnson as a poet, they certainly are none as a discerner of the times, or as a political economist.

427 Proud. Why does he use this epithet?

428 As ocean, &c. Explain this *Simile*.

Laboured mole. Lat. *moles*, a mass. Hence any massive pile which has been constructed by labor.

Cf. *Traveller*, l. 288 :—"The firm connected bulwark."

429 Self-dependent power, i.e., a nation that becomes rich by developing its own resources, not as England is represented is doing, by depending upon trade with foreign countries.

Time=lapse of time.

430 Sky, by *Metonymy* for storms and atmospheric action.

LIFE OF COWPER.

WILLIAM COWPER was born on the 26th of November, 1731, at Great Birkhamstead, in Hertfordshire. On both sides he was well descended. His father, the Rev. John Cowper, D.D., rector of that parish, was chaplain to George II. His grandfather was a Judge of the Court of Common Pleas, and one of his grand-uncles was Lord-Chancellor, and afterwards Earl Cowper. His mother was a descendant of the family of the celebrated Dean of St. Paul's, Dr. Donne, the poet. While yet at the tender age of six years, he suffered an irreparable loss in the death of his kind and loving mother. From her, as he himself thinks, he had inherited a nervous and sensitive nature, which the lack of a mother's soothing sympathy rendered much more impressible. So greatly did this gentle nature feel the dark shadow cast over its young years by this sad bereavement that the remembrance of the tenderness of her who was gone, was, after the lapse of nearly fifty years, daily in his thoughts.

To add to the gloom of his situation, the child was sent from home to a large boarding-school kept by Dr. Pitman, at the small town of Market Street. Here his timid and quivering nature sank before the bullying of the larger boys. Particularly was he in terror of one large lad of fifteen, by whom, he tells us "I was singled out as a proper object upon whom he might let loose the cruelty of his temper.   His savage treatment of me impressed such a dread of his figure upon my mind that I remember well being afraid to lift my eyes upon him higher than his knee ; and that I knew him better by his shoe-buckles than by any other part of his dress."

After spending two years in this school, he was removed on account of a disease of his eyes, and placed under the care of Mrs. Disney, a female oculist, where, if his eyes were but little improved, he was free from the suffering of the boarding-school.   He was next sent to Westminster School.   Here he spent seven of his happiest years.   He entered with zest into the sports as well as the studies of the school ; by the former he improved his health, relieved his melancholy and became popular amongst his fellows, being quite a distinguished football-player and cricketer ; by the latter he gained favor with his masters and reputation as a scholar.   His closest friend was Lloyd, a son of one of the masters, and among his other class-mates were names destined to take prominent places in the history of their country : Churchill, the poet, Colman, the translator of Terence, Cumberland, Thornton, Impey and Hastings were then forming character and collecting strength for their future career.   Yet, noted as some of them became, none will be longer or more affectionately remembered than Cowper.

On leaving Westminster, at the age of eighteen, he returned to his father's house, where he spent about nine months.   Owing to family connections, the profession of law was chosen for him, and he was articled to Mr. Chapman, an attorney in London.   Here he lived for three years professedly studying law, but in reality spending

" his leisure hours, which were well-nigh all his time,"
with his young cousins, Harriet and Theodora Cowper,
and his fellow-clerk, Edward, afterwards Lord, Thurlow.
The chief occupation of this happy quartette, the poet, for
already he had tuned his lyre, tells us, was " giggling and
making giggle." The " Delia," to whom his muse now
addressed her song, was his cousin Theodora. The elder
sister, Harriet, afterwards Lady Hesketh, was his corres-
pondent in later years ; but Theodora had awakened the
tender passion of his heart, which she as truly recipro-
cated. Her father, Ashley Cowper, Clerk of Parliament,
forbade a union, and closed his doors against his nephew.
The lovers parted never to meet again, and in 1755
Cowper took a last farewell of " Delia " in his Poem on
Disappointment. She remained, throughout life, faithful
to her early attachment, and when he became dependent
on his family, " a person who had tenderly loved him,"
offered to supply any reduction in his income, and from
this same unknown friend, who, he never seemed to suspect, was Theodora, he frequently received presents that
only the delicacy and tenderness of a woman's thoughtful
mind could have devised. She died unmarried in 1825,
and then his love effusions to her—his only poems on tha
theme—were given to the public. It was unfortunate
that Cowper never married. Had there been another to
fill, in his warm and loving heart, the place rendered
vacant by the death of his mother, she might have charmed
his melancholy spirit into happiness, and healed his
wounded heart with the sympathy it craved.

At the end of his three years with the attorney, Cowper
took chambers in the Middle Temple, which he afterwards

changed for the Inner Temple.   Here he studied law as
he had previously done with Mr. Chapman, for his time
was spent chiefly in literature and poetry.   However, he
was called to the Bar in 1754.   It was shortly after taking
up his residence here that he was seized with the first of
those attacks of depression to which he was more or less
subject till the end of his life.   The cause of his insanity
has been variously sought for, in his boarding-school sorrow, in the refusal of his uncle's consent to his marriage
with Theodora, in his religious views, and in his family.
There can be little doubt that he was correct when he
thought it was constitutional.   This first attack was of
short duration, and he became fully restored during. a
short visit to Southampton.   The death of his father,
which occurred in 1756, was the occasion of his last
visit to the scenes of his childhood, scenes to which
he was very deeply attached, though his having been sent
from home so young had prevented the growth of any
strong affection for his father.   The next four years of his
life were spent nominally in chambers ; but in order to
prevent a recurrence of his malady, he engaged in a continued circle of diversions, mostly of a literary character.
He was a member of the " Nonsense Club," which met
every Thursday to dine and discuss literary matters, contributed some articles to the *Connoisseur*, assisted his
brother John in translating Voltaire's *Henriade*, and the
Duncombes in their *Horace*.   He was now thirty-two.
His law had yet brought him no income, and family influence had so far secured for him only a Commissionership
of Bankrupts, with a salary of £60 a year.   His father
had left him but an inconsiderable patrimony, so that, al-

though he labored to hide it, he became reasonably alarmed about his future. Just at this juncture, the clerkship of the House of Lords fell vacant. The nomination was vested with Major Cowper, who conferred it on his kinsman, William. An examination at the Bar of the House had to be undergone before entering upon the duties of the office. Cowper sank before the thoughts of such an ordeal. Nearly six months were spent in attempting to become acquainted with the journals. His melancholy again returned. He fancied opposition from the Lords, thought he had wickedly hoped for the death of the former occupant, and imagined a libel in every newspaper. He was thoroughly mad, and made several attempt to take his own life. He bought laudanum, proposed to escape to France, returned to the laudanum, rode down to the Tower Wharf to drown himself, lay, the night before his examination, with a penknife at his heart, and then tried to strangle himself with a garter. For his recovery, he was placed in a private asylum, under the care of Dr. Cotton, where, for the first five months, he seemed hopelessly lost ; but by kind and judicious treatment he began to improve. One day he took up his Bible which, in his madness, he always threw aside, and his eye caught the 25th verse of the third chapter of Romans. He immediately " received strength to believe, and the full beams of the Sun of Righteousness fell upon him. In a moment he believed and received the Gospel." Prior to this, he had not led more than a moral life ; he now became deeply religious, and it is clear, from his own minute account of his restoration to health, and from his sudden conversion, that religion was not the cause, if, indeed it was not the cure, of his madness. On his recovery, his brother, who was residing at Cambridge, provided him a lodging at Huntingdon, fifteen miles distant. The brothers were able to visit each other on horse-back each alternate week. Cowper

"Found here that leisure and that ease he wished."

His happiness was greatly enhanced through an acquaintance he made with a kind and pious family, the Unwins. Mr. Unwin was the non-resident rector of Grimston, in Norfolk. His wife, a son and daughter made up this happy family. After some little time, Cowper was received as a boarder. He soon became a real member of the household. The Unwins were Evangelicals, and Cowper had earnestly desired to enjoy fuller religious intercourse with them. He had lately been obliged to resign the Commissionership of Bankrupts, and being unfit to live by his profession, he became entirely dependent on his family for support. They, however, generously subscribed a sufficient allowance for his comfortable maintenance. Cowper had lived in this happy home for eighteen months, when it was broken up by the death of the father, in 1767. At Olney, in Buckingham, Mrs. Unwin found a new home, and, accompanied by Cowper, she took up her residence there. The chief reason for selecting this place was that they might enjoy the ministration of a clergyman who preached the Gospel as received by the Evangelicals, and Mr. Newton had been recommended to them as one "who had been baptized by the same baptism." Mr. Newton was one of the foremost preachers of the revival. His mother, who was a pious dissenter, had given him a careful religious training ; but a rough sea-life, and the writings of Shaftesbury, had for a time led him into a profligate, blasphemous and reckless mode of life. He fell in love with a girl of thirteen, and left home because his father disapproved of the connection. He was impressed, deserted and was flogged. Being released from the navy, he went on board a slave-ship, where he suffered every kind of abuse and privation. Even here he was studying Euclid and Latin. A narrow escape from shipwreck, stirring up vivid recollections of his mother's teachings, and consequently a strong conviction of his wicked life, led to his conversion. He now became captain of a slave-ship, on which he made several voyages ; but, as he disliked the trade, although he did not consider it wrong, he gave it up, and after a short interval was ordained by the Bishop of Lincoln. He threw himself with great enthusiasm into the work of reforming the irreligion and brutality of Olney. In this employment Cowper was induced to take part. He visited the sick, prayed with the dying and even led in public prayer-meetings. He now gave up riding on horseback which he had enjoyed at Huntingdon. His only exercise besides visiting among the poor, fever-stricken inhabitants of the village, was pacing a gravel walk thirty yards long, for eight months in the year. The greater part of his time was spent with Mr. Newton, indeed, " for six years they were seldom separate, when at home and awake." He had not been three years at Olney when his brother John died. To his affectionate nature this was a severe trial, but he was greatly relieved by knowing that his brother died a true convert to saving grace. Close confinement, exhausting labor in the parish, lack of lively company, a perhaps somewhat morbid religious belief, and sorrow at the death of his brother, could have but one effect on the despondent, sensitive nature of Cowper. Mr. Newton noticed the returning gloom, and in order to raise his spirits induced him to assist in the preparation of the Olney Hymns. Of these hymns Cowper wrote sixty-seven, some of which still retain their popularity, as : " God moves in a mysterious way ; " " Oh, for a closer walk with God ; " " There is a fountain filled with blood." The return of his dreadful malady was not, however, to be prevented by such means ; for early in 1773, he was " suddenly reduced from his wonted rate of understanding to an almost childish imbecility." His mind was racked by all sorts of imaginings. " He believed that everybody hated him, and Mrs. Unwin most of all." He went to Mr. Newton's, and refused to leave. For sixteen months he suffered all the agony and distress of his previous attack. At last Dr. Cotton was applied to, and the patient began slowly to recover. He now returned to Mrs. Unwin's. During all this period she had watched over him with the fondness and care of a mother. Indeed, a still tenderer bond drew her to him, for it had been arranged that they should be united in marriage, had not the recurrence of his malady precluded all thought of its consummation. As he slowly recovered, he began to seek for employment and diversion. He returned to his favorite pursuit, gardening ; took a boyish pleasure in building himself a green-house ; found recreation in landscape-painting, and especially delighted in tending his pet animals, of which he had at one time nearly twenty. About this time some one kindly gave him three hares—Puss, Tiney and Bess. These he tamed, and afterwards immortalized in his verse. His correspondence, too, which had entirely ceased, was renewed.

In 1780, Mr. Newton left Olney to take charge of the United Rectories of St. Mary Woolnoth and St. Mary Woolchurch Haw; but before his departure, he commended his dependent friend to the Rev. Mr. Bull, a Congregational minister residing five miles from Olney. He and Cowper became fast friends, and remained so as long as the latter continued at Olney. For some time past the invalid had found great pleasure and mental benefit in composing short poems on passing events of private or public interest. The keen eye of love was quick to observe the quieting effect which this occupation produced on his still troubled mind, and Mrs. Unwin desired him to undertake a long poem. In answer to his request for a subject she gave him *The Progress of Error.* He at once set energetically to work, and in the short interval between December and March produced not only a poem on that subject, but also *Truth, Table Talk* and *Expostulation.* Through Mr. Newton he found a publisher in Johnson, of St. Paul's Churchyard, at whose suggestion *Hope, Charity, Conversation, Retirement* and a few minor pieces were added. Early in 1782, the volume appeared. *Table Talk*, which seemed the least distasteful to the unregenerated world, was put first, and the author awaited, with no little anxiety, the success of his venture. Cowper tells us that he had read only one English poet for the past twenty years, and further asserts "that he never in his life designed an imitation of Young or of any other writer; for mimicry was his abhorrence, at least in poetry." Perhaps this one poet was Churchill, traces of whose manner may be seen in the satire of these poems. They likewise bear evident marks of the poetical peculiarities of the preceding age, as well as of the religious tendencies of his own. There is manifest throughout a fervent desire to improve mankind, and to this end, they all have a distinctly religious purpose, a purpose, no doubt, begotten of the influence of Mr. Newton. For ten years he had seen nothing of the world; never had he had anything like a thorough acquaintance with it, yet he attacks the vices and errors of the time with all the fervor of an Evangelical preacher of his day. The fox-hunter, the gambler, the *dilettante* preacher, the drunkard and the fop, all come in for a share of his angry reproofs. Directly opposite opinions have been expressed regarding Cowper's satirical powers. Some deny him the character of satirist altogether, while others assert that he has produced some of our most potent, pungent and pointed satire. It is true that his attacks sometimes resemble pulpit denunciations, and that he may be open to the charge of " damning sins he has no mind to." But if satire consists in exposing vice and folly that they may be reformed, then Cowper is no mean satirist, though his anger may always be tempered with kindness. Nor are his writings destitute of that wit and humor which render satire effective.

To Mrs. Unwin we owe the *Moral Satires;* to Lady Austen we are vastly more indebted for the *Task.* In 1781 she came to Clifton, a mile from Olney, to visit her sister, Mrs. Jones. She was the widow of Sir Robert Austen, a baronet, with whom she had lived in France until his death, eleven years previous. Sprightly, gay, vivacious and accustomed to the best society, she threw a spell of delight over the gloomy life of the recluse, such as he had never enjoyed before. A passion for retirement had taken possession of her, and she, strangely enough, determined to establish herself at Olney, with these two Puritans as her companions ; for the two families became so intimate that "a practice obtained at length of dining with each other alternately every day, Sundays excepted." For Lady Austen's harpsichord, *The Loss of the Royal George*, and other poems were written. One evening, when Cowper appeared unusually gloomy, she related to him the story of John Gilpin, which he turned into verse before morning. This ballad was published in the *Public Advertiser*, and became immensely popular. Lady Austen frequently had urged him to write a long poem in blank verse, and one day he said " I will, if you give me a subject." " Oh ! " she replied, " you can write on any subject— write upon this sofa." The *Sofa* grew into the *Task*, in six books. The whole was written in a little more than a year, and published in 1785, in one volume, along with a poem called *Tirocinium*, or a *Review of Schools*, and the *History of John Gilpin*. The *Task* immediately raised Cowper to celebrity. His friends who had neglected him, opened up correspondence with him, sent him presents and complimentary letters, while the general public outdid them in their emulous endeavors to honor the man who had been able to supply a deeply-felt want by pouring forth his heart in these strains at once strongly religious, manly and human.

While the composition of the *Task* was in progress, the

cheering and inspiring presence which had given birth to the poem, and which had added so much to the mental health and social happiness of the poet, was to his very grave loss separated from him.   The cause of the rupture of this friendship has been the fertile source of dispute, and various theories are still held as to its true origin ; but whether it arose from jealousy on the part of Mrs. Unwin, dissimilar temperament, or too great a demand on the poet's time, " forcing him to neglect *The Task* to attend upon the muse who had inspired the subject," Lady Austen left Olney in May, 1784, and this singular friendship was ended forever.   The loss was in part made up to Cowper by an acquaintance which he made with the Throckmortons, who lived on an estate near Olney, and by the renewal of his correspondence with Lady Hesketh. This amiable person visited him and Mrs. Unwin about two years afterwards, and wisely thinking that the gloomy surroundings were unfavorable to the health and spirits of the poet, induced him and Mrs. Unwin to remove to Weston Lodge.   Accordingly, after nineteen years' residence at Olney, they left it on the 15th of November, 1786.   Scarcely had they settled in their new abode when it was saddened by the death of the Rev. Mr. Unwin, Mrs. Unwin's only son.   Shortly after finishing the *Tirocinium*, Cowper had undertaken the laborious task of translating Homer, and was still busily engaged upon it when the gloom of the season and overwork brought on another attack of insanity, in January, 1787.   This time, however, it was only six months till he suddenly recovered, and went to work at his translating.   He received, at this period, numerous visitors, among others, Mr. and Mrs.

Newton and Mr. Rose, a student from Scotland, who brought him a copy of Burns' poems. His cousin, Mrs. Bodman, sent him his mother's picture, " the only one in the world." It called forth that effusion of tenderness, pathos and endearing affection which is unsurpassed in these qualities by any poem in the language. Numerous other short poems, all characterized by delicacy of conception, tenderness of sentiment and beauty of execution, flowed from his pen about this time during his intervals of translation.

After seven years of toil, his *Homer* was at last given to the world in June, 1791. Johnson, the publisher, paid him £1,000 for the manuscript, and allowed him to retain the copyright. Cowper has avoided the faults of Pope, who had stiffened the simplicity, ease and nature of the ancient bard into the flashing brilliancy and elegant correctness of the eighteenth century ; but he, too, has failed where it is impossible to succeed, in rendering into our harsh tongue the sound and sense of that grand hymn of nature.

Homer finished, he began to cast about for other subjects. Lady Hesketh suggested the *Mediterranean Sea ;* Buchanan, *The Four Ages,* and he himself selected *Yardley Oak.* Of the first a few fragments were written, of the next an outline sketch was drawn, while the last was carried further ; and if the whole had been finished, so as to be equal to the stanzas that are produced, it would have been the crowning glory of his fame. Its completion was prevented by a proposition from his publisher that he should edit a magnificent edition of Milton, which the former proposed to bring out, with splendid illustrations by Fuseli. From this undertaking, all that we have is a few translations of Milton's Italian and Latin poems. The work of annotating was uncongenial to him, and was never completed. Hayley, a poet of the time, was also engaged upon an edition of the great Puritan poet. He wrote to Cowper to disclaim anything like rivalry, and this introduction led to a sincere friendship between Cowper and his admirer, Hayley.

In December, 1791, Mrs. Unwin was seized by a stroke of paralysis, and after a second attack, in the next year, her mind, which had since the first shown signs of decline, rapidly sank into second childhood. The long and affectionate attentions which had been so endearingly bestowed upon Cowper, it was now his to return. And with all the tenderness of affection he set himself to gratify every whim of the exacting and querulous sufferer. The task was more than he could long perform. He once more sank beneath the dark cloud of despair, which never again, except at brief intervals, lifted its shroud of blackness from his horror-stricken mind. His kinsman, the Rev. J. Johnson, and his friend Mr. Hayley, on the advice of the famous Dr. Willis, who had benefited George III., provided him a change of residence. He was removed to Norfolk, and, after several changes, finally settled at East Dereham. Here his much-loved and long-tried friend, Mrs. Unwin, died on the 17th of December, 1796. Both were unconscious of the separation about to take place. When taken in to look his last upon the lifeless form of her he had loved so long, he uttered one wild shriek of despair, and was never heard to mention her name again. During his lucid intervals, Cowper was able occasionally to receive visitors, to revise his *Homer*, and even to throw off short poems. In the autumn of 1793, he wrote those beautiful verses " To Mary," and six years later he penned those sweet, sad lines, *The Castaway*. They were founded upon an incident in *Anson's Voyages*; but the gloomy despair which enshrouded the poet's mind, led him to connect the fate of the perishing sailor with his own. Early in the next year, signs of dropsy began to appear; and about three months later he died peacefully on the 25th of April, 1800, in the sixty-ninth year of his age. His friends had fondly hoped that the dark veil of spiritual despair would have been raised from his beclouded reason before the lamp of life had ceased to burn. Such, however, was not the case; but his blameless, useful, pious life, and his firm faith in Christ, could have but one reward before the " Judge of all the earth."

Cowper has vividly stamped his personality upon all his works, and poured into them the thoughts that stirred his own heart. Like Byron and Wordsworth, he is one of the most subjective of our poets. Not only his thoughts, but his feelings and tastes are everywhere present in his writings. As the reader peruses his page, he can never fail to be struck with the sincere love of nature in which the poet seems to revel. Not its forms and appearances alone, but even its sounds attract his notice, and delight us in his copy. Not less intense is his love for his race. If any motive other than his own pleasure prompted him to the production of his poems, it assuredly was that he might benefit his fellow-men, that he might assist them in "virtue and piety," for this he considered the most important of all the aims of life, and to this he was especially moved by his own deep and ardent piety. He is the most decidedly religious of all our poets, and with him religion is something more than doctrine and creed—it is an actual daily experience of the heart. It must be confessed that his religious views were sometimes narrow and fanatical, but they are always manly and profound. He is seldom betrayed into harshness towards those whose theory or practice he condemns. His satire is always generous and kindly, intended to heal wherever it may wound. In truth, he possessed a most tender and sympathetic nature, and into some of his poems he has breathed all the tenderness and pathos of his heart. Some of his poetry has lost its force, as the occasions which gave it birth are passed away. Some of it, too, is tedious and dull, but none of it is weak, twaddling or sentimental. His masculine sense and nervous, mental vigor are only equalled by the felicity of his diction, his simplicity, naturalness and wealth of imagination.

Southey has pronounced Cowper the best of English letter-writers, a praise not undeserved. In his private correspondence we see the man as he is. His letters are all ease and familiarity, the unaffected, cheerful and humorous conversation of a man of ability and character. They lay open the bosom of a friend, attractive, human and genial. Like his poetry, they are an expression of his own thoughts and feelings. They were not written to be published, and if they have not all the brilliancy of the eloquent epistles of Lord Macaulay, they teach us to love as well as esteem

> " That teeming, grand poetic mind,
>   Which God saw fit in chains to bind."

THE TASK.

BOOK III.—THE GARDEN.

INTRODUCTION.

COWPER, like Wordsworth, owed much to his lady
friends. It was Mrs. Unwin who inspired the *Moral
Satires*, and but for Lady Austen, he might never have
penned a line of the *Task*. The former lady suggested
the *Progress of Error* as a subject, and it proved only
the commencement of a series of poems on a variety of
topics ; the latter was likewise instrumental in kindling
into flame a long galaxy of coruscations that outshone the
earlier scintillations of his genius, as the brightness of
noon-day outshines the morning dawn. For this poem,
Lady Austen proposed the *Sofa* as the subject, and prescribed blank verse as the form. The terms were accepted,
and the poet set to work with such vigor that, though
the work grew on his hands to dimensions never intended
at first, yet, in little more than a year, he finished the
whole poem, which comprises six books : *The Sofa, The
Timepiece, The Garden, The Winter Evening, The
Winter Morning Walk*, and *The Winter Walk at Noon*.
He began *The Sofa* in June or July, 1783, and by " working sometimes an hour a day, sometimes half a one and
sometimes two," he completed the entire *Task* in August

or September, 1784. During a delay in the publication, he wrote, or rather finished, another poem, *The Tirocinium*, which, along with *The History of John Gilpin*, was added to the volume, and the whole brought out by Johnson, a publisher, in St. Paul's Churchyard, in July, 1785. The name was not intended by the author to indicate the matter of the poem, but "it seemed almost necessary to accommodate the name to the incident that gave it birth." "Nor does it appear to me," he adds "that because I performed more than my task, that therefore 'The Task' is not a suitable title."

If to write what he did on the *Sofa*, was his *Task*, he certainly "performed more"—vastly more, and it is well that he did. In a semi-comic way, he toyed for a little with his theme, then wandered off into the green fields and rural scenes that he loved, whence he returned to satirize the follies of his age. Then, through the whole of the second book, he continues to attack the vices and errors of the time. It is here that he brandishes with the best effect the " satiric thong." In the third book, the plan of the poem takes definite shape. He here reaches his true theme—domestic happiness, and, though he exhibits the worst features of his narrow religious creed in abusing the pioneers of science, he becomes really interesting when he begins to tell us of himself and his occupations. The *Winter Evening* is a gallery of exquisite pictures, the postman, the poet's brown study, the suffering poor and others of equal beauty. These pictures continue in the beginning of the next book ; but icicles carry him away to the Russian ice-palace, from which he rather awkwardly launches off into a long and somewhat tiresome discussion on liberty, ending with the happiness of him whom grace makes free so that he can enjoy the works of his Creator. In the last book, the variety is, if possible, greater than usual, a bell, a walk, books, spring and its flowers, animals and their rights are delightfully discoursed upon, and the poem closes with a sublime invocation to him who is to restore all things, and with a vindication of retirement.

Mr. Goldwin Smith, in his excellent Life of Cowper, most justly says : " As *Paradise Lost* is to militant Puritanism, so is the *Task* to the religious movement of its author's time. To its character as the poem of a sect it no doubt owed and still owes much of its popularity. Not only did it give beautiful and effective expression to the sentiments of a large religious party, but it was about the only poetry that a strict Methodist or Evangelical could read ; while to those whose worship was unritualistic and who were debarred by their principles from the theatre and the concert, anything in the way of art that was not illicit, must have been eminently welcome. But the *Task* has merits of a more universal and enduring kind. Its author himself, says of it :—' If the work cannot boast a regular plan (in which respect, however, I do not think it altogether indefensible), it may yet boast, that the reflections are naturally suggested always by the preceding passage, and that, except the fifth book, which is rather of a political aspect, the whole has one tendency, to discountenance the modern enthusiasm after a London life, and to recommend rural ease and leisure as friendly to the cause of piety and virtue.'" A regular plan, assuredly the *Task* has not. It rambles through a vast variety of subjects, religious, political, social, philosophical, and horticultural, with as little of method as its author used in taking his morning walks. Nor as Mr. Benham has shown, are the reflections, as a rule, naturally suggested by the preceding passage. From the use of a sofa by the gouty to those, who, being free from gout, do not need sofas,—and so to country walks and country life is hardly a natural transition. It is hardly a natural transition from the ice-palace, built by a Russian despot, to despotism and politics in general. But if Cowper deceives himself in fancying that there is a plan or a close connection of parts, he is right as to the existence of a pervading tendency. The praise of retirement and of country life as most friendly to piety and virtue, is the perpetual refrain of the *Task*, if not its definite theme. From this idea immediately flow the best and most popular passages : those which please apart from anything peculiar to a religious school ; those which keep the poem alive ; those which have found their way into the heart of the nation, and intensified the taste for rural and domestic happiness, to which they most winningly appeal. In these Cowper pours out his inmost feelings, with the liveliness of exhilaration, enhanced by contrast with previous misery. The pleasures of the country and of home, the walk, the garden, but above all the " intimate delights " of the winter evenings, the snug parlour, with its close-drawn curtains shutting out the stormy night, the steaming and bubbling tea-urn, the cheerful circle, the book read aloud, the newspaper, through which we look out into the unquiet world, are painted by the writer with a heartfelt enjoyment, which infects the reader."

It was this earnest and cordial love of nature and determined persistence, notwithstanding the fashion of the times, in painting her, and in painting her as she is, not with the Arcadianism of Thomson, but with the plainness and even the coarseness in which she appears in English rural life, along with his use in poetry of the common language of conversation, that were the distinctive characteristics of Cowper, as he appeared to the age in which he lived, and that made *The Task* so popular. The heart of the nation had been longing once more to hear those tones of natural music which had so long given place to metaphysical disquisitions, to personal envy or to the song of polite society. On closer examination, we find that, observant as he was, his observations were superficial. He looks only on the exterior surface of the scene—the most familiar and easy survey, the field and lawns, the snow, the woodman and his dog. It is all easy observation, calm meditation, and quiet reflection on what he sees. There is little strong feeling, emotion is subdued, if, indeed, emotion is present; yet, as he leads us on in wrapt delight, attracted by our attachment to him personally, we become delighted with the sweet, the real humanity with which he invests his subject, and charms his listener. It is not the astounding creation of a lofty imagination; it is the clear, quiet unfolding of a picture with which every eye is already familiar, a revelation of what every sensitive soul had felt, but yet had never found words to express. It is the power which transmutes nature into such a form that it is appreciated and enjoyed by the affectionate and tender part of our nature. In striking contrast to his broad, genial and loving description of rural scenes, stand his views of human life and humanity. He sees these objects with very different eyes—the one, with the clear vision of his natural eye, the other, with the jaundiced eye of his narrow creed.

Religion, too, as a subject for poetry, had, for several generations, been almost entirely abandoned. It was deemed totally unsuitable as a theme for any sublime hymn ; but religion, practical, experimental religion, that which transforms the heart and ennobles the life, was selected as the special theme of this devoted bard. And as he saw that the practices of society, as indulged at that day, were unfriendly to the cultivation of exalted piety, he dwelt with enraptured strain on rural retirement, as the true sphere for developing the Christian graces. This is the real inspiration of the *Task*. The poet sets before all things the intention of doing good to his fellow-men ; and as the practice of piety is the noblest vocation of men, he exerts himself to the utmost to arouse them to this work. It is for this he lauds rural life and rural scenery. Here men may be free from the baneful influences of depraved modern society. Here they may, by meditation and devotion, be led up from nature to the "soul that lives and moves in all things," and which " is God."

The *Garden*, which is our special study, exhibits all the best and worst features of Cowper's poetry. The worst arise from the narrowness and hardness of his religious creed, which leads him into a violent and unreasonable attack on those who follow pursuits of which he is ignorant. He seems to forget that the occupations of the philosopher, the historian, and the astronomer, may be not less noble than his own—poetry and cucumbers. But, as we turn from the prosaic minuteness of the one, and the fanatical bigotry of the other, we are charmed with the unobtrusive egotism that delights us as we harken with interest to the relation of his own religious experiences, to a description of his employments and pleasures, and smile at the sense of quiet superiority with which he looks out upon the vain turmoil of the eager world he has left, and the self-gratulatory contempt with which he regards the pursuits of the deluded multitude. But he is not always wrong, for he administers some well-merited rebuke in his satire on the gaities and frivolities of London life. Yet, the theme which warms him most is domestic happiness ; and "nature, enchanting nature," is the "charmer," whose pleasures he loves to depict as entirely beyond the false joys wrung from an assiduous attendance on fashionable society.

There is, in the *Garden*, the same simple, direct and straightforward language, giving expression to strong, manly and independent sentiments, that is found throughout the other books of the *Task*. Though, at times, it falls below the subject, yet it has a fulness and flow that gives easy and happy utterance to the copious stream of ideas and the masculine common sense of the writer. It possesses, too, a clearness, a vigor and a certain melody and richness of swell that, in some of the loftier passages, remind us of the music of the great Puritan poet.

THE TASK.

BOOK III.—THE GARDEN.

As one who, long in thickets and in brakes
Entangled, winds now this way and now that
His devious course uncertain, seeking home ;
Or, having long in miry ways been foiled
And sore discomfited, from slough to slough   5
Plunging, and half despairing of escape ;
If chance at length he find a greensward smooth
And faithful to the foot, his spirits rise,
He chirrups brisk his ear-erecting steed,
And winds his way with pleasure and with ease ;   10
So I, designing other themes, and called
To adorn the Sofa with eulogium due,
To tell its slumbers and to paint its dreams,
Have rambled wide.   In country, city, seat
Of academic fame (howe'er deserved)   15
Long held, and scarcely disengaged at last.
But now with pleasant pace, a cleanlier road
I mean to tread.   I feel myself at large,
Courageous, and refreshed for future toil,
If toil await me, or if dangers new.   20

Since pulpits fail, and sounding-boards reflect
Most part an empty ineffectual sound,
What chance that I, to fame so little known,
Nor conversant with men or manners much,
Should speak to purpose, or with better hope   25
Crack the satiric thong? 'Twere wiser far
For me, enamoured of sequestered scenes,
And charmed with rural beauty, to repose,
Where chance may throw me, beneath elm or vine
My languid limbs, when summer sears the plains;   30
Or when rough winter rages, on the soft
And sheltered Sofa, while the nitrous air
Feeds a blue flame and makes a cheerful hearth;
There, undisturbed by folly, and apprized
How great the danger of disturbing her,   35
To muse in silence, or at least confine
Remarks that gall so many to the few,
My partners in retreat. Disgust concealed
Is ofttimes proof of wisdom, when the fault
Is obstinate, and cure beyond our reach.   40

Domestic happiness, thou only bliss
Of Paradise that hast survived the fall
Though few now taste thee unimpaired and pure,
Or, tasting, long enjoy thee, too infirm
Or too incautious, to preserve thy sweets   45
Unmixed with drops of bitter, which neglect

Or temper sheds into thy crystal cup.
Thou art the nurse of virtue.   In thine arms
She smiles, appearing, as in truth she is,
Heaven-born and destined to the skies again   50
Thou art not known where pleasure is adored,
That reeling goddess with the zoneless waist
And wandering eyes, still leaning on the arm
Of Novelty, her fickle, frail support ;
For thou art meek and constant, hating change,   55
And finding in the calm of truth-tried love
Joys that her stormy raptures never yield.
Forsaking thee, what shipwreck have we made
Of honour, dignity, and fair renown,
Till prostitution elbows us aside   60
In all our crowded streets, and senates seem
Convened for purposes of empire less,
Than to release the adultress from her bond.
The adultress ! what a theme for angry verse !
What provocation to the indignant heart   65
That feels for injured love ! but I disdain
The nauseous task to paint her as she is,
Cruel, abandoned, glorying in her shame !
No : let her pass, and charioted along
In guilty splendour shake the public ways ;   70
The frequency of crimes has washed them white,
And verse of mine shall never brand the wretch,
Whom matrons now, of character unsmirched,

And chaste themselves, are not ashamed to own.
Virtue and vice had boundaries in old time   75
Not to be passed ; and she that had renounced
Her sex's honour, was renounced herself
By all that prized it ; not for prudery's sake,
But dignity's, resentful of the wrong.
'Twas hard, perhaps, on here and there a waif   80
Desirous to return, and not received ;
But was a wholesome rigour in the main,
And taught the unblemished to preserve with care
That purity, whose loss was loss of all.
Men too were nice in honour in those days,   85
And judged offenders well. Then he that sharped,
And pocketed a prize by fraud obtained,
Was marked and shunned as odious. He that sold
His country, or was slack when she required
His every nerve in action and at stretch,   90
Paid with the blood that he had basely spared,
The price of his default. But now,—yes, now,
We are become so candid and so fair,
So liberal in construction, and so rich
In Christian charity, (good-natured age !)   95
That they are safe, sinners of either sex,
Transgress what laws they may. Well-dressed, well-bred.
Well-equipaged, is ticket good enough
To pass us readily through every door.
Hypocrisy, detest her as we may,   100

(And no man's hatred ever wronged her yet)
May claim this merit still—that she admits
The worth of what she mimics with such care,
And thus gives virtue indirect applause ;
But she has burned her mask, not needed here,   105
Where vice has such allowance, that her shifts
And specious semblances have lost their use.

I was a stricken deer that left the herd
Long since ; with many an arrow deep infixed
My panting side was charged, when I withdrew   110
To seek a tranquil death in distant shades.
There was I found by One who had himself
Been hurt by the archers.   In his side He bore,
And in his hands and feet, the cruel scars.
With gentle force soliciting the darts,   115
He drew them forth, and healed and bade me live.
Since then, with few associates, in remote
And silent woods I wander, far from those
My former partners of the peopled scene ;
With few associates, and not wishing more.   120
Here much I ruminate, as much I may,
With other views of men and manners now
Than once, and others of a life to come.
I see that all are wanderers, gone astray
Each in his own delusions ; they are lost   125
In chase of fancied happiness, still wooed

And never won.   Dream after dream ensues,
And still they dream that they shall still succeed,
And still are disappointed. Rings the world
With the vain stir.   I sum up half mankind   130
And add two-thirds of the remaining half,
And find the total of their hopes and fears
Dreams, empty dreams.   The million flit as gay,
As if created only, like the fly
That spreads his motley wings in the eye of noon,   135
To sport their season and be seen no more.
The rest are sober dreamers, grave and wise,
And pregnant with discoveries new and rare.
Some write a narrative of wars, and feats
Of heroes little known, and call the rant   140
A history ; describe the man, of whom
His own coevals took but little note,
And paint his person, character, and views,
As they had known him from his mother's womb.
They disentangle from the puzzled skein,   145
In which obscurity has wrapped them up,
The threads of politic and shrewd design
That ran through all his purposes, and charge
His mind with meanings that he never had,
Or having, kept concealed.   Some drill and bore   150
The solid earth, and from the strata there
Extract a register, by which we learn
That He who made it and revealed its date

To Moses, was mistaken in its age.
Some, more acute, and more industrious still,   155
Contrive creation ; travel nature up
To the sharp peak of her sublimest height,
And tell us whence the stars ; why some are fixed,
And planetary some ; what gave them first
Rotation ; from what fountain flowed their light.   160
Great contest follows, and much learned dust
Involves the combatants, each claiming truth,
And truth disclaiming both.   And thus they spend
The little wick of life's poor shallow lamp
In playing tricks with nature, giving laws   165
To distant worlds, and trifling in their own.
Is't not a pity now, that tickling rheums
Should ever tease the lungs, and blear the sight
Of oracles like these ?   Great pity too,
That having wielded the elements, and built   170
A thousand systems, each in his own way,
They should go out in fume and be forgot ?
Ah ! what is life thus spent ? and what are they
But frantic who thus spend it all for smoke ?
Eternity for bubbles proves at last   175
A senseless bargain.   When I see such games
Played by the creatures of a Power who swears
That he will judge the earth, and call the fool
To a sharp reckoning that has lived in vain ; ·
And when I weigh this seeming wisdom well,   180

And prove it in the infallible result
So hollow and so false—I feel my heart
Dissolve in pity, and account the learned,
If this be learning, most of all deceived.
Great crimes alarm the conscience, but it sleeps   185
While thoughtful man is plausibly amused.
Defend me therefore, common sense, say I,
From reveries so airy, from the toil
Of dropping buckets into empty wells,
And growing old in drawing nothing up !   190

    'Twere well, says one sage, erudite, profound,
Terribly arched and aquiline his nose,
And overbuilt with most impending brows,
'Twere well, could you permit the world to live
As the world pleases.   What's the world to you ?   195
Much.   I was born of woman, and drew milk
As sweet as charity from human breasts.
I think, articulate, I laugh and weep
And exercise all functions of a man.
How then should I and any man that lives   200
Be strangers to each other ?   Pierce my vein,
Take of the crimson stream meandering there,
And catechise it well.   Apply your glass,
Search it, and prove now if it be not blood
Congenial with thine own ; and if it be,   205
What edge of subtlety canst thou suppose

Keen enough, wise and skilful as thou art,
To cut the link of brotherhood, by which
One common Maker bound me to the kind?
True, I am no proficient, I confess,   210
In arts like yours.   I cannot call the swift
And perilous lightnings from the angry clouds,
And bid them hide themselves in earth beneath;
I cannot analyse the air, nor catch
The parallax of yonder luminous point   215
That seems half quenched in the immense abyss:
Such powers I boast not—neither can I rest
A silent witness of the headlong rage,
Or heedless folly by which thousands die,
Bone of my bone, and kindred souls to mine.   220

God never meant that man should scale the heavens
By strides of human wisdom.   In his works,
Though wondrous, he commands us in his word
To seek him rather where his mercy shines.
The mind indeed, enlightened from above,   225
Views him in all; ascribes to the grand cause
The grand effect; acknowledges with joy
His manner, and with rapture tastes his style.
But never yet did philosophic tube,
That brings the planets home into the eye   230
Of observation, and discovers, else
Not visible, his family of worlds,

Discover him that rules them ; such a veil
Hangs over mortal eyes, blind from the birth,
And dark in things divine.   Full often too   235
Our wayward intellect, the more we learn
Of nature, overlooks her Author more ;
From instrumental causes proud to draw
Conclusions retrograde, and mad mistake.
But if his word once teach us, shoot a ray   240
Through all the heart's dark chambers, and reveal
Truths undiscerned but by that holy light.
Then all is plain.   Philosophy, baptised
In the pure fountain of eternal love,
Has eyes indeed ; and, viewing all she sees   245
As meant to indicate a God to man,
Gives him his praise, and forfeits not her own.
Learning has borne such fruit in other days
On all her branches.   Piety has found
Friends in the friends of science, and true prayer   250
Has flowed from lips wet with Castalian dews.
Such was thy wisdom, Newton, childlike sage !
Sagacious reader of the works of God,
And in his word sagacious.   Such too thine,
Milton, whose genius had angelic wings, ·   255
And fed on manna.   And such thine in whom
Our British Themis gloried with just cause,
Immortal Hale ! for deep discernment praised,
And sound integrity not more, than famed

For sanctity of manners undefiled.   260

   All flesh is grass, and all its glory fades
Like the fair flower dishevelled in the wind ;
Riches have wings, and grandeur is a dream.
The man we celebrate must find a tomb,
And we that worship him, ignoble graves.   265
Nothing is proof against the general curse
Of vanity, that seizes all below.
The only amaranthine flower on earth
Is virtue ; the only lasting treasure, truth.
But what is truth ? 'twas Pilate's question put   270
To Truth itself, that deigned him no reply.
And wherefore ? will not God impart his light
To them that ask it ?—Freely—'tis his joy,
His glory and his nature to impart.
But to the proud, uncandid, insincere,   275
Or negligent inquirer, not a spark.
What's that which brings contempt upon a book
And him that writes it, though the style be neat,
The method clear, and argument exact ?
That makes a minister in holy things   280
The joy of many, and the dread of more,
His name a theme for praise and for reproach ?
That, while it gives us worth in God's account
Depreciates and undoes us in our own ?
What pearl is it that rich men cannot buy,   285

That learning is too proud to gather up,
But which the poor and the despised of all
Seek and obtain, and often find unsought?
Tell me, and I will tell thee what is truth.

   Oh, friendly to the best pursuits of man,   290
Friendly to thought, to virtue and to peace,
Domestic life in rural leisure passed !
Few know thy value, and few taste thy sweets,
Though many boast thy favours, and affect
To understand and choose thee for their own.   295
But foolish man foregoes his proper bliss,
Even as his first progenitor, and quits,
Though placed in paradise, (the earth has still
Some traces of her youthful beauty left)
Substantial happiness for transient joy.   300
Scenes formed for contemplation, and to nurse
The growing seeds of wisdom ; that suggest,
By every pleasing image they present,
Reflections such as meliorate the heart,
Compose the passions, and exalt the mind ;   305
Scenes such as these, 'tis his supreme delight
To fill with riot and defile with blood.
Should some contagion, kind to the poor brutes
We persecute, annihilate the tribes
That draw the sportsman over hill and dale   310
Fearless, and rapt away from all his cares ;

Should never game-fowl hatch her eggs again,
Nor baited hook deceive the fish's eye ;
Could pageantry and dance, and feast and song
Be quelled in all our summer-month retreats ;   315
How many self-deluded nymphs and swains,
Who dream they have a taste for fields and groves,
Would find them hideous nurseries of the spleen,
And crowd the road, impatient for the town !
They love the country, and none else, who seek   320
For their own sake its silence and its shade ;
Delights which who would leave, that has a heart
Susceptible of pity, or a mind
Cultured and capable of sober thought,
For all the savage din of the swift pack,   325
And clamours of the field ?   Detested sport,
That owes its pleasures to another's pain,
That feeds upon the sobs and dying shrieks
Of harmless nature, dumb, but yet endued
With eloquence that agonies inspire,   330
Of silent tears and heart-distending sighs !
Vain tears, alas ! and sighs that never find
A corresponding tone in jovial souls.
Well—one at least is safe.   One sheltered hare
Has never heard the sanguinary yell   335
Of cruel man, exulting in her woes.
Innocent partner of my peaceful home,
Whom ten long years' experience of my care

Has made at last familiar ; she has lost
Much of her vigilant instinctive dread,   340
Not needful here, beneath a roof like mine.
Yes—thou may'st eat thy bread, and lick the hand
That feeds thee ; thou may'st frolic on the floor
At evening, and at night retire secure
To thy straw couch, and slumber unalarmed ;   345
For I have gained thy confidence, have pledged
All that is human in me, to protect
Thine unsuspecting gratitude and love.
If I survive thee I will dig thy grave,
And when I place thee in it, sighing say,   350
I knew at least one hare that had a friend.

How various his employments, whom the world
Calls idle, and who justly in return,
Esteems that busy world an idler, too !
Friends, books, a garden, and perhaps his pen,   355
Delightful industry enjoyed at home,
And nature in her cultivated trim
Dressed to his taste, inviting him abroad—
Can he want occupation who has these ?
Will he be idle who has much to enjoy ?   360
Me, therefore, studious of laborious ease,
Not slothful ; happy to deceive the time,
Not waste it ; and aware that human life
Is but a loan to be repaid with use,

When He shall call his debtors to account,   365
From whom are all our blessings, business finds
Even here : while sedulous I seek to improve,
At least neglect not, or leave unemployed,
The mind he gave me ; driving it, though slack
Too oft, and much impeded in its work   370
By causes not to be divulged in vain,
To its just point—the service of mankind.
He that attends to his interior self,
That has a heart and keeps it ; has a mind
That hungers and supplies it ; and who seeks   375
A social, not a dissipated life,
Has business ; feels himself engaged to achieve
No unimportant, though a silent task.
A life all turbulence and noise may seem
To him that leads it, wise and to be praised ;   380
But wisdom is a pearl with most success
Sought in still water, and beneath clear skies.
He that is ever occupied in storms,
Or dives not for it, or brings up instead,
Vainly industrious, a disgraceful prize.   385

    The morning finds the self-sequestered man
Fresh for his task, intend what task he may.
Whether inclement seasons recommend
His warm but simple home, where he enjoys,
With her who shares his pleasures and his heart,   390

Sweet converse, sipping calm the fragrant lymph
Which neatly she prepares ; then to his book
Well chosen, and not sullenly perused
In selfish silence, but imparted oft
As aught occurs that she may smile to hear,   395
Or turn to nourishment, digested well ;
Or if the garden with its many cares,
All well repaid, demand him, he attends
The welcome call, conscious how much the hand
Of lubbard labour needs his watchful eye,   400
Oft loitering lazily if not o'erseen,
Or misapplying his unskilful strength.
Nor does he govern only or direct,
But much performs himself ; no works indeed
That ask robust tough sinews, bred to toil,   405
Servile employ ; but such as may amuse,
Not tire, demanding rather skill than force.
Proud of his well-spread walls, he views his trees
That meet (no barren interval between)
With pleasure more than even their fruits afford,   410
Which, save himself who trains them, none can feel.
These therefore are his own peculiar charge,
No meaner hand may discipline the shoots,
None but his steel approach them. What is weak,
Distempered, or has lost prolific powers,   415
Impaired by age, his unrelenting hand
Dooms to the knife. Nor does he spare the soft

And succulent that feeds its giant growth,
But barren, at the expense of neighbouring twigs
Less ostentatious, and yet studded thick   420
With hopeful gems.   The rest, no portion left
That may disgrace his art, or disappoint
Large expectation, he disposes neat
At measured distances, that air and sun
Admitted freely may afford their aid,   425
And ventilate and warm the swelling buds.
Hence Summer has her riches, Autumn hence,
And hence even Winter fills his withered hand
With blushing fruits, and plenty not his own.
Fair recompense of labour well bestowed   430
And wise precaution, which a clime so rude
Makes needful still, whose Spring is but the child
Of churlish Winter, in her froward moods
Discovering much the temper of her sire.
For oft, as if in her the stream of mild   435
Maternal nature had reversed its course,
She brings her infants forth with many smiles,
But, once delivered, kills them with a frown.
He, therefore, timely warned, himself supplies
Her want of care, screening and keeping warm   440
The plenteous bloom, that no rough blast may sweep
His garlands from the boughs.   Again, as oft
As the sun peeps and vernal airs breathe mild,
The fence withdrawn, he gives them every beam,

And spreads his hopes before the blaze of day.   445

   To raise the prickly and green-coated gourd
So grateful to the palate, and when rare
So coveted, else base and disesteemed—
Food for the vulgar merely—is an art
That toiling ages have but just matured,   450
And at this moment unessayed in song.
Yet gnats have had, and frogs and mice long since,
Their eulogy ; those sang the Mantuan bard,
And these the Grecian, in ennobling strains ;
And in thy numbers, Phillips, shines for aye   455
The solitary Shilling.   Pardon then,
Ye sage dispensers of poetic fame,
The ambition of one meaner far, whose powers,
Presuming an attempt not less sublime,
Pant for the praise of dressing to the taste   460
Of critic appetite, no sordid fare,
A cucumber, while costly yet and scarce.

   The stable yields a stercoraceous heap,
Impregnated with quick fermenting salts,
And potent to resist the freezing blast ;   465
For ere the beech and elm have cast their leaf
Deciduous, and when now November dark
Checks vegetation in the torpid plant
Exposed to his cold breath, the task begins.

Warily therefore, and with prudent heed   470
He seeks a favoured spot, that where he builds
The agglomerated pile, his frame may front
The sun's meridian disk, and at the back
Enjoy close shelter, wall, or reeds, or hedge
Impervious to the wind.   First he bids spread   475
Dry fern or littered hay, that may imbibe
The ascending damps ; then leisurely impose,
And lightly, shaking it with agile hand
From the full fork, the saturated straw.
What longest binds the closest, forms secure   480
The shapely side, that as it rises takes
By just degrees an overhanging breadth,
Sheltering the base with its projected eaves.
The uplifted frame, compact at every joint,
And overlaid with clear translucent glass   485
He settles next upon the sloping mount,
Whose sharp declivity shoots off secure
From the dashed pane the deluge as it falls.
He shuts it close, and the first labour ends.
Thrice must the voluble and restless earth   490
Spin round upon her axle, ere the warmth,
Slow gathering in the midst, through the square mass
Diffused, attain the surface ; when, behold !
A pestilent and most corrosive steam,
Like a gross fog Bœotian, rising fast,   495
And fast condensed upon the dewy sash,

Asks egress ; which obtained, the overcharged
And drenched conservatory breathes abroad,
In volumes wheeling slow, the vapour dank,
And purified, rejoices to have lost   500
Its foul inhabitant.   But to assuage
The impatient fervour which it first conceives
Within its reeking bosom, threatening death
To his young hopes, requires discreet delay.
Experience, slow preceptress, teaching oft   505
The way to glory by miscarriage foul,
Must prompt him, and admonish how to catch
The auspicious moment, when the tempered heat
Friendly to vital motion, may afford
Soft fermentation, and invite the seed.   510
The seed selected wisely, plump and smooth
And glossy, he commits to pots of size
Diminutive, well filled with well-prepared
And fruitful soil that has been treasured long,
And drunk no moisture from the dripping clouds.   515
These on the warm and genial earth that hides
The smoking manure, and overspreads it all,
He places lightly, and, as time subdues
The rage of fermentation, plunges deep
In the soft medium, till they stand immersed.   520
Then rise the tender germs, upstarting quick
And spreading wide their spongy lobes, at first
Pale, wan and livid, but assuming soon

If fanned by balmy and nutritious air,
Strained through the friendly mats, a vivid green.		525
Two leaves produced, two rough indented leaves,
Cautious he pinches from the second stalk
A pimple that portends a future sprout,
And interdicts its growth.   Thence straight succeed
The branches, sturdy to his utmost wish,			530
Prolific all, and harbingers of more.
The crowded roots demand enlargement now
And transplantation in an ampler space.
Indulged in what they wish, they soon supply
Large foliage, overshadowing golden flowers,		535
Blown on the summit of the apparent fruit.
These have their sexes, and when summer shines
The bee transports the fertilizing meal
From flower to flower, and even the breathing air
Wafts the rich prize to its appointed use.			540
Not so when winter scowls.   Assistant art
Then acts in nature's office, brings to pass
The glad espousals and ensures the crop.

Grudge not, ye rich, (since luxury must have
His dainties, and the world's more numerous half	545
Lives by contriving delicates for you)
Grudge not the cost.   Ye little know the cares,
The vigilance, the labour, and the skill
That day and night are exercised, and hang

Upon the ticklish balance of suspense   550
That ye may garnish your profuse regales
With summer fruits, brought forth by wintry suns.
Ten thousand dangers lie in wait to thwart
The process.   Heat and cold, and wind and steam,
Moisture and drought, mice, worms, and swarming flies 555
Minute as dust and numberless, oft work
Dire disappointment that admits no cure,
And which no care can obviate.   It were long,
Too long, to tell the expedients and the shifts
Which he that fights a season so severe,   560
Devises, while he guards his tender trust,
And oft, at last, in vain.   The learned and wise
Sarcastic would exclaim, and judge the song
Cold as its theme, and like its theme, the fruit
Of too much labour, worthless when produced.   565

Who loves a garden loves a greenhouse too.
Unconscious of a less propitious clime,
There blooms exotic beauty, warm and snug,
While the winds whistle and the snows descend.
The spiry myrtle with unwithering leaf   570
Shines there and flourishes.   The golden boast
Of Portugal and Western India there,
The ruddier orange and the paler lime,
Peep through their polished foliage at the storm,
And seem to smile at what they need not fear.   575

The amomum there with intermingling flowers
And cherries hangs her twigs.   Geranium boasts
Her crimson honours, and the spangled beau,
Ficoides, glitters bright the winter long.
All plants, of every leaf, that can endure   580
The winter's frown, if screened from his shrewd bite,
Live there and prosper.   Those Ausonia claims,
Levantine regions these, the Azores send
Their jessamine, her jessamine remote
Caffraria ; foreigners from many lands,   585
They form one social shade, as if convened
By magic summons of the Orphean lyre.
Yet just arrangement, rarely brought to pass
But by a master's hand, disposing well
The gay diversities of leaf and flower,   590
Must lend its aid to illustrate all their charms,
And dress the regular yet various scene.
Plant behind plant aspiring, in the van
The dwarfish, in the rear retired, but still
Sublime above the rest, the statelier stand.   595
So once were ranged the sons of ancient Rome,
A noble show ! while Roscius trod the stage ;
And so, while Garrick as renowned as he,
The sons of Albion, fearing each to lose
Some note of Nature's music from his lips,   600
And covetous of Shakspeare's beauty, seen
In every flash of his far-beaming eye.

Nor taste alone and well-contrived display
Suffice to give the marshalled ranks the grace
Of their complete effect.   Much yet remains   605
Unsung, and many cares are yet behind,
And more laborious ; cares on which depends
Their vigour, injured soon, not soon restored.
The soil must be renewed, which often washed
Loses its treasure of salubrious salts,   610
And disappoints the roots ; the slender roots,
Close interwoven where they meet the vase,
Must smooth be shorn away ; the sapless branch
Must fly before the knife ; the withered leaf
Must be detached, and where it strews the floor   615
Swept with a woman's neatness, breeding else
Contagion, and disseminating death.
Discharge but these kind offices, (and who
Would spare, that loves them, offices like these ?)
Well they reward the toil.   The sight is pleased,   620
The scent regaled, each odoriferous leaf,
Each opening blossom freely breathes abroad
Its gratitude, and thanks him with its sweets.

So manifold, all pleasing in their kind,
All healthful are the employs of rural life,   625
Reiterated as the wheel of time
Runs round ; still ending, and beginning still.
Nor are these all.   To deck the shapely knoll

That, softly swelled and gaily dressed, appears
A flowery island, from the dark green lawn   630
Emerging, must be deemed a labour due
To no mean hand, and asks the touch of taste.
Here also grateful mixture of well matched
And sorted hues (each giving each relief,
And by contrasted beauty shining more)   635
Is needful.   Strength may wield the ponderous spade,
May turn the clod, and wheel the compost home,
But elegance, chief grace the garden shows
And most attractive, is the fair result
Of thought, the creature of a polished mind.   640
Without it, all is Gothic as the scene
To which the insipid citizen resorts
Near yonder heath ; where industry misspent,
But proud of his uncouth, ill-chosen task,
Has made a heaven on earth ; with suns and moons 645
Of close-rammed stones has charged the encumbered soil,
And fairly laid the zodiac in the dust.
He, therefore, who would see his flowers disposed
Sightly and in just order, ere he gives
The beds the trusted treasure of their seeds,   650
Forecasts the future whole ; that when the scene
Shall break into its preconceived display,
Each for itself, and all as with one voice
Conspiring, may attest his bright design.
Nor even then, dismissing as performed   655

His pleasant work, may he suppose it done.
Few self-supported flowers endure the wind
Uninjured, but expect the upholding aid
Of the smooth-shaven prop, and neatly tied,
Are wedded thus, like beauty to old age,   660
For interest sake, the living to the dead.
Some clothe the soil that feeds them, far diffused
And lowly creeping, modest and yet fair,
Like virtue, thriving most where little seen.
Some, more aspiring, catch the neighbour shrub   665
With clasping tendrils, and invest his branch,
Else unadorned, with many a gay festoon
And fragrant chaplet, recompensing well
The strength they borrow with the grace they lend.
All hate the rank society of weeds,   670
Noisome, and ever greedy to exhaust
The impoverished earth ; an overbearing race
That, like the multitude made faction-mad,
Disturb good order, and degrade true worth.

   Oh blest seclusion from a jarring world,   675
Which he, thus occupied, enjoys ! Retreat
Cannot, indeed, to guilty man restore
Lost innocence, or cancel follies past ;
But it has peace, and much secures the mind
From all assaults of evil, proving still   680
A faithful barrier, not o'erleaped with ease

By vicious custom, raging uncontrolled
Abroad, and desolating public life.
When fierce temptation, seconded within
By traitor appetite, and armed with darts   685
Tempered in hell, invades the throbbing breast,
To combat may be glorious, and success
Perhaps may crown us, but to fly is safe.
Had I the choice of sublunary good,
What could I wish that I possess not here?   690
Health, leisure, means to improve it, friendship, peace,
No loose or wanton, though a wandering muse,
And constant occupation without care.
Thus blest, I draw a picture of that bliss ;
Hopeless, indeed, that dissipated minds,   695
And profligate abusers of a world
Created fair so much in vain for them,
Should seek the guiltless joys that I describe,
Allured by my report ; but sure no less
That self-condemned they must neglect the prize,   700
And what they will not taste must yet approve.
What we admire we praise, and when we praise,
Advance it into notice, that its worth
Acknowledged, others may admire it too.
I therefore recommend, though at the risk   705
Of popular disgust, yet boldly still
The cause of piety and sacred truth
And virtue, and those scenes which God ordained,

Should best secure them and promote them most ;
Scenes that I love, and with regret perceive   710
Forsaken, or through folly not enjoyed.
Pure is the nymph, though liberal of her smiles,
And chaste, though unconfined, whom I extol.
Not as the prince in Shushan, when he called,
Vain-glorious of her charms, his Vashti forth,   715
To grace the full pavilion.   His design
Was but to boast his own peculiar good,
Which all might view with envy, none partake.
My charmer is not mine alone ; my sweets,
And she that sweetens all my bitters too,   720
Nature, enchanting Nature, in whose form
And lineaments divine I trace a hand
That errs not, and find raptures still renewed,
Is free to all men—universal prize.
Strange that so fair a creature should yet want   725
Admirers, and be destined to divide
With meaner objects even the few she finds.
Stripped of all her ornaments, her leaves and flowers,
She loses all her influence.   Cities then
Attract us, and neglected Nature pines   730
Abandoned as unworthy of our love.
But are not wholesome airs though unperfumed
By roses, and clear suns though scarcely felt,
And groves, if unharmonious, yet secure
From clamour, and whose very silence charms,   735

To be preferred to smoke, to the eclipse
That metropolitan volcanoes make,
Whose Stygian throats breathe darkness all day long ;
And to the stir of commerce, driving slow,
And thundering loud, with his ten thousand wheels ? 740
They would be, were not madness in the head
And folly in the heart ; were England now
What England was, plain, hospitable, kind,
And undebauched.   But we have bid farewell
To all the virtues of those better days,   745
And all their honest pleasures.   Mansions once
Knew their own masters, and laborious hinds
That had survived the father, served the son.
Now the legitimate and rightful lord
Is but a transient guest, newly arrived   750
And soon to be supplanted.   He that saw
His patrimonial timber cast its leaf,
Sells the last scantling, and transfers the price
To some shrewd sharper, ere it buds again.
Estates are landscapes, gazed upon awhile,   755
Then advertised, and auctioneered away.
The country starves, and they that feed the o'ercharged
And surfeited lewd town with her fair dues,
By a just judgment strip and starve themselves
The wings that waft our riches out of sight   760
Grow on the gamester's elbows, and the alert
And nimble motion of those restless joints

That never tire, soon fans them all away.
Improvement too, the idol of the age,
Is fed with many a victim.   Lo ! he comes—   765
The omnipotent magician, Brown, appears.
Down falls the venerable pile, the abode
Of our forefathers, a grave whiskered race,
But tasteless.   Springs a palace in its stead,
But in a distant spot, where, more exposed,   770
It may enjoy the advantage of the North
And aguish East, till time shall have transformed
Those naked acres to a sheltering grove.
He speaks.   The lake in front becomes a lawn,
Woods vanish, hills subside, and valleys rise,   775
And streams, as if created for his use,
Pursue the track of his directing wand,
Sinuous or straight, now rapid and now slow,
Now murmuring soft, now roaring in cascades,
Even as he bids.   The enraptured owner smiles.   780
'Tis finished, and yet, finished as it seems,
Still wants a grace, the loveliest it could show,
A mine to satisfy the enormous cost.
Drained to the last poor item of his wealth,
He sighs, departs and leaves the accomplished plan   785
That he has touched, retouched, many a long day
Laboured, and many a night pursued in dreams,
Just when it meets his hopes, and proves the heaven
He wanted, for a wealthier to enjoy.

And now perhaps the glorious hour is come, 790
When having no stake left, no pledge to endear
Her interests, or that gives her sacred cause
A moment's operation on his love,
He burns with most intense and flagrant zeal
To serve his country.   Ministerial grace 795
Deals him out money from the public chest ;
Or, if that mine be shut, some private purse
Supplies his need with an usurious loan,
To be refunded duly, when his vote,
Well-managed, shall have earned its worthy price. 800
Oh innocent, compared with arts like these,
Crape and cocked pistol and the whistling ball
Sent through the traveller's temples ! He that finds
One drop of heaven's sweet mercy in his cup,
Can dig, beg, rot, and perish well content, 805
So he may wrap himself in honest rags
At his last gasp ; but could not for a world
Fish up his dirty and dependent bread
From pools and ditches of the commonwealth,
Sordid and sickening at his own success. 810

   Ambition, avarice, penury incurred
By endless riot, vanity, the lust
Of pleasure and variety, despatch,
As duly as the swallows disappear,
The world of wandering knights and squires to town. 815

London engulfs them all.   The shark is there,
And the shark's prey ; the spendthrift, and the leech
That sucks him.   There the sycophant, and he
That with bare-headed and obsequious bows,
Begs a warm office, doomed to a cold jail   820
And groat per diem if his patron frown.
The levee swarms, as if in golden pomp
Were charactered on every statesman's door,
" BATTERED AND BANKRUPT FORTUNES MENDED
       HERE."
These are the charms that sully and eclipse   825
The charms of nature.   'Tis the cruel gripe
That lean hard-handed poverty inflicts,
The hope of better things, the chance to win,
The wish to shine, the thirst to be amused,
That, at the sound of Winter's hoary wing,   830
Unpeople all our counties of such herds
Of fluttering, loitering, cringing, begging, loose
And wanton vagrants, as make London, vast
And boundless as it is, a crowded coop.

   Oh thou resort and mart of all the earth,   835
Chequered with all complexions of mankind,
And spotted with all crimes ; in whom I see
Much that I love, and more that I admire,
And all that I abhor ; thou freckled fair
That pleases and yet shocks me ; I can laugh   840

And I can weep, can hope, and can despond,
Feel wrath and pity when I think on thee !
Ten righteous would have saved a city once,
And thou hast many righteous.—Well for thee !
That salt preserves thee ; more corrupted else,   845
And therefore more obnoxious at this hour,
Than Sodom in her day had power to be,
For whom God heard his Abraham plead in vain.

NOTES.

THE GARDEN.

EPITOME.

The poet begins this Book by comparing himself to a traveller who returns to the route he had lost. He will abandon his satiric strain, since, if pulpits fail to reform the world, it is vain for him to try. He then invokes domestic happiness, which he grieves to find is so impaired by the vices of the time that have led men away from the old chastity and honor of the country. This brings him to advert to his own "retreat" from the "vain stir" of life, and to reprove what he considers the foolish pursuits of others, such as pleasure, history, geology and astronomy. His objections may seem strange to some, but his interest in his fellow-man must justify his censure. The question, What is Truth, is next answered, and then the poet returns to domestic happiness. This is best enjoyed in the country, yet even rural life is not loved for its own sake, but because it affords opportunities to enjoy the cruel chase. From the "savage din," one sheltered hare is safe. How variously and usefully the idle man may be employed, is then discussed, and his particular occupations dwelt upon, conversation, gardening, pruning fruit trees and raising cucumbers. After describing the last with tiresome minuteness, the poet regretfully leaves it to set forth the pleasures and cares of a green-house. From the green-house, he naturally goes to the garden, and after pointing out how it should be managed, he goes on into the country, and having shewn how far its pleasures surpass those of the town even in winter, he tells how some gamble away their estates, how others ruin themselves by fancied improvements and then cringe for "money from the public chest." But men will not be charmed with nature's joys, they will hasten off to London, the centre of fashion and vice.

1-20 The influence of Milton, who was one of Cowper's favorite poets, is clearly perceptible in these opening lines. The long sentence, the involved construction, the abundant use of participles, the transpositions as well as the somewhat majestic swell of the verse, all recall the great Puritan poet. These lines resemble parts of the description of Satan's journey from pandemonium to earth in Paradise Lost, Bk. II.

1 The Thickets and brakes in which the poet has been so *long entangled* are the follies and vices of his age, which in the preceding book led him so far from his original task, the *Sofa.*

2 Entangled. The caesural pause coming after this word, adds greatly to the *Harmony.* In the preceding line, the difficulty of the action is well expressed by the difficulty of pronouncing the line which is formed of so large a proportion of consonants, but with *entangled,* the voice, of necessity, pauses, like the traveller caught in a thicket.

3 His devious course uncertain=his devious, uncertain course. This collocation of words is frequent in Milton. The clauses *long - - entangled* and *seeking home,* are complements of *who* in l. 1.

4 Before *having,* supply *one who. Who* is then grammatically the subject of *chirrups* in l. 9, and of *winds* in l. 10. *He* is inserted to make the sense clearer, but it confuses the construction.

Each of the clauses, *having - - - foiled, sore discomfited, from - - plunging,* and *half - - - - escape,* is a complement of *who,* to be supplied in l. 4.

7 Chance=by chance, or by *Aphaeresis* for perchance. Cf. Gray's *Elegy,* l. 95, "If chance, by lonely contemplation led."

8 His should, grammatically, be *whose,* and the clause adjectival to *one* (understood) in l. 4. *His* is used to refer to *he* in the preceding line.

1-10 When the construction is changed in the course of a sentence, as, for example, in this case from a relative to a principal clause, it is customary to call such an arrangement an *Anacoluthon.*

9 Chirrups. Probably onomatopoetic, like *chirp.* Some consider it a contraction of *cheer up.* It is sometimes spelled *cherup.*

Ear-erecting. This is called a *proleptic* epithet. The erecting of the ears takes place after the chirruping.

10 Is *way* the object of *winds?* See *How to Parse*, pars, 130-1.

11 So I have rambled, &c. This is the principal clause of the sentence, and *as one, &c.*, is adverbial to it.

Called to adorn, &c., alluding to the manner in which he was led to undertake the *Task.* See *Introduction.*

14 Have rambled wide. This refers particularly to the subjects discussed in the Second Book, which by no degree of courtesy can be regarded as arising naturally from the original subject of the *Task*, the Sofa.

14-16 See note above.

15 Howe'er deserved. See Book II., also the *Tirocinium*, for the poet's opinion of how well the schools and universities of England deserved their fame. All were not "regardless of their charge," his brother was a noble exception. See note on ll. 191-260, also, *Life.*

16 Long held, i.e., *I was long held.*

17 A cleanlier road. He now proposes to leave the vices of the age for the rural nature that he loves.

22 Sounding-boards. These are boards or structures placed over pulpits to diffuse the speaker's voice through the church.

23 To fame, &c. He, as is the fashion with poets, professes self-depreciation, and affects to believe himself obscure. He had already published, in 1782, his first volume of poems, which had attracted considerable attention. Cf. Scott, *L. of L.* I. I.

24 Nor conversant, &c. This is literally true. For upwards of twelve years he had lived in complete isolation from the great world ; nor had he ever seen much society beyond a narrow circle of literary friends.

30-1 Observe how the *Harmony* is improved by the *s* sounds in the one clause and the *r* sounds in the other.

For analysis, supply *to repose my languid limbs* before *on the soft, &c.*

32 Nitrous air, "the name given by Priestly to oxygen gas, whose researches into its nature were nearly contemporaneous with the writing of these lines."—Benham.

35 The poet affects to think that his attacks on folly and vice rather than the character of his verse had brought upon him the censure of the *Critical Review.* He had, however, the pleasure of seeing his poems favorably criticised in the *Gentleman's* and

London Magazines, as well as in the *Monthly*, the chief Review of the time.

37 That gall. Cowper seems to have had the impression that his *Progress of Error*, and other satirical poems, wielded a very cutting lash. To his gentle nature it probably appeared much more severe than it does to the ordinary reader.

41-107 In this passage the poet expatiates with more than his ordinary excellence on two themes, which of all others he loved to dwell upon—domestic happiness and popular vice, the former of these he was at this time thoroughly enjoying in the company of Mrs. Unwin and Lady Austen, the latter he but dimly saw as reflected in the columns of *St. James' Chronicle*. The great religious revival whose effects Cowper rather felt than saw, was at this very time renovating society. He was himself, if unconsciously, a potent factor in this revolution, which purified the social and moral life of England. It colored his own views and to its influence, we owe these very lines. The strong feeling, affectionate love for his race, a noble outburst of passion at the departure from the stern morality of the good old Puritan days, all set forth in language terse and clear, in verse rich, smooth and melodious, exhibit some of the finest qualities of this true Christian poet. See *General Introduction*.

46 Neglect i.e., of one another.

47 Temper=ill temper. *Crystal cup*=cup of perfect happiness.

52 Zoneless. A hybrid word. Lat., *zona*, a girdle and A. S. *laes*, less, without. Not having on the girdle worn by respectable young women.

56 Truth-tried=tried and found true. Poetry, for brevity or ornament, often assumes the liberty of inventing terse and euphonious *Epithets*.

58 Forsaking. A. S. *for*, not ; and *secan*, to seek.

63 Bond=the marriage-tie.

68 Abandoned=given up to wickedness.

70 Guilty splendour. Cf. Goldsmith, *D. V.* l. 105 : "Guilty state."

72 Of Mine. Dr. Abbott thinks *of mine* is instead of *of me* to avoid harshness. See *How to Parse*, pars. 432-5.

Shall never, &c. An example of *Aposiopesis*, a figure by which the writer pretends to pass over what he is most strongly enforcing.

77 Renowned. The repetition of the chief term in successive clauses, has the effect of the *Balanced Sentence.*

80 Waif. Law Lat. *waivium*, Law Fr. *weif.* Something thrown away by the thief who had stolen it. *Waived* was applied to a woman in the same sense as outlaw to a man.

81 To return to the society of those who had not *renounced their sex's honour.*

84 Whose loss was loss of all. See note on l. 77.

85 Nice. This word dates from the French period. It first meant foolish, next whimsical, then subtle, and afterwards fastidious. It then fell into its present social use. See Earle's *Philology*, par. 424.

86 Sharped = won by sharp practice.

91 There may be an allusion to Admiral Byng, who was shot in 1757.

93-5 Notice the *Irony* of these lines.

94 In construction = in attributing good motives to other people.

97 Transgress, &c. Emphatic arrangement for *whatever laws they may transgress.*

100 Detest. See note on l. 97.

104 Cf. Rochefoucauld, *Reflex. Mor.*, No 223 :—" Hypocrisy is a homage that vice pays to virtue."

108-190 The poet now proceeds to compare himself and his religious standing with the rest of mankind, greatly to the disadvantage of the latter. His conversion was, in his opinion, the cure of his madness, and to the same cause, he owes, as he thinks, just views of himself and of the engagements of the world. The originators of the revival movement had been rousing England to think that the affairs of this life were of small importance, compared with the issues of the life to come. Some of their followers, pushing these ideas to extremes, had begun to regard literature and science as antagonistic to spiritual life.

This attack on history and science is the worst part of the *Task*—the worst outcome of a fanatical view of the concerns of this life. No doubt, the influence of his friend and protector, Mr. Newton, had done much to narrow down Cowper's creed, while his entire ignorance of the subjects he assailed, tended to lead him to despise them. It seems never to have struck him that the pursuits of others might be not less harmless than his own.

As he always relaxed this austerity towards any systems he opposed, when he became acquainted with persons who espoused
them it is a matter of regret that some of the pioneers of science
had not fallen within the circle of his private friends.

108 After his first attack of insanity, he gave up all thought of
following his profession in the busy world of men.   He here refers also to his conversion. With the Revivalists, "coming out
from the world," as it was termed, was a favorite theme.

112. One, i. e., Christ.   See Gen. xlix. 23 :—"The archers
have sorely grieved him, and shot him, and hated him."   See
also Isaiah liii. 4.

115 Soliciting = tenderly moving, so as to loosen and draw
out.   Imitated from Virgil, *Aen.* xii. 404.

116 Note the *Climax.*

117 Since.   "Down to the middle of the sixteenth century,
and indeed somewhat later, *sith, seththe, syth, sithe, sythen, sithen,
sithan, sythan, sithence, since, syns, sens.* were indifferently employed, both in the signification of *seeing that, inasmuch as, considering,* and of *after* or *afterwards,*   About that period, good
authors established a distinction between the forms, and used
sith only as a logical word, an illative, while, *sithence, since,*
whether as prepositions or as adverbs, remained mere narrative
words, confined to the signification of *time after.*   Immediately
after this time, all the forms of the word except *since* went out
of use, and of course the distinction perished with them—an exception to the general tendency of English."   Marsh's *English
Language,* p. 584 et seq.

Few associates.   See *Life.*

120 Recalling an expression in order to add something further
is called *Epanorthosis.*

128 Shall. Will, not shall, is used in the third person to express futurity.

128-9 Still - - - still - - - still = ever - - - yet - - - ever.   This
repetition of the same word is a blemish, as the same meaning
is not retained in each case.

133 See note on l. 120.

The million = the great majority.   A definite number for an
indefinite—*Metonymy.*

The Ephemeridae or Day-flies, to which the poet appears to refer, are so called because some species of them, at least, exist in

the perfect state for but a single day. They are often called May-flies in England, from the season in which they appear.

144 As=as if.

147 Shrewd. The history of this word illustrates how the feeble moral indignation of men against wrong becomes often weaker, or even entirely vanishes. To do a *shrewd* turn was once to do a wicked turn ; now it is applied to men to express a highly commendable sharpness. Other examples are flirt, luxury, peevish, and uncivil. See Trench's *English Past and Present*, page 297.

155 Contrive creation=devise and set forth the scheme by which the world was made.

156 Travel, &c. Nature, by which is here meant not only this earth, but the universe of which it forms a part, is compared to a precipitous mountain which these sages explore to its "sublimest height ;" and who, not satisfied with inventing mistaken theories about the creation of this globe, profess to explain the origin and movements of the stars. He probably refers to the theories of Descartes, La Place and Whiston.

160 Rotation. Referring to the discovery of gravitation by Sir Isaac Newton. See note on l. 252.

162-3 Each - - - both. These clauses are so *balanced* as to form a species of *Antithesis*.
Cowper appears to think more favorably of astronomy, in the *Tirocinium*, where he approves of teaching it to the young. See ll. 630 et seq.

165-6 Observe the *Antithesis* and gently sarcastic *Innuendo.*

169 Oracles, i.e., in their own estimation.

170 Wielded=discovered the manner in which the elements are controlled.
Having - - - elements and *built - - - way.* These clauses are complements of *they* in l. 172.

174 But frantic=but frantic persons, or if they are not frantic.

175 Eternity. Spent or lost *for bubbles, proves,* &c.

178 The relative clause should immediately follow the antecedent *fool*, and might do so without injuring either line.

183 Be. A present supposition, unless contrary to fact, should be expressed by the Indicative Mood ; few writers are consistent in their use of the Subjunctive. The Indicative is now used in many cases in which the Subjunctive was formerly employed.

189-90 One cannot but regret to find so choice a *Metaphor* gracing the exposition of such mistaken views of history and science.

202 Meandering is derived from Meander, a river in Phrygia, noted for its windings. It is one of an interesting class of words formed from proper names. Cf. labyrinth, palace, mausoleum, hector, tantalize, stentorian and cereal.

205 Congenial from Lat. *con*, together, and *genitus*, born. Hence, born of the same race, having the same origin.

207 Wise and skilful as. Dr. Abbott (*How to Parse*, par. 464) thinks that *as* is used for *though*, and that the fuller construction would be *as wise and skilful as thou art*, which is itself a contraction for *be thou as wise, &c.*

212-16 As Franklin, Priestley and Newton.

191-260 The previous severe criticism of the pleasures and pursuits of others is defended, on the grounds that the poet is himself a man, and a man desirous of saving his fellow-men from ruin ; but he cannot think that " philosophy " is of any value unless consecrated by piety, as in the case of Newton, Milton and Hale. Indeed, God himself is the object after which men should seek, and in his word, not in his works, are they to seek him. Cowper can always find some excuse for his friends. Newton may " scale the heavens " uncensured ; Warren Hastings may oppress India, uncondemned, because he and the poet had been school-fellows, and the attack on Popery has to be expunged after an acquaintance is made with the Throckmortons.

215 Parallax. The parallax (major) of a star is the difference in its apparent position as viewed from opposite points in the earth's orbit.

Luminous is to be reckoned a dissyllable in scansion.

217 Neither can I rest, &c. The poet wishes to intimate that he, as a moralist, has as strong claims to the privilege of exercising himself in reclaiming his " kind," from " headlong rage and heedless folly," as men of science have to investigate nature.

222 The clause *in his works* naturally comes after *shines*. Thus *To seek him rather where his mercy shines than to seek him in his works, though they are wondrous.*

226 Grand. See note on l. 77.

228 Manner=method.

Tastes his style, i.e., approvingly enjoys his method of working. In such an application, this word is now become vulgar. Cf. to dub, pate, to punch, to wag and to buss.

229 Philosophic tube. Poetry avoids common and familiar names, using instead of the ordinary designation some feature, or quality, or part of the object, by which it is readily suggested.

The telescope is believed to have been invented and applied to astronomical investigations, by Galileo about the year 1609.

234 The term *birth* may be justified by remembering that *mortal eyes* is by *Synecdoche* for *men*.

236 The is here an adverb. It is said to be derived from *thy* the ablative case of the A. S. definite article ; hence the phrase properly means *more by that* quantity.

We should be *she*. No good purpose is served by introducing a new subject.

238 Instrumental=secondary. See Book ii, ll. 174 et seq.

239 Retrograde. That lead away from, instead of leading up to the Creator.

To draw cannot strictly be used with *mistake*; *to make* would be the proper term. When a word is thus to be supplied in one clause in a sense different from that which it bears in the clause in which it is expressed, we have what is called *Zeugma*. *Proud to make a mad mistake.*

240 Once. In old English, spelt *ones*, an adverb formed from a genitive case. Cf. also needs, perhaps, eftsoons, unawares, here, there and whence.

Throughout Cowper's poems, are found passages strongly, and in some cases, bluntly, asserting the ideas prevalent among the leaders of the great religious movement of the time. In the lines before us, he means to tell us that if the heart is renewed by grace, the regenerate one is no longer subject to " mad mistake," but unerringly sees the Creator in all his works.

242 But is here a preposition governing the clause *by that holy light*, which may be expanded into a proposition.

243 Philosophy, &c. The poet would have us believe that the study of science when pursued by truly pious men, is the highest glory of human genius ; but that in the hands of those " unbaptised in the pure fountain of eternal love" it is but "bubbles and smoke," since it does not lead them to God himself.

247 Observe the *Antithesis*.

248 Has borne instead of *bore*, probably for the sake of the measure.

251 Castalian dews. Castalia, a celebrated fountain in Greece, which rises at the foot of Mount Parnassus, in the neighborhood of Delphi. It was sacred to Apollo and the Muses, and is frequently referred to both by classical and modern poets as a source of inspiration.

252 Newton. Sir Isaac Newton (1642-1727), a distinguished mathematician. He spent most of his life in his College. He sat in Parliament for his University, and presided over the Mint under Montague. He published, besides his *Principia* and *Optics, Discourses on Prophecy*. The latter are written in English, in a plain, manly style, and breathe a spirit of deep piety.

255 Milton. The great epic poet of England (1608-1674). See note on l. 1.

256 Fed on manna, i.e., received its inspiration from heaven.

257 Themis, the daughter of Uranus and Ge, was in Greek mythology regarded as the personification of order and justice. In modern art she is represented with bandaged eyes, and holding a pair of balanced scales in her hands. In this passage the word stands for law personified—*Antonomasia*.

Hale. " Sir Matthew Hale (1609-1676), the celebrated Chief Justice of the King's Bench in the reign of Charles II., wrote several works, many of them of a moral and religious character, of which his *Contemplations Moral and Divine*, are the best known."—Smith.

261 Psalm ciii. 15, 16 ; Isaiah xl. 6.

262 Dishevelled. Dis, *asunder*, and Fr. *cheveu*, hair.

The *Simile* is not properly carried out. There can be no comparison between *fading*, and having the leaves (hairs) *scattered* by the wind.

263 Proverbs xxiii. 5.

264 Observe that the term, *tomb* is here used, and correctly so, to denote a burial place superior to that denoted by the word *graves*. This is a common distinction between Anglo-Saxon and classical words.

265 Worship, A. S. *weorthscipe*, worthship, formerly meant *honor*, as " with my body I thee worship." Its signification is now much stronger, but more limited.

268-9 A good example of *Balanced Sentence*. Amaranthine. Gr. α, not, and μαραίνειν, to fade. In poetry, the amaranth is an imaginary flower that never fades.

271 John xiv. **6.**

276 Not qualifies *a*, which is here a genuine adjective = one.

277-289 " Truth" is the answer understood to be given to each of these questions. In the second question, the poet refers to the irreligion so prevalent in his time.

278 Be. See note on l. 183.

283-4 It is a peculiarity of our minds that the higher we rise in moral purity, the less highly we think of ourselves.

285 Matt. xiii. 46.

300 That the retirement of the country. is more favorable to virtue than the activity of the town, is a favorite theme with the poet.

301 Scenes is governed by *to fill* in l. 307.

To nurse may be parsed as an adverbial infinitive, qualifying the participle *formed.* See *How to Parse*, par. 99. Others regard *to=for*, a preposition and *nurse = nursing*, a gerundial noun.

304 Meloriate for ameloriate, by *Aphaeresis.*

305 Compose = soothe.

306 'Tis &c. This clause would naturally come before L 301. So great a transposition is called *Anastrophe.*

311 Rapt = hurried.

312-3 Since Cowper's time, cock-fighting has been forbidden by law, but angling, which he places in the same category, is still legal.

316 Self-deluded. " Who imagine themselves nymphs and swains, i. e., real rusties."—Storr.

318 Spleen. Dr. Johnson says :—The spleen is supposed the seat of anger, melancholy and mirth." Now that this theory is exploded, it means simply melancholy, ill-humour. See note on *D. V.* l. 33.

320 Who seek, &c. This clause is adjectival to *they.*

321 To what does *their* refer ?

322 Who would leave ? This adjectival clause is thrown into the interrogative form, instead of the negative assertion *none would leave.* The clauses *that . . . . . pity* and *that . . . . . thought*, are each adjectival to *who.*

333 Jovial. See note on *D. V.*, l. 33.

334-51 " ' The Poet's favorite hare, Puss, given to him in 1774. See his ' Account of the Treatment of his Hares,' inserted in the ' Gentleman's Magazine,' for June, 1784. Puss died March 9, 1786, 'aged eleven years, eleven months, of mere old age.'"—Griffith.

340 Mine. In Anglo-Saxon, *min* was used both as the genitive case of I (*ic*), and as an adjective pronoun. In the latter form it was declined through all the cases in the same way as other adjectives. Hence it may here be parsed as an adjective, used substantively, in the objective case after *like* or after *to* understood.

351 Cf. *Task*, Bk. VI., 719-728.

352-445 We are apt to call that the highest poetry which, dealing with the sublimest topics, strikes us with the greatest awe, but it should not be forgotten that, though such subjects demand the handling of a master genius, yet he who can afford to select the common-place affairs of every day life as his subject, and who can exalt them in such ennobling strains of simple grandeur as these lines display, falls but little short of the highest praise. Cf. Bk. VI., 908 et seq.

357 Trim = neat and elegant form. Cf. Milton, *The Nativity* :—

> " Nature, in awe to him,
> Had doff'd her gaudy trim ;"

Also *Table Talk* ;—

> " In him,
> Humour in holiday and slightly trim."

361 Me is the object of *finds*, in l. 366.

Laborious ease. To thus join together two terms that express opposite ideas is called *Oxymoron*.

362 To deceive. To pass away. Cf. Shakes., *Macbeth* ; I. 6. 61 : " To beguile the time, look like the time."

364 Use = usage, interest.

369 *Though too oft* (*it is driven*) *slack and* (*though it is*) *much impeded, &c.*

370-1 The poet here feelingly alludes to his times of melancholy and mental aberration.

373 Cf. Bk. VI., 933 et seq.

384 **Or—or,** poetic license for either—or.

387 **Intend—may** = whatever task he may intend **or** purpose to accomplish.

388 **Whether** is correlative with *or* in l. 397.

389 **He enjoys with her.** In the description which follows, it is easy to recognise the original of the portrait in the poet himself. At Olney, he spent nineteen years of his life with her whom he affectionately called his "second mother," pruning his garden, studying, writing poetry, and sipping by his evening fire "the cups that cheer but not inebriate." See *Life.*

390 **Fragrant lymph.** *Lympha,* water, and *nympha,* a bride, a goddess of fountains, are said to have been originally the same word. The muses being of a like nature are often called nymphs. Hence *lymph* here contains an *Allusion* to the cheering effects of tea-drinking. *Fragrant* is an ornamental epithet.

400 **Lubbard.** *Ard* from Germ. *hart,* Gothic *hardus,* has come to us through the Italian and French. Many words of this form have fallen out of use, such as blinkard, musard, dizzard, bosard, stinkard and shreward.

402 **His** refers to *labour. Its* would remove the ambiguity caused by *his* in l. 400.

404-7 Is there lurking in the sentiment of those lines any of that subordination of class and race that constitutes the spirit of slavery?

409 After *than* supply *that pleasure is much which.*

411 **Save.** See note on *except* in *D. V.* l. 233.

419 **Barren.** This position of the adjective is, no doubt, imitated from Milton.

421 **Gems**=buds, from Lat. *gemma,* a bud.

427 **Hence.** Note the effect of repeating the same term. To what does *hence* refer?

428 **Withered,** contains an *Allusion,* a figure by which something more is suggested by the words than is expressed.

430 **Fair recompense.** The fruits which are produced by the careful pruning above described are a *fair recompense of (this) labour well bestowed and (of this) wise precaution.*

431 **Rude** = severe.

433 **Churlish,** A. S. *ceorl,* a husbandman. See Trench, *Study of Words,* p. 56.

434 Discovering = showing, exhibiting. Lat. *dis*, not, *co*, together, and *operire*, to cover; Fr. *découvrir*, to uncover.

439 He, therefore, &c. The poet built himself a greenhouse at Olney.

444 Fence = defence, by *Aphaeresis*.

445 Hopes, for the plants on which he builds his hopes of a crop. Cf. Virgil's "Spes agricolæ."

446 To raise, &c. We confess to be unable to enter with such zest into the "stercoraceous" minuteness of this cucumber raising as some of the poet's admirers. It is usual to confine poetic description to such objects as can be clearly placed before the mind by a few bold dashes, but Cowper sometimes rides rough shod over all the rules of art.

Gourd. Gourd is here used for cucumber. It is properly a name given to various plants of the order *cucurbitaceae*. Cucumber (*cucumis*) is a genus under this order of which there are many species as the *cucumis sativus* or common cucumber.

448 Else base. Observe the *Sarcasm*.

452 Gnats. In the *Culex*, an early poem by Virgil, the *Mantuan bard*.

Frogs and mice. In the *Batrachomyomachia* (battle of the frogs and mice), a poem which is usually attributed to Homer.

452-6 The poet's method of apologizing by quoting these examples, calls to mind the remark of Addison in the *Spectator*, No. 122: "A man is more sure of his conduct, when the verdict which he passes upon his own behaviour, is thus warranted and confirmed by the opinion of all who know him."

455 Phillips. Phillips (1676-1708) is remembered chiefly for his poem, the *Splendid Shilling*, a parody in which he attempts to ridicule Milton's pompous style, by applying it to a trifling subject. The imitation is very felicitous. Phillips was a great favorite with Cowper, whose earliest verses that have survived, were written to imitate him. They are On Finding the Heel of a Shoe, 1748.

Shrines. Note the double meaning.

457 Dispensers. The reviewers whom he had reason to fear. See note on l. 35.

460 Dressing is here used for *describing how the dressing is managed—Metonymy*.

463 **Stercoraceous.** Cowper never could resist the temptation to use a long sonorous Latin word. This practice frequently mars his otherwise clear and natural style.

467 **Deciduous.** Probably this position of the adjective is imitated from Milton.

477 **Damps** for *damp*, by *Enallage*. The plural for the singular is more frequent in Latin than in English.

Impose. This infinite is in the same construction as *spread*.

Shaking = by shaking. On the adverbial use of the participle, see *How to Parse*, par. 261.

479 **Saturated straw** = *stercoraceous heap* of l. 463.

480-9 This part of the description is somewhat obscure. The heap of "saturated straw," gradually widening as it rises, is piled up to a suitable height. Upon it is placed the frame which is covered with a glass roof of sharp pitch.

What is longest = that which is longest, i.e., the longest of the *straw*.

481 **Shapely** is one of a number of words that went out of use, but afterwards became again familiar. Others are interlace, plumage, anthem, sphere.

483 **Eaves** is used in the plural, but was, originally, singular, from A. S. *efese*, eaves. Cf. riches from Fr. *richesse*.

484 **Uplifted**, rather awkward, = which had been lifted up.

486 **Sloping.** In what direction?

487 **Whose, &c.** This clause is adjectival to *frame*, and to prevent ambiguity should be placed nearer its antecedent.

Sharp declivity. One of the characteristics of the roof is, by *Synecdoche*, put for the roof.

490 **Thrice, &c.,** A *Periphrasis* for three days. Cf. Milton, *P. L.* Bk. 1. 50:

> " Nine times the space that measures day and night
> To mortal men."

Voluble. Lat. *volvere*, to roll. Revolving.

493-501 The *personal interest* which is introduced into these lines by the *personification* of *steam* and *conservatory*, aids greatly in elevating this prosaic subject.

495 **Gross fog Bœotian.** See note on l. 3. Owing to the number of the lakes in Bœotia, the air was thick and foggy.

497 Which is in the nominative absolute.

504 Hopes.   See note on l. 445.

509 Vital motion = germination.

517 Manure.   Lat. *manus*, the hand and *opera*, works , **Fr.** *main*, and *œuvre*.   Hence *manœuvre*, first meant work done by hand.   So *manure* was to cultivate with the hand (Milton, *P. L.* iv. 626), then applied to a particular branch of the art.   It is here accented in the first syllable, in Milton it is accented on the second, according to present usage.

525 Mats.   The glass roof with which the "frame" is covered.

531 Prolific.   Lat. *proles*, offspring, and *facere*, to make. Here simply, of luxurious growth.

531 Harbingers.   Forerunners.   A. S. *here*, an army and *hœrg*, a shelter.   Formerly applied to the officer whose duty it was to go before and arrange lodgings for the king and his attendants in a progress.

536 Apparent = that is beginning to appear.

In the cucumber, the fruit is of the class called *Simple Fruits*, which consist of a seed-vessel formed by the ripening of one *pistil*.

537 These, i.e., the flowers. In imperfect flowers, one flower has stamens only and another pistils only.   When both kinds are borne on the same plant, they are called *monœcious*, and when on different plants, *diœcious*.   In such plants, the seed will not ripen unless the pollen of the stamens of one flower is transported by some means to the pistils of the sterile flower. This is done as stated by the poet.   In the open air, the wind, insects and other things perform the work, but in the greenhouse it is necessary to rub the flowers together with the hand In most plants of the *Gourd* family, the flowers are *monœcious*.

These subjects are poetically dealt with by Dr. Erasmus Darwin in his *Botanic Garden*, which was published about the same time as the *Task*.   It is written in the artificial style of the preceding age, and is, in this respect, the very opposite of the freshness and ease of Cowper.

538 Fertilizing meal.   The *pollen*; Lat. *pollen*, meal.

546 Delicates.   The use of the adjective for the noun is rare.   It is very harsh, and, though it suits the metre, it injures the line.

549 Cares, &c., can scarcely be said to *hang, &c.* The poet might more correctly have said, *and their results hang, &c.*

551 Regales. Seldom used as a noun in English, though quite common in French.

552 Wintry. To be understood literally as "the task begins" in November.

558 Were = would be. This use of one mood for another is usually called *Enallage.* It may be regarded as an *Archaism.*

560 Fights, here used transitively. This license is frequently permitted, in order to give terseness to the diction. See *How to Parse,* par. 532.

563 Exclaim. This line is rendered very harsh by using *exclaim* without an object.

The strong sense of Cowper could not fail to discover the weakness of this cucumber episode. As it was introduced with one apology, it ends with another. Although he flatters himself that great poets have sung even humbler themes, yet he forecasts a lack of appreciation in the "learned and wise." It furnishes us, however, with a fine example of his command of language. Many parts of the description seem rather to resemble rich melodious prose than deliberate verse.

568 Exotic. Gr. ἔξω, without, ἐξωτικός, foreign.

570 Myrtle. The common myrtle is a beautiful evergreen shrub that bears white flowers. It is a native of the countries around the Mediterranean Sea.

573 Orange. The native country of the orange is not known. It is an evergreen tree, and in the South of England it is sometimes cultivated in the open air.

Lime. The lime is a shrub, usually about eight feet in height, with many prickly branches. It is a native of India and China. The fruit resembles a lemon, has a thin rind and a very acid juice.

574-5 The *personification* of *orange* and *lime* adds greatly to the beauty of these happy lines.

576 Amomum, a genus of plants of the order *Sitamineae.* The stems are perennial, and the flowers rise by themselves from the roots. Some species yield the spice called *grains of paradise.*

577 Geranium, or rather **Pelargonium,** is very abundant at the Cape of Good Hope. Gr. γέρανος, a crane. Popularly called Crane's-bill in England.

578 **Beau** = beauty. Lat. *bellus*, beautiful ; Fr. *beau*. *Spangled*. Ger. *spang*. See note on next line.

579 **Ficoides**, Lat. *ficus*, a fig, and Gr. όιδος, form ; so called from the nature of the seeds, which are sometimes ground into flour. It is usually called the Ice-plant, from the watery particles with which the surface is covered. It is an annual, a native of Africa and Southern Europe.

582-4 Observe the antithetical arrangement.

582 **Ausonia**, i.e., Italy.—Poetry prefers the ancient names of places to the modern, as being less familiar and frequently more euphonious.

584 **Jessamine.** A shrub with exquisitely fragrant flowers. It is a native of the South of Africa.

586 **Shade.** Gathered so closely together as to overshadow the same spot.

587 **Orphean lyre.** The story of the trees following the lyre of Orpheus, is often alluded to by the poets. Cf. Dryden.

> " And trees uprooted, left their place
> Sequacious of the lyre."

Summons. Lat. *sub* and *moneo*, I admonish. Fr. *semonce*. See note on l. 483.

591 **Illustrate** = display to advantage.

592 **Dress.** By contraction from Lat. *dirigere*, to put straight; It. *drizzare*. Here, adorn by giving order and neatness to the scene.

597 **Roscius** was in the time of Cicero and Sulla, the greatest comic actor at Rome. Before his death in B. C. 62, he had attained such perfection in his art, that his name became a synonym for superiority in any profession.

598 After *so*, supply *were ranged*.

Garrick. Garrick (1716-1779) " trod the stage" in London from 1741-76. He was Dr. Johnson's pupil, came with him to London, and became the greatest actor of his day. He also wrote plays. The *Lying Valet* and *Miss in her Teens* are the best. His naturalness, the chief beauty of his acting is referred to in l. 600. See note on line 582.

601 **Shakespeare.** The representation of Shakespeare's plays

which had been almost entirely banished from the stage in the age of Augustan artificiality, was revived with great success by Garrick.

615 Where—floor is a noun clause the subject of (*must be*) *swept.*

616 Breeding else=*or else it will breed.*

Else, old English *elles,* is an example of an adverb formed from a genitive case. Cf. needs, eftsoons, perhaps, once.

637 Wheel—home, i.e., wheel the fertilizing mixture to the place where it is required.

640 Creature=creation, production.

641 Gothic first signified barbarous, compared with Roman civilization.

642 Insipid=tasteless. Lat., *in* not, and *sapio,* I am wise.

643 Heath. "Probably Hampstead Heath; but it may be any of the numerous places of amusement in the suburbs of London."—Storr.

Misspent, i.e., if without the guidance of the "polished mind."

644 Uncouth. A. S. *un,* not, and *cuth,* the past participle of *cunnan,* to know; hence literally, unknown. Render it here *rude.*

645 Heaven, i.e., in form.

646 Encumbered. Cf. the *Epitaph :—*

> " Lie heavy on him, earth, for he
> Laid many a heavy load on thee."

647 Has made his garden a map of the entire heavens.

654 Bright. Brilliant in conception, and brilliantly bedecked with flowers.

658 Expect. What is the subject?

661 Interest sake. Is not truth here cut short to make a *figure* round ?

664 A notion of Cowper's, from which we have already had occasion to demur.

665 Neighbour, as an adjective, has at present given place to "neighboring."

668 Fragrant. The addition of this *ornamental epithet* shews how poetry seeks to unite as many pleasing ideas as possible with the subject with which it deals.

671 Noisome. Words in *some* seem more than ordinarily mortal. Many have disappeared, as mightsome, hearsome, thoughtsome, friendsome, likesome and laboursome.

657-74 Neatness and appropriateness of language, smoothness of versification and richness of imagery, are here united, to form a very attractive description.

683 Public life, Life spent in society and business. It is here opposed to " blest seclusion."

" Addison pronounced it an unquestionable truth that there was 'less appearance of religion in England than any neighbouring state or kingdom,' whether it be Protestant or Catholic ; Sir John Barnard complained that ' it really seems to be the fashion for a man to declare himself of no religion,' and Montesquieu summed up his observations on English life by declaring, no doubt with great exaggeration, that there was no religion in England, that the subject, if mentioned in society, excited nothing but laughter, and that not more than four or five members of the House of Commons were regular attendants at church."— Lecky's *England in the 18th Century.*

687-8 Cf. *D. V.* ll, 101-2.

692-3 This line very aptly states the design and matter of Cowper's poems. For his occupations and his pecuniary resources, see *Life.*

697 Much qualifies *in vain.*

Cowper was, perhaps, the greatest reformer that English poetry has ever seen ; in religion and morality, too, he was in the strongest sympathy with the most advanced views of his time, yet all the while he fancies himself the sternest Cato.

707 Piety and - - and - - and. " It is a general rule that excess of the connecting parts of speech—as pronouns and conjunctions—enfeebles the style. Yet emphasis sometimes requires their multiplication ; as in the verses in Paul, ' For I am persuaded that *neither* life, *nor* death, *nor* —, &c."—Bain.

709 A life of retirement is more favorable to virtue than an active one. " God made the country, and man made the town." Such is the perpetual refrain of the *Task.*

714 See Esther i. 10.

718 Alone is an adjective qualifying *mine*, which is here an adjective used substantially. See note on l. 340.

720 Bitters. See note on l. 546.

721 Nature, enchanting nature. For figure, see note on *Traveller*, l. 277.

One of the distinguishing features of Cowper's poetry, and that of the school of which he was the real founder, is a genuine love of nature.

727 Meaner objects. Geology and history, for example.

730 Wander from it as he may, the poet ever again returns to this, the real object of the *Task*, to show how much better fitted for the cultivation of piety and virtue is rural than city life.

738 Stygian. Styx, one of the rivers of the lower world. Here put for the infernal regions themselves, with, of course, a Christian idea added to the pagan.

" In 1853, an Act was passed to abate the smoke nuisance proceeding from chimney shafts and steamers above London Bridge. In 1856, its provisions were to steamers below the bridge, and to potteries and glass factories, by a second Act, which came into operation January 1, 1858. By these Acts, the ' metropolitan volcanoes ' are compelled to consume their own smoke."— Griffith.

742 England, for Englishmen, by *Metonymy.* The poet sighs for the days of Puritanism.

746 Honest, from Lat. *honor,* formerly applied in a wide sense to whatever was honorable, is now usually narrowed down in its application to one kind of honor.

747 Hinds = servants. A. S. *hine,* a servant, a peasant.

Fair, i.e., honestly earned by the town that gives a return, such as it is, for what it charges those who come from the country.

760. The wings, &c. Gambling was, at this time, one of the most common vices of fashionable society. Some years previously, Parliament had, by special Acts, suppressed, as far as possible, all gaming-houses and gaming-tables, and people of quality had established private clubs where they indulged their fondness for gambling. Lord Sandwich, one of the most inveterate gamblers of the time, is said to have sat at his game on one occasion for twenty-four hours, with no food except " a bit of beef between two slices of bread."

765 He. This anticipatory use of the pronoun is here adopted with excellent effect. As the mind is held in suspense awaiting the announcement of the name, the impression is much stronger than if introduced without first awakening expectation.

766 Brown. "Lancelot Brown, a famous landscape-gardener (born 1715, died 1773). He was called 'Capability Brown,' from his favourite phrase about 'great capability of improvement.' He laid out the grounds and park at Weston for Sir Robert Throckmorton, the grandfather of Cowper's 'Benevolus.'"—Griffith.

768 Whiskered. "Beards in England declined with the Commonwealth, and the court of Charles was the last in which even a small one was grown. After the Restoration mustachios or whiskers continued, but the rest of the face was shaven; in a short time the custom of shaving the whole face became universal. It was not till the Crimean war that beards again grew fashionable."—Storr.

769 Tasteless. Observe the sly *Innuendo*.

772 Aguish east. The east wind in England is considered to be promotive of fevers.

788 Proves = becomes.

794 Burns, &c. Note the *Irony*.

795-800. Bribery did not become conspicuous in England till the early part of the eighteenth century. In the beginning of the reign of George III., especially when Fox was Paymaster of the Forces, it was practised without scruple. Speaking of the peace of 1763, Lord Macaulay says: "The Pay-office was turned into a mart for votes. Hundreds of members were closeted there with Fox, and, as there is too much reason to believe, departed carrying with them the wages of infamy. It was affirmed by persons who had the best opportunities of obtaining information that £25,000 were thus paid away in a single morning. The lowest bribe given, it is said, was a bank-note for £200."

802 Crape. The mask worn by highwaymen. "The highwayman was an institution especially connected with the stage-coach. He had been growing into a power for many years. He was in his most high and palmy state when Fielding had ceased to write and George III. began to reign. In 1761, 'the Flying Highwayman engrosses the conversation of most of the towns within twenty miles of London. He robs upon three different horses—a gray, a sorrel, and a black one. He has leaped over

Colnbrook turnpike a dozen times within this fortnight.'"—Knight's *Popular History of England*, p. 938.

805 Probably intended for a *Climax*.

Observe the effect of the monosyllables and of the harsh consonants.

So=if, or provided that. Cf. Shakes., *J. C.* I. 2 :—

"I would not, so with love I might entreat you."

814 **Swallows** generally leave England early in October.

815 Not to the country as in the palmy days of knight-errantry.

Squires. "The attendant of a knight. Latin *scutum*, a shield, and *gero*, to carry ; hence, scutifer, a shield-bearer. To this the French added a euphonic initial *e*, making it *escuyer*, from which we get *esquire* and *squire*, and ' Esq ,' now used as a general title of respect. This French *e* is seen also in estate espy (spy, Lat. specio), etc."—Armstrong's *Lady of the Lake*, p. 197.

817 **Spendthrift.** See note on *D. V.*, l. 153.

818 **Sycophant.** On this word, see Trench's *English Past and Present*, p. 296.

820 **Cold jail.** If there is a particular reference, it may be to the *Fleet*, which was a debtors' prison as early as the twelfth century.

821 **Groat.** See note on l. 582.

822 **Levee.** In Cowper's time, ministers as well as sovereigns held their levees. Then, however, these assemblies were rather for business than for affording opportunities to ladies and gentlemen to pay their compliments to the sovereign.

833 This *Accumulation* of epithets is very happy. The repetition of the *ng* sound strengthens the tone of contempt.

843 See Genesis xviii. 23-33.

845 Cf. Matt. v. 13.

CHRONOLOGICAL PARALLEL.

A. D.	ENGLISH HISTORY AND LITERATURE.	LIFE OF ADDISON.	LIFE OF STEELE.
1672	Declaration of Indulgence.	Born at Milston, Wilts	
1675	Treaty with Louis.		Born in Dublin.
1683	Russel and Sidney executed	At Lichfield Grammar School.	
1684		Enters Charter-house	
1685	Monmouth's rebellion.		At Charter-house.
1687	Newton's *Principia*.	Enters Queen's College, Oxford.	
1692	Massacre of Glencoe.		At Merton College, Oxford.
1693	Congreve's *Old Bachelor*.	Takes his M. A. degree Wrote *Verses to Dryden*.	
1694	Tillotson *d.* The first English Ministry.	*English Poets*. *Fourth Georgic*.	
1695	Triennial Bill.	*A Poem to His Majesty*.	
1698	Sir W. Temple *d.*	Fellow of Magdalen College.	
1699	Stillingfleet *d.*	Travels on the Continent.	
1701	Act of Settlement.	*Letter from Italy to Halifax*.	Christian Hero.
1702	Queen Anne.		*The Funeral*.
1703	Swift's *Tale of the Tub*.	Returns to England.	*Tender Husband*.
1704	Harley and St. John. Locke *d.* Battle of Blenheim.	*The Campaign*. Commissioner of Appeals.	*Lying Lover*.
1705		*Remarks on Italy*.	
1706	Battle of Ramillies.	Under-Secretary of State.	
1707	Union. Farquhar *d.*	*Rosamond*.	
1709	Dr. S. Johnson *b.*	Chief Sec. for Ireland Writes for the *Tatler*.	Begins *Tatler*, 12th April.
1710	Trial of Sacheverell.	Loses all his employments. Writes for *Whig Examiner*.	
1711	Pope's *Essay on Criticism*.	*Spectator*.	*Spectator* begun, 1st March.
1712	Dismissal of Marlborough.		Seventh volume ends 6th December.
1713	Shaftesbury *d.* Sterne *b.* Pope's *Windsor Forest*.	*Cato*. Writes for the *Guardian*.	Writes for the *Englishman* and *Guardian*.

K

A. D.	ENGLISH HISTORY AND LITERATURE.	LIFE OF ADDISON.	LIFE OF STEELE.
1714	George the First. Budgell's *Characters.*	*Spectator* resumed. Secreary to Council of State. Again Chief Secretary for Ireland.	Expelled from the House of Commons for writing the *Crisis.*
1715	Bishop Burnet *d.* Rowe, Laureate.	*Drummer.* Returns from Ireland. Commences the *Freeholder.*	
1716	Septennial Bill. Gray *b.*	Marries Countess of Warwick	
1717	Triple Alliance.	Secretary of State. *Treatise on Christian Religion.*	
1719	*Robinson Crusoe.*	Writes for *Old Whig.* Death, 17th June.	Writes for *Plebeian.*
1721	Walpole's Ministry. Burnet's *Own Times.*	*Dialogue on Medals* (posthumous).	
1722	Atterbury banished.		*Conscious Lovers.*
1726	Thomson's *Winter.* Gulliver's *Travels.*		
1727	George the Second. Newton *d.*		
1729	Congreve *d.*		Death, 1st Sept.

DE COVERLEY PAPERS,

From the "Spectator."

INTRODUCTION.

The honor of originating the periodical essay containing short sketches of character, criticisms of manners, vices, and modes of life is due to Defoe. Like all inventors, he had little idea of the improvements which would be made in his plan, of the purpose to which it would be applied, or of the perfection to which it would so soon be brought. Few men have the genius of invention, many have that of improvement. Of the latter class, were Steele and Addison. Once give them a plan upon which to work, and there never have been geniuses better adapted to add the finer touches and nicer beauties which go to make any invention perfect. And this they did with the social essay. In 1704, the year of Blenheim, a time when news of the French campaigns was as eagerly devoured by the patriotic and office-loving Whigs as by the dissatisfied and sullen Tory Opposition, Defoe struck the happy thought of publishing a *Weekly Review of the Affairs of France*, to which was to be added, in every issue, a "little diversion," consisting of a column detailing the most inter-

esting reports of the doings of the Scandalous Club.
Hence, at first, these essays were only a new feature introduced into the newspaper of the day. Defoe's *Review*,
for the first two years and a half, was simply a newspaper,
differing from others chiefly by this column of editorial
matter.   At the end of that period its name was changed
to *Review of the Affairs of the English Nation*, and
from that time it was more fully devoted to social matters.
Its pleasing and humorous expositions of the follies and
extravagances of the men and women of the time are the
direct predecessors of the delightful fancies of the *Tatler*
and *Spectator*. The idea struck the quick and lively mind
of Steele, who had been appointed Government Gazetteer,
that the opportunities he possessed for obtaining the earliest authentic news from the continent would enable him
to issue a journal which would have an advantage over
the numerous newspapers then published in London ; and
that the certainty of thus obtaining a hearing would enable
him to greatly extend the usefulness, interest and pleasure
of papers written in the manner and upon the topics suggested by the essays in Defoe's *Review*. Steele belonged,
by birth, to a family that had been settled by Cromwell on
the confiscated estate of some Irish rebel ; but he possessed all the warm-heartedness, impetuosity and reckless-
ness of the Irish Celt. For some years, but with quite
ordinary results, he had been before the public as a writer
in a somewhat varied character. In his *Christian Hero*,
he had taught virtues he could not practise ; and in
his comedies, *The Tender Husband*, and *The Lying
Lover*, he thought to interest the town without sparkling
dialogue or engaging plot. Need of money drove him, as

it has driven many others, to grasp at the first means of bettering his financial condition. The French war still continued, and its prosecution was creating more intense feeling between the two political parties. Accordingly, on the 12th of April, 1709, Steele sent forth the first number of the *Tatler*. It was a small folio half-sheet of four columns, published three times a week, and purporting to be edited by Isaac Bickerstaff, Esq., a name popularized by Swift ; it was to contain news and advertisements as well as " advices and reflexions ;" to teach " politic persons what to think," and " to afford something of entertainment to the fair sex." " All accounts of gallantry," says the first number, "pleasure and entertainment, shall be under the article of White's Chocolate-house ; poetry, under that of Will's Coffee-house ; learning, under the title of " The Grecian " ; foreign and domestic news you will have from St. James's Coffee-house ; and what else I shall on any other subject offer, shall be dated "from my own apartment." Addison was, in Ireland, as secretary to Lord-Lieutenant Wharton when the *Tatler* appeared. He soon recognised the voice of his old Charterhouse school-fellow, and joined him in his venture, contributing, it is said, sixty-nine of the two hundred and seventy-one papers the *Tatler* contained. They are chiefly visions, dreams or allegories, and form the most charming and vigorous pages of the paper. In January, 1711, the *Tatler* ceased to appear ; and when Steele proposed that a new periodical should be begun and conducted in the same manner, with the improvements which experience had suggested, Addison willingly consented, and the first number of the *Spectator* was issued on the first of March of the same

year. It continued to be published daily, till it had reached
the 555th number, making seven volumes, when it ceased,
on the 6th December, 1712.   It was again revived by Addison on the 18th of June, 1714, and continued to be issued three times a week till the 20th of December of that
year, when, with the completion of the eighth volume and
eightieth number, the new club, which had been less successful than its predecessor, was closed. The price was at
first a penny, but when Bolingbroke's Act came in force,
on the 1st of August, 1712, it was raised to two-pence. The
Spectator does not, like the *Tatler*, go from one coffee-
house to another for its various topics, but is supposed to
be issued by a club, the members of which represent the
chief classes of society.   This club, however, seems to
serve little other purpose than passively to supply materials for Mr. Spectator to discourse upon, and to leave on
the public mind the impression that .there would be such
variety of subjects, interests and modes of treatment, as
would make the paper interesting to every class of readers.
The papers all appear as if written by Mr. Spectator himself, who is president of the club.   Sir Roger de Coverley
figures most prominently, but does not contribute a single
paper, though he affords matter for several of the most delightful essays in the book ; nor do the other members
lend more assistance than the occasional contribution of
a letter.

Of the 635 papers which the *Spectator* contains, it has
been calculated that Addison wrote 274 ; Steele, 240 ; Budgell, 37; Hughes, 11 ; Grove, 4 ; Pope, two or three. About a
score of other papers have been credited to different writers
—Tickell, Swift, Parnell, Phillips, and others ; while there

are over fifty the authorship of which is unknown. Most of the original papers are marked by signatory letters ; those written by Steele by R or T. T was also used by other contributors. Budgell signed X or Z, Pope, Z, and Mr. Addison one of the letters of the word CLIO.

The *Spectator* was at first printed for Sam. Buckley at the Dolphin, and sold by A. Baldwin, in Warwick Lane. From No. 18 appears, in addition, "Charles Lillie [perfumer, bookseller, and secretary to the Tatler's ' Court of Honour '], at the corner of Beaufort Buildings, in the Strand." From August 5th, 1712 (No. 449), Jacob Tonson's imprint is appended. About that time he removed from Gray's Inn Gate to the " Strand, over against Catherine Street."

It seems probable that when Steele and Addison concerted the plan of the *Spectator*, they intended fully to develop the characters of all the members of the club, in order to expose to ridicule many of the follies and vices of the age, and to hold up to public admiration the moderation, morality, and social virtues which they themselves appreciated. If so, this design was never carried out, but, as is pointed out in another place, the different members are disposed of, in some cases at least, before they are more than mere names. Of those that have been more fully portrayed, the chief are from the lively and inventive pen of Steele. The original sketch of all of them, except Mr. Spectator himself, was drawn by his quaint humor. It is to him (assisted by some of the other contributors), that we owe the solid old merchant, Sir Andrew Freeport, and the outline of the member of the Inner Temple. He drew the brave and modest Captain Sentry, and, from his experience in the world, was evolved the well-dressed, genteel Will Honeycomb. With none of these has the public been as fully familiarized as was at first intended; nor was the character of Sir Roger, who is by far the most famous member, carried out as originally proposed. The first sketch of this last was likewise drawn by Steele, but the filling up was left entirely to Addison. He conceived a peculiar fancy for the old knight, and ffave his choicest wit, humor, and pathos to the perfecting of his cherished ideal. The weakness and foibles of the old knight, his superstition, loyalty, bigotry, ignorance and generosity furnish themes upon which his airy fancy, nimble wit, kindly satire and descriptive power seem to revel in sportive glee.

At no period of English history have class-lines been more distinctly drawn than in the reign of Anne and George I. In the country, as well as in the city, the people were divided into classes that were separated from one another by gulfs almost impassable. The lowest was composed of domestics and laborers, who received poor wages, and lived, when not required about the master's house, in miserable unfurnished hovels, without one of the minor comforts of even the modern English farm laborer. Next to these, but scarcely above them, came the farmers and small freeholders. Socially, they held no intercourse with the classes above them. They possessed no learning, resisted all improvement in methods of tilling the land, and lived in a rude and often comfortless domestic condition.

Then followed forty thousand "freeholders of the better sort," possessing an average income of about a hundred pounds per annum. These enjoyed many of the comforts of life unknown to the less wealthy farmers, but socially they had no rank, and were not recognised even by the "gentlemen" and esquires immediately above them, because they could not shew

> " Their ancient, but ignoble blood
> Had crept thro' scoundrels since the flood."

Yet his genealogy upon which the esquire especially prided himself had no power to introduce him to the circles of the nobility, the highest class, from which he was as distinctly and completely separated as from all below him. To this class of country esquires, Sir Roger belongs. His character, as presented in the essays selected for our study, was drawn by the most delicate moralist of that day, and gives, to say the least, the most favorable view of the country gentleman of the period. In Addison's papers all the coarser features of the character have been softened down, or entirely omitted, and the old Tory fox-hunter, who in those days of religious and political animosity looked with contempt and hatred upon the opposite party, is so delineated by the hand of a leading Whig politician as not to court ridicule, much less scorn. In the papers (not included in this selection) written by Steele, a much coarser and more vulgar side of the character is unfolded—a side, it is true, little in keeping with the fine and delicate strokes of Addison's picture, but which, if Steele had been allowed to complete, as he described Sir Roger's love affair and pride of ancestry, not to mention his doubtful London escapade, would have been nearer a real description of the actual squire of Queen Anne's reign. The picture must be regarded as intended to show rather the ideal character

Mr. Spectator considered should be aimed at, than the esquires as they really were. The barbarous hospitality of the period trembled for the " honor of the house if the guest went out sober," but Sir Roger never regaled his friends with anything stronger than Widow Trueby's Water. He fell in with the custom then becoming prevalent of going periodically to London, but while the squire of history is drinking more punch than he can carry and learning to whisper obscene compliments in the ears of ladies in Spring Gardens, or gambling with sharpers, the old knight is at his club or walking in company with a gentleman of most refined literary tastes. Bishop Burnet says " the gentry were ill-taught and ill-bred, haughty and insolent, without patriotism or love of liberty, earnestly desiring the return of tyranny, provided they might be the under-tyrants ; " but our typical old country gentleman reads history, appreciates the learned eloquence of Dr. Barrow, loves a widow who is "a reading lady," "a desperate scholar," belongs to a club of educated gentlemen, has an almost absurd pride in his country and a genuine love for its ancient constitution. He has his little oddities, to be sure, but he has lived alone, and has had his crosses, too —experiences that could not fail to leave effects on the strongest mind. Once more, while the historian's squire is carousing, gambling or horse-racing, Sir Roger is at home providing for the temporal happiness or spiritual welfare of his dependants. It must be admitted that his religious views are rather intolerant towards Dissenters, but comparatively mild when it is remembered that he lived at a time when both Houses of Parliament, as well as the clergy, were so blinded by bigotry and intolerance that they could be satisfied with nothing less than the Occasional Conformity Bill. It must not be forgotten either that much of his apparent political exclusiveness and violence arose from the force of circumstances. We are all compelled, by the customs of society, to be what we would not. Sir Roger deplored the pernicious effects of party divisions; they injured the land-tax and the Game Act, and made "honest gentlemen hate one another;" but in times of such agitation, when important principles (as he thought) were at stake, it behoved him to do all in his power to strengthen the hands of his political friends and weaken their opponents. Then, too, if sincerity is a redeeming feature, he must have full credit for the best intentions. He was no political trickster, but held his views from conviction, and conscientiously supported his church and party.

"When," says Dr. J. R. Green, in the introduction to his *Essays of Addison*, "we cease to study Addison as a statesman or a critic, or a theologian or a moralist, what of him remains? Well, I think we may fairly answer, all that is individually and distinctively Addison. There remains his light and playful fancy. There remains his incomparable humor. There remains, pervading all, his large and generous humanity. I know no writer whose moral temper so perfectly reflects itself in his work. His style, with its free, unaffected movement, its clear distinctness, its graceful transitions, its delicate harmonies, its appropriateness of tone; the temperance and moderation of his treatment, the effortless self-mastery, the sense of quiet power, the absence of exaggeration or extravagance, the perfect keeping with which he deals with his subjects ; or, again, the exquisite reserve, the subtle tenderness, the geniality, the pathos of his humor—what are these but the literary reflexion of Addison himself, of that temper so pure and lofty yet so sympathetic, so strong yet so loveable ? In the midst of that explosion of individuality, of individual energy and force, which marked the eighteenth century, Addison stands out individually, full of force, but of a force harmonious, self-controlled, instinct with the sense of measure, of good taste, good humor, culture, urbanity. It seems natural to him that this temper should find its expression in the highest literature. ' The greatest wits I have conversed with,' he says, ' were men eminent for their humanity ; ' and it is this for which he himself is so eminent as a wit, he is humane. Man is the one interesting thing to him ; he is never weary of tracking out human character into its shyest recesses, of studying human conduct, of watching the play of human thought and feeling, and of contrasting man's infinite capacities of greatness with his infinite capacities of littleness. But the sight stirs in him not only interest, but sympathy ; he looks on it with eyes as keen as those of Swift, but with a calmer and juster intelligence ; and as he looks it moves him not to the ' sæva indignatio ' of the Dean, but to that mingled smile and tear, that blending of ' how wonderful a thing is man,' with, ' but oh ! the pity of it !' which had found equal utterance but once before in Shakespeare. It was the sense of this that won him so wide a love in his own day ; and it is the sense of this that still makes his memory so dear to Englishmen."

ADDISON'S
SIR ROGER DE COVERLEY.

THE AUTHOR'S PREFACE.

[No. 1.

Non fumum ex fulgore, sed ex fumo dare lucem
Cogitat, ut speciosa dehinc miracula promat.
—Hor.

I have observed that a reader seldom peruses a
book with pleasure until he knows whether the writer
of it be a black or a fair man, of a mild or choleric
disposition, married or a bachelor, with other particulars of the like nature, that conduce very much to   5
the right understanding of an author.   To gratify
this curiosity, which is so natural to a reader, I
design this paper, and my next, as prefatory discourses to my following writings, and shall give some
account in them of the several persons that are   10
engaged in this work.   As the chief trouble of com-
piling, digesting, and correcting will fall to my
share, I must do myself the justice to open the
work with my own history.

I was born to a small hereditary estate, which,   15

according to the tradition of the village where it
lies was bounded by the same hedges and ditches
in William the Conqueror's time that it is at present, and has been delivered down from father to
son whole and entire, without the loss or acquisition
of a single field or meadow, during the space of six
hundred years.   My mother has often told me, I
threw away my rattle before I was two months old,
and would not make use of my coral till they had
taken away the bells from it.

As for the rest of my infancy, there being nothing
in it remarkable, I shall pass it over in silence.   I
find, that, during my nonage, I had the reputation of
a very sullen youth, but was always a favourite of
my schoolmaster, who used to say, that my parts
were solid, and would wear well.   I had not been
long at the university, before I distinguished myself
by a most profound silence : for, during the space
of eight years, excepting in the public exercises of
the college, I scarce uttered the quantity of an hundred words ; and indeed do not remember that I
ever spoke three sentences together in my whole life.
Whilst I was in this learned body, I applied myself
with so much diligence to my studies, that there are
very few celebrated books, either in the learned or
the modern tongues, which I am not acquainted
with.

Upon the death of my father I was resolved to
travel into foreign countries, and therefore left the
university with the character of an odd unaccount-
able fellow, that had a great deal of learning, if I

would but show it. An insatiable thirst after knowledge carried me into all the countries of Europe,
in which there was any thing new or strange to be
seen ; nay, to such a degree was my curiosity raised, 50
that having read the controversies of some great men
concerning the antiquities of Egypt, I made a voyage
to Grand Cairo, on purpose to take the measure of a
pyramid ; and, as soon as I had set myself right in
that particular, returned to my native country with 55
great satisfaction.

I have passed my latter years in this city, where
I am frequently seen in most public places, though
there are not above half-a-dozen of my select friends
that know me ; of whom my next paper shall give a 60
more particular account. There is no place of
general resort wherein I do not often make my
appearance : sometimes I am seen thrusting my head
into a round of politicians at Will's, and listening
with great attention to the narratives that are made 65
in those little circular audiences. Sometimes I smoke
a pipe at Child's, and whilst I seem attentive to nothing but the postman, overhear the conversation
of every table in the room. I appear on Sunday
nights at St. James's coffee-house, and sometimes 70
join the little committee of politics in the inner
room, as one who comes there to hear and improve.
My face is likewise very well known at the Grecian,
the Cocoa-Tree, and in the theatres both of Drury-
Lane and the Haymarket. I have been taken for a 75
merchant upon the exchange for above these ten
years, and sometimes pass for a Jew in the assembly

of stock-jobbers at Jonathan's : in short, where-
ever I see a cluster of people, I always mix with
them, though I never open my lips but in my own   80
club.

Thus I live in the world rather as a spectator of
mankind, than as one of the species, by which
means I have made myself a speculative statesman,
soldier, merchant, and artizan, without ever meddling   85
with any practical part in life.   I am very well
versed in the theory of a husband, or a father,
and can discern the errors in the economy, business, and diversion of others, better than those who
are engaged in them ; as standers-by discover blots,   90
which are apt to escape those who are in the game.
I never espoused any party with violence, and am
resolved to observe an exact neutrality between the
Whigs and Tories, unless I shall be forced to declare
myself by the hostilities of either side.   In short, I   95
have acted in all the parts of my life as a looker-on,
which is the character I intend to preserve in this
paper.

I have given the reader just so much of my history and character, as to let him see I am not alto-   100
gether unqualified for the business I have undertaken.   As for other particulars in my life and
adventures, I shall insert them in following papers,
as I shall see occasion.   In the meantime, when I
consider how much I have seen, read, and heard, I   105
begin to blame my own taciturnity ; and since I have
neither time nor inclination to communicate the
fulness of my heart in speech, I am resolved to do

it in writing; and to print myself out, if possible, before I die. I have been often told by my friends 110 that it is a pity so many useful discoveries which I have made, should be in the possession of a silent man. For this reason, therefore, I shall publish a sheet-full of thoughts every morning, for the benefit of my contemporaries : and if I can any way con- 115 tribute to the diversion or improvement of the country in which I live, I shall leave it, when I am summoned out of it, with the secret satisfaction of thinking that I have not lived in vain.

There are three very material points which I have 120 not spoken to in this paper ; and which, for several important reasons, I must keep to myself, at least for some time : I mean, an account of my name, my age, and my lodgings. I must confess I would gratify my reader in any thing that is reasonable ; 125 but as for these three particulars, though I am sensible they might tend very much to the embellishment of my paper, I cannot yet come to a resolution of communicating them to the public. They would indeed draw me out of that obscurity which I have 130 enjoyed for many years, and expose me in public places to several salutes and civilities, which have been always very disagreeable to me ; for the greatest pain I can suffer is the being talked to, and being stared at. It is for this reason, likewise, that I keep 135 my complexion and dress as very great secrets ; though it is not impossible but I may make discoveries of both in the progress of the work I have undertaken.

L

After having been thus particular upon myself, I 140 shall in to-morrow's paper give an account of those gentlemen who are concerned with me in this work. For, as I have before intimated, a plan of it is laid and concerted, as all other matters of importance are, in a club. However, as my friends have 145 engaged me to stand in the front, those who have a mind to correspond with me may direct their letters to the Spectator, at Mr. Buckley's, in Little Britain. For I must further acquaint the reader, that though our club meets only on Tuesdays and Thursdays, 150 we have appointed a committee to sit every night, for the inspection of all such papers as may contribute to the advancement of the public weal.

C.

SIR ROGER DE COVERLEY.

CHAPTER I.

SIR ROGER AND THE CLUB.

——————*Ast alii sex*
Et plures uno conclamant ore.
—Juv.

The first of our society is a gentleman of Worcestershire, of ancient descent, a baronet, his name Sir Roger de Coverley. His great grandfather was inventor of that famous country-dance which is called after him. All who know that shire are very well acquainted with the parts and merits of Sir Roger. He is a gentleman that is very singular in his behaviour, but his singularities proceed from his good sense, and are contradictions to the manners of the world, only as he thinks the world is in the wrong. However, this humour creates him no enemies, for he does nothing with sourness or obstinacy; and his being unconfined to modes and forms, makes him but the readier and more capable to please and oblige all who know him. When he is in town he lives in Soho Square. It is said, he keeps himself a bachelor by reason he was crossed in love by a perverse beautiful widow of the next county to him.

Before this disappointment, Sir Roger was what you call a fine gentleman, had often supped with my Lord Rochester and Sir George Etherege, fought a duel upon his first coming to town, and kicked Bully Dawson in a public coffee-house for calling him youngster. But being ill-used by the above-mentioned widow, he was very serious for a year and a half; and though his temper being naturally jovial, he at last got over it, he grew careless of himself and never dressed afterwards; he continues to wear a coat and doublet of the same cut, that were in fashion at the time of his repulse, which, in his merry humours, he tells us, has been in and out twelve times since he first wore it. He is now in his fifty-sixth year, cheerful, gay, and hearty; keeps a good house in both town and country; a great lover of mankind; but there is such a mirthful cast in his behaviour, that he is rather beloved than esteemed. His tenants grow rich, his servants look satisfied, all the young women profess love to him, and the young men are glad of his company; when he comes into a house he calls the servants by their names, and talks all the way up stairs to a visit. I must not omit that Sir Roger is a justice of the *quorum;* that he fills the chair at a quarter-session with great abilities, and three months ago, gained universal applause by explaining a passage in the game-act.

The gentleman next in esteem and authority among us, is another bachelor, who is a member of the Inner Temple ; a man of great probity, wit,

and understanding; but he has chosen his place of 50
residence rather to obey the direction of an old
humoursome father, than in pursuit of his own inclinations. He was placed there to study the laws
of the land, and is the most learned of any of the
house in those of the stage. Aristotle and Longinus 55
are much better understood by him than Littleton
or Coke. The father sends up every post questions
relating to marriage-articles, leases, and tenures,
in the neighbourhood; all which questions he agrees
with an attorney to answer and take care of in the 60
lump. He is studying the passions themselves,
when he should be inquiring into the debates among
men which arise from them. He knows the argument of each of the orations of Demosthenes and
Tully; but not one case in the reports of our own 65
courts. No one ever took him for a fool, but none,
except his intimate friends, know he has a great
deal of wit. This turn makes him at once both
disinterested and agreeable; as few of his thoughts
are drawn from business, they are most of them fit 70
for conversation. His taste of books is a little too
just for the age he lives in; he has read all, but
approves of very few. His familiarity with the customs, manners, actions, and writings of the ancients,
makes him a very delicate observer of what occurs 75
to him in the present world. He is an excellent
critic, and the time of the play is his hour of
business; exactly at five he passes through New Inn,
crosses through Russell Court; and takes a turn at
Wills' till the play begins; he has his shoes rubbed 80

and his periwig powdered at the barber's, as you go
into the Rose. It is for the good of the audience
when he is at a play, for the actors have an ambition to please him.

The person of next consideration is Sir Andrew   85
Freeport, a merchant of great eminence in the
city of London. A person of indefatigable industry,
strong reason, and great experience. His notions
of trade are noble and generous, and (as every rich
man has usually some sly way of jesting, which   90
would make no great figure were he not a rich man)
he calls the sea the British Common. He is acquainted with commerce in all its parts, and will tell
you that it is a stupid and barbarous way to extend
dominion by arms; for true power is to be got by   95
arts and industry. He will often argue, that if this
part of our trade were well cultivated, we should
gain from one nation,—and if another, from another.
I have heard him prove that diligence makes more
lasting acquisitions than valour, and that sloth has   100
ruined more nations than the sword. He abounds
in several frugal maxims, amongst which the greatest
favourite is, " A penny saved is a penny got." A
general trader of good sense is pleasanter company
than a general scholar; and Sir Andrew having a   105
natural unaffected eloquence, the perspicuity of his
discourse gives the same pleasure that wit would in
another man. He has made his fortunes himself;
and says that England may be richer than other
kingdoms, by as plain methods as he himself is   110
richer than other men; though at the same time I can

say this of him, that there is not a point in the compass but blows home a ship in which he is an
owner.

Next to Sir Andrew in the club-room sits Cap- 115
tain Sentry, a gentleman of great courage, good
understanding, but invincible modesty.   He is one
of those that deserve very well, but are very awkward
at putting their talents within the observation of
such as should take notice of them.   He was some 120
years a captain, and behaved himself with great
gallantry in several engagements, and at several
sieges ; but having a small estate of his own, and
being next heir to Sir Roger, he has quitted a way
of life in which no man can rise suitably to his 125
merit, who is not something of a courtier as well as
a soldier.   I have heard him often lament, that in a
profession where merit is placed in so conspicuous a
view, impudence should get the better of modesty.
When he has talked to this purpose, I never heard 130
him make a sour expression, but frankly confess that
he left the world, because he was not fit for it.   A
strict honesty, and an even regular behaviour, are in
themselves obstacles to him that must press through
crowds, who endeavour at the same end with him- 135
self, the favour of a commander.   He will, however,
in his way of talk, excuse generals, for not disposing according to men's desert, or enquiring into
it : for, says he, that great man who has a mind
to help me, has as many to break through to come at 140
me, as I have to come at him : therefore he will
conclude, that the man who would make a figure,

especially in a military way, must get over all false
modesty, and assist his patron against the importu-
nity of other pretenders, by a proper assurance in 145
his own vindication. He says it is a civil cowardice
to be backward in asserting what you ought to expect,
as it is a military fear to be slow in attacking when
it is your duty. With this candour does the gentleman speak of himself and others. The same frank- 150
ness runs through all his conversation. The military
part of his life has furnished him with many adventures, in the relation of which he is very agreeable
to the company; for he is never over-bearing, though
accustomed to command men in the utmost degree 155
below him ; nor ever too obsequious, from an habit
of obeying men highly above him.

But that our society may not appear a set of hu-
mourists unacquainted with the gallantries and pleasures of the age, we have among us the gallant 160
Will Honeycomb, a gentleman who, according to
his years, should be in the decline of his life, but
having ever been very careful of his person, and
always had a very easy fortune, time has made but
a very little impression, either by wrinkles on his 165
forehead, or traces in his brain. His person is
well turned, and of a good height. He is very
ready at that sort of discourse with which men
usually entertain women. He has all his life
dressed very well, and remembers habits as others 170
do men. He can smile when one speaks to him,
and laughs easily. He knows the history of every
mode, and can inform you from what French

women our wives and daughters had this man-
ner of curling their hair, that way of placing their 175
hoods, and whose vanity to show her foot made
that part of the dress so short in such a year.   In
a word, all his conversation and knowledge have
been in the female world.   As other men of his
age will take notice to you what such a minister 180
said upon such and such an occasion, he will tell
you when the Duke of Monmouth danced at court
such a woman was then smitten, another was taken
with him at the head of his troop in the Park.   For
all these important relations, he has ever about the 185
same time received a kind glance, or a blow of a
fan, from some celebrated beauty, mother of the present lord such-a-one.   This way of talking of his,
very much enlivens the conversation among us of a
more sedate turn ; and I find there is not one of the 190
company but myself, who rarely speak at all, but
speaks of him as of that sort of man, who is usually
called a well-bred fine gentleman.   To conclude his
character, where women are not concerned, he is an
honest worthy man.   195

I cannot tell whether I am to account him whom I
am next to speak of, as one of our company ; for he
visits us but seldom, but when he does, it adds to
every man else a new enjoyment of himself.   He is
a clergyman, a very philosophic man, of general 200
learning, great sanctity of life, and the most exact
good breeding.   He has the misfortune to be of a
very weak constitution, and consequently cannot
accept of such cares and business as preferments in

his function would oblige him to ; he is therefore 205
among divines what a chamber-counsellor is among
lawyers. The probity of his mind, and the integrity of his life, create him followers, as being eloquent or loud advances others. He seldom introduces the subject he speaks upon ; but we are so 210
far gone in years that he observes, when he is among
us, an earnestness to have him fall on some divine
topic, which he always treats with much authority,
as one who has no interests in this world, as one
who is hastening to the object of all his wishes, and 215
conceives hope from his decays and infirmities. ·
These are my ordinary companions.

R.

CHAPTER II.

[No. 106.

COVERLEY HALL.

> ————————*Hic tibi copia*
> *Manabit ad plenum, benigno*
> *Ruris honorum opulenta cornu.*
>
> —Hor.

Having often received an invitation from my friend
Sir Roger de Coverley to pass away a month with him
in the country, I last week accompanied him thither,
and am settled with him for some time at his country-
house, where I intend to form several of my ensuing 5
speculations. Sir Roger, who is very well acquainted
with my humour, lets me rise and go to bed when I
please, dine at his own table or in my chamber as I

think fit, sit still and say nothing without bidding me
be merry. When the gentlemen of the county come
to see him, he only shows me at a distance. As I
have been walking in his fields, I have observed them
stealing a sight of me over an hedge, and have heard
the knight desiring them not to let me see them, for
that I hated to be stared at.

I am the more at ease in Sir Roger's family, because
it consists of sober and staid persons; for, as the
knight is the best master in the world, he seldom
changes his servants; and, as he is beloved by all
about him, his servants never care for leaving him;
by this means his domestics are all in years, and grown
old with their master. You would take his *valet-de-chambre* for his brother, his butler is grey-headed, his
groom is one of the gravest men that I have ever seen,
and his coachman has the looks of a privy-councillor.
You see the goodness of the master even in the old
house-dog, and in a grey pad that is kept in the stable
with great care and tenderness out of regard to his
past services, though he has been useless for several
years.

I could not but observe with a great deal of pleasure
the joy that appeared in the countenances of these
ancient domestics, upon my friend's arrival at his
country seat. Some of them could not refrain from
tears at the sight of their old master; every one of
them pressed forward to do something for him, and
seemed discouraged if they were not employed. At
the same time the good old knight, with the mixture
of the father and master of the family, tempered the

inquiries after his own affairs with several kind ques- 40
tions relating to themselves. This humanity and good
nature engages everybody to him, so that when he is
pleasant upon any of them, all his family are in good
humour, and none so much as the person whom he
diverts himself with ; on the contrary, if he coughs, 45
or betrays any infirmity of old age, it is easy for a
stander-by to observe a secret concern in the looks of
all his servants.

My worthy friend has put me under the particular
care of his butler, who is a very prudent man, and, as 50
well as the rest of his fellow-servants, wonderfully desirous of pleasing me, because they have often heard
their master talk of me as of his particular friend.

My chief companion, when Sir Roger is diverting
himself in the woods or the fields, is a very venerable 55
man, who is ever with Sir Roger, and has lived at his
house in the nature of a chaplain above thirty years.
This gentleman is a person of good sense and some
learning, of a very regular life and obliging conversation. He heartily loves Sir Roger, and knows that 60
he is very much in the old knight's esteem, so that
he lives in the family rather as a relation than a de-
pendant.

I have observed in several of my papers, that my
friend Sir Roger, amidst all his good qualities, is 65
something of an humorist ; and that his virtues, as
well as imperfections, are as it were tinged by a certain extravagance, which makes them particularly his,
and distinguishes them from those of other men. This
cast of mind, as it is generally very innocent in itself, 70

so it renders his conversation highly agreeable, and
more delightful than the same degree of sense and
virtue would appear in their common and ordinary
colours. As I was walking with him last night, he
asked me how I liked the good man whom I have just 75
now mentioned; and without staying for my answer,
told me that he was afraid of being insulted with Latin
and Greek at his own table; for which reason he desired a particular friend of his at the university to find
him out a clergyman rather of plain sense than much 80
learning, of a good aspect, a clear voice, a sociable
temper, and, if possible, a man that understood a little
of backgammon. "My friend," says Sir Roger,
"found me out this gentleman, who, besides the endowments required of him, is, they tell me, a good 85
scholar, though he does not show it. I have given
him the parsonage of the parish; and because I know
his value, have settled upon him a good annuity for
life. If he outlives me, he shall find that he was higher
in my esteem than perhaps he thinks he is. He has 90
now been with me thirty years; and though he does
not know I have taken notice of it, has never in all
that time asked anything of me for himself, though he
is every day soliciting me for something in behalf of
one or other of my tenants, his parishioners. There 95
has not been a lawsuit in the parish since he has lived
among them; if any dispute arises, they apply themselves to him for the decision; if they do not acquiesce
in his judgment, which I think never happened above
once or twice at most, they appeal to me. At his first 100
settling with me, I made him a present of all the

good sermons which have been printed in English, and only begged of him, that every Sunday he would pronounce one of them in the pulpit. Accordingly, he has digested them into such a series, that they follow one another naturally, and make a continued system of practical divinity." 105

As Sir Roger was going on with his story, the gentleman we were talking of came up to us; and upon the knight's asking him who preached to-mor- 110 row (for it was Saturday night), told us, the Bishop of St. Asaph in the morning, and Dr. South in the afternoon. He then showed us his list of preachers for the whole year, where I saw with a great deal of pleasure Archbishop Tillotson, Bishop Saunderson, 115 Dr. Barrow, Dr. Calamy, with several living authors, who have published discourses of practical divinity. I no sooner saw this venerable man in the pulpit, but I very much approved of my friend's insisting upon the qualifications of a good aspect and a clear voice ; 120 for I was so charmed with the gracefulness of his figure and delivery, as well as with the discourses he pronounced, that I think I never passed any time more to my satisfaction. A sermon repeated after this manner is like the composition of a poet in the 125 mouth of a graceful actor.

I could heartily wish that more of our country clergy would follow this example, and instead of wasting their spirits in laborious compositions of their own, would endeavour after a handsome elocution, and all 130 those other talents that are proper to enforce what has been penned by greater masters. This would not only be more easy to themselves, but more edifying to the people.

L.

CHAPTER III.

[No. 108.

THE COVERLEY GUEST.

Gratis anhelans, multa agendo nihil agens.
—Phæd.

As I was yesterday morning walking with Sir Roger before his house, a country-fellow brought him a huge fish, which, he told him, Mr. Will Wimble had caught that morning; and that he presented it, with his service to him, and intended to come and dine with him. At the same time he delivered a letter, which my friend read to me as soon as the messenger left him :—

"Sir Roger,

"I desire you to accept of a jack, which is the best I have caught this season. I intend to come and stay with you a week, and see how the perch bite in the Black River. I observed with some concern, the last time I saw you upon the bowling-green, that your whip wanted a lash to it; I will bring half a dozen with me that I twisted last week, which I hope will serve you all the time you are in the country. I have not been out of the saddle for six days past, having been at Eton with Sir John's eldest son. He takes to his learning hugely. I am,

"Sir, your humble servant,

"Will Wimble."

This extraordinary letter, and message that accompanied it, made me very curious to know the character and quality of the gentleman who sent them ; which I found to be as follows : Will Wimble is younger brother to a baronet, and descended of the ancient family of the Wimbles.   He is now between forty and fifty : but being bred to no business, and born to no estate, he generally lives with his elder brother as superintendent of his game.   He hunts a pack of dogs better than any man in the country, and is very famous for finding out a hare.   He is extremely well versed in all the little handicrafts of an idle man : he makes a May-fly to a miracle ; and furnishes the whole country with angle-rods.   As he is a good-natured officious fellow, and very much esteemed upon account of his family, he is a welcome guest at every house, and keeps up a good correspondence among all the gentlemen about him.   He carries a tulip-root in his pocket from one to another, or exchanges a puppy between a couple of friends that live perhaps in the opposite sides of the county. Will is a particular favourite of all the young heirs, whom he frequently obliges with a net that he has weaved, or a setting-dog that he has made himself. He now and then presents a pair of garters of his own knitting to their mothers or sisters ; and raises a great deal of mirth among them, by enquiring as often as he meets them, how they wear ? These gentleman-like manufactures and obliging little humours, make Will the darling of the country.

Sir Roger was proceeding in the character of

him, when we saw him make up to us with two or
three hazel-twigs in his hand that he had cut in Sir 55
Roger's woods, as he came through them, in his
way to the house. I was very much pleased to observe on one side the hearty and sincere welcome
with which Sir Roger received him, and on the
other, the secret joy which his guest discovered at 60
sight of the good old knight. After the first salutes
were over, Will desired Sir Roger to lend him
one of his servants to carry a set of shuttlecocks
he had with him in a little box, to a lady that lived
about a mile off, to whom it seems he had pro- 65
mised such a present for above this half-year. Sir
Roger's back was no sooner turned but honest
Will began to tell me of a large cock-pheasant
that he had sprung in one of the neighbouring
woods, with two or three other adventures of the 70
same nature. Odd and uncommon characters are
the game that I look for, and most delight in ; for
which reason I was as much pleased with the novelty of the person that talked to me, as he could be
for his life with the springing of a pheasant, and 75
therefore listened to him with more than ordinary
attention.

In the midst of his discourse the bell rung to
dinner, where the gentleman I have been speaking
of had the pleasure of seeing the huge jack he had 80
caught served up for the first dish in a most sumptu-
ous manner. Upon our sitting down to it he gave
us a long account how he had hooked it, played with
it, foiled it, and at length drew it out upon the bank,

with several other particulars that lasted all the first 85
course. A dish of wild fowl that came afterwards
furnished conversation for the rest of the dinner,
which concluded with a late invention of Will's for
improving the quail-pipe.

Upon withdrawing into my room after dinner, I 90
was secretly touched with compassion towards the
honest gentleman that had dined with us ; and could
not but consider with a great deal of concern, how
so good an heart and such busy hands were wholly
employed in trifles ; that so much humanity should 95
be so little beneficial to others, and so much industry
so little advantageous to himself. The same temper
of mind and application to affairs might have recommended him to the public esteem, and have
raised his fortune in another station of life. What 100
good to his country or himself might not a trader
or merchant have done with such useful though ordinary qualifications !

Will Wimble's is the case of many a younger
brother of a great family, who had rather see their 105
children starve like gentlemen, than thrive in a
trade or profession that is beneath their quality.
This humour fills several parts of Europe with
pride and beggary. It is the happiness of a trad-
ing nation, like ours, that the younger sons, though 110
incapable of any liberal art or profession, may be
placed in such a way of life, as may perhaps enable
them to vie with the best of their family : accordingly we find several citizens that were launched
into the world with narrow fortunes, rising by an 115

honest industry to greater estates than those of their elder brothers. It is not improbable but Will was formerly tried at divinity, law, or physic; and that finding his genius did not lie that way, his parents gave him up at length to his own inven- 120 tions. But certainly, however improper he might have been for studies of a higher nature, he was perfectly well turned for the occupations of trade and commerce.

L.

CHAPTER IV.

[No. 110.

THE COVERLEY GHOST.

Horror ubique animos, simul ipsa silentia terrent.
—Virg.

At a little distance from Sir Roger's house, among the ruins of an old abbey, there is a long walk of aged elms; which are shot up so very high, that when one passes under them, the rooks and crows that rest upon the tops of them seem to be 5 cawing in another region. I am very much delighted with this sort of noise, which I consider as a kind of natural prayer to that Being who supplies the wants of his whole creation, and who, in the beautiful language of the Psalms, feedeth the young ravens 10 that call upon him. I like this retirement the better, because of an ill report it lies under of being haunted; for which reason (as I have been told in the family) no living creature ever walks in it be-

sides the chaplain. My good friend the butler desired me with a very grave face not to venture myself in it after sunset, for that one of the footmen
had been almost frightened out of his wits by a
spirit that appeared to him in the shape of a black
horse without an head ; to which he added, that
about a month ago one of the maids coming home
late that way with a pail of milk upon her head,
heard such a rustling among the bushes that she let
it fall.

I was taking a walk in this place last night between the hours of nine and ten, and could not but
fancy it one of the most proper scenes in the world
for a ghost to appear in. The ruins of the abbey
are scattered up and down on every side, and half
covered with ivy and elder bushes, the harbours of
several solitary birds, which seldom make their appearance till the dusk of the evening. The place
was formerly a churchyard, and has still several
marks in it of graves and burying-places. There is
such an echo among the old ruins and vaults, that
if you stamp but a little louder than ordinary, you
hear the sound repeated. At the same time the
walk of elms, with the croaking of the ravens,
which, from time to time, are heard from the tops of
them, looks exceedingly solemn and venerable. These
objects naturally raise seriousness and attention ;
and when night heightens the awfulness of the
place, and pours out her supernumerary horrors upon
everything in it, I do not at all wonder that weak
minds fill it with spectres and apparitions.

Mr. Locke, in his chapter of the Association of Ideas,* has very curious remarks to shew how by the prejudice of education one idea often introduces into the mind a whole set that bear no resemblance to one another in the nature of things. Among several examples of this kind, he produces the following instance:—The ideas of goblins and sprites have really no more to do with darkness than light ; yet let but a foolish maid inculcate these often on the mind of a child, and raise them there together, possibly he shall never be able to separate them again so long as he lives ; but darkness shall ever afterwards bring with it those frightful ideas, and they shall be so joined, that he can no more bear the one than the other.

As I was walking in this solitude, where the dusk of the evening conspired with so many other occasions of terror, I observed a cow grazing not far from me, which an imagination that is apt to startle might easily have construed into a black horse without an head ; and I daresay the poor footman lost his wits upon some such trivial occasion.

My friend Sir Roger has often told me, with a great deal of mirth, that at his first coming to his estate he found three parts of his house altogether useless ; that the best room in it had the reputation of being haunted, and by that means was locked up ; that noises had been heard in his long gallery, so

---

* Locke's " Essay on the Human Understanding." Book II., chap. 33.

that he could not get a servant to enter it after eight o'clock at night ; that the door of one of his cham- 75 bers was nailed up, because there went a story in the family that a butler had formerly hanged himself in it ; and that his mother, who lived to a great age, had shut up half the rooms in the house, in which either her husband, a son, or daughter had died. 80 The knight seeing his habitation reduced to so small a compass, and himself in a manner shut out of his own house, upon the death of his mother ordered all the apartments to be flung open, and exorcised by his chaplain, who lay in every room 85 one after another, and by that means dissipated the fears which had so long reigned in the family.

I should not have been thus particular upon these ridiculous horrors, did I not find them so very much prevail in all parts of the country. At the same time 90 I think a person who is thus terrified with the ima- gination of ghosts and spectres much more reason- able than one who, contrary to the reports of all historians sacred and profane, ancient and modern, and to the traditions of all nations, thinks the 95 appearance of spirits fabulous and groundless. Could not I give myself up to this general testimony of mankind, I should to the relations of particular persons who are now living, and whom I cannot dis- trust in other matters of fact. I might here add, 100 that not only the historians, to whom we may join the poets, but likewise the philosophers of antiquity, have favoured this opinion. Lucretius himself, though by the course of his philosophy he was

obliged to maintain that the soul did not exist sepa-   105
rate from the body, makes no doubt of the reality
of apparitions, and that men have often appeared
after their death.   This I think very remarkable ;
he was so pressed with the matter of fact, which he
could not have the confidence to deny, that he was 110
forced to account for it by one of the most absurd
unphilosophical notions that was ever started.   He
tells us, that the surfaces of all bodies are perpetually flying off from their respective bodies, one after
another ; and that these surfaces or thin cases that 115
included each other whilst they were joined in the
body like the coats of an onion, are sometimes seen
entire when they are separated from it ; by which
means we often behold the shapes and shadows of
persons who are either dead or absent.   120

L.

CHAPTER V.

[No 112.

THE COVERLEY SUNDAY.

'Αθανάτους μεν πρῶτα θεοὺς, νόμῳ ὡς διάκειται.
Τιμᾰ————   —Pyth.

I am always very well pleased with a country Sunday ; and think, if keeping holy the seventh day
were were only a human institution, it would be
the best method that could have been thought of for
the polishing and civilizing of mankind. It is certain   5
the country people would soon degenerate into a

kind of savages and barbarians, were there not such frequent returns of a stated time, in which the whole village meet together with their best faces, and in their cleanliest habits, to converse with one another upon indifferent subjects, hear their duties explained to them, and join together in adoration of the Supreme Being. Sunday clears away the rust of the whole week, not only as it refreshes in their minds the notions of religion, but as it puts both the sexes upon appearing in their most agreeable forms, and exerting all such qualities as are apt to give them a figure in the eye of the village. A country fellow distinguishes himself as much in the churchyard, as a citizen does upon the 'Change, the whole parish politics being generally discussed in that place either after sermon or before the bell rings.

My friend Sir Roger, being a good churchman, has beautified the inside of his church with several texts of his own choosing. He has likewise given a handsome pulpit-cloth, and railed in the communion table at his own expense. He has often told me, that at his coming to his estate he found his parishioners very irregular; and that in order to make them kneel and join in the responses, he gave every one of them a hassock and a Common Prayer Book; and at the same time employed an itinerant singing-master, who goes about the country for that purpose, to instruct them rightly in the tunes of the psalms; upon which they now very much value themselves, and indeed outdo most of the country churches that I have ever heard.   .

As Sir Roger is landlord to the whole congregation, he keeps them in very good order, and will suffer nobody to sleep in it besides himself; for if by chance he has been surprised into a short nap at sermon, upon recovering out of it he stands up and looks about him, and if he sees anybody else nodding, either wakes them himself, or sends his servant to them. Several other of the old knight's particularities break out upon these occasions. Sometimes he will be lengthening out a verse in the singing-psalms, half a minute after the rest of the congregation have done with it; sometimes, when he is pleased with the matter of his devotion, he pronounces Amen three or four times to the same prayer; and sometimes stands up when everybody else is upon their knees, to count the congregation, or see if any of his tenants are missing.

I was yesterday very much surprised to hear my old friend, in the midst of the service, calling out to one John Matthews to mind what he was about, and not disturb the congregation. This John Matthews, it seems, is remarkable for being an idle fellow, and at that time was kicking his heels for his diversion. This authority of the knight, though exerted in that odd manner which accompanies him in all circumstances of life, has a very good effect upon the parish, who are not polite enough to see any thing ridiculous in his behaviour; besides that the general good sense and worthiness of his character makes his friends observe these little singularities as foils that rather set off than blemish his good qualities. 70

As soon as the sermon is finished, nobody presumes to stir till Sir Roger is gone out of the church. The knight walks down from his seat in the chancel between a double row of his tenants, that stand bowing to him on each side ; and every now and then 75 enquires how such an one's wife, or mother, or son, or father do, whom he does not see at church ; which is understood as a secret reprimand to the person that is absent.

The chaplain has often told me, that upon a cate- 80 chising day, when Sir Roger has been pleased with a boy that answers well, he has ordered a Bible to be given him next day for his encouragement ; and sometimes accompanies it with a flitch of bacon to his mother. Sir Roger has likewise added five 85 pounds a year to the clerk's place ; and that he may encourage the young fellows to make themselves perfect in the church service, has promised, upon the death of the present incumbent, who is very old, to bestow it according to merit. 90

The fair understanding between Sir Roger and his chaplain, and their mutual concurrence in doing good, is the more remarkable, because the very next village is famous for the differences and contentions that rise between the parson and the squire, who 95 live in a perpetual state of war. The parson is always preaching at the squire, and the squire to be revenged on the parson never comes to church.

The squire has made all his tenants atheists and
tithe-stealers; while the parson instructs them every 100
Sunday in the dignity of his order, and insinuates
to them in almost every sermon that he is a better
man than his patron.   In short, matters are come
to such an extremity, that the squire has not said
his prayers either in public or private this half year; 105
and that the parson threatens him, if he does not
mend his manners, to pray for him in the face of the
whole congregation.

Feuds of this nature, though too frequent in the
country, are very fatal to the ordinary people; who 110
are so used to be dazzled with riches, that they pay
as much deference to the understanding of a man
of an estate, as of a man of learning; and are very
hardly brought to regard any truth, how important
soever it may be, that is preached to them, when they 115
know there are several men of five hundred a year
who do not believe it.

L.

CHAPTER VI.

[No. 115.

THE COVERLEY EXERCISE.

> ———*Ut sit mens sana in corpore sano.*
> —Juv.

Bodily labour is of two kinds, either that which
a man submits to for his livelihood, or that which
he undergoes for his pleasure.   The latter of them

generally changes the name of labour for that of
exercise, but differs only from ordinary labour as it
rises from another motive.

A country life abounds in both these kinds of
labour, and for that reason gives a man a greater
stock of health, and consequently a more perfect
enjoyment of himself, than any other way of life.
I consider the body as a system of tubes and glands,
or, to use a more rustic phrase, a bundle of pipes
and strainers, fitted to one another after so wonderful
a manner as to make a proper engine for the soul to
work with. This description does not only comprehend the bowels, bones, tendons, veins, nerves and
arteries, but every muscle and every ligature, which
is a composition of fibres, that are so many imper-
ceptible tubes or pipes interwoven on all sides with
invisible glands or strainers.

This general idea of a human body, without considering it in its niceties of anatomy, lets us see how
absolutely necessary labour is for the right preservation of it. There must be frequent motions and agi-
tations, to mix, digest, and separate the juices contained in it, as well as to clear and cleanse that
infinitude of pipes and strainers of which it is composed, and to give their solid parts a more firm and
lasting tone. Labour or exercise ferments the humours,
casts them into their proper channels, throws off re-
dundancies, and helps nature in those secret distribu-
tions, without which the body cannot subsist in its
vigour, nor the soul act with cheerfulness.

I might here mention the effects which this has

upon all the faculties of the mind, by keeping the
understanding clear, the imagination untroubled, and
refining those spirits that are necessary for the proper
exertion of our intellectual faculties, during the present laws of union between soul and body. It is to a
neglect in this particular that we must ascribe the
spleen, which is so frequent in men of studious and
sedentary tempers, as well as the vapours, to which
those of the other sex are so often subject.

Had not exercise been absolutely necessary for our
well-being, nature would not have made the body so
proper for it, by giving such an activity to the limbs,
and such a pliancy to every part, as necessarily produce those compressions, extensions, contortions,
dilatations, and all other kinds of motions that are
necessary for the preservation of such a system of
tubes and glands as has been before mentioned. And
that we might not want inducements to engage us in
such an exercise of the body as is proper for its welfare, it is so ordered that nothing valuable can be procured without it. Not to mention riches and honour,
even food and raiment are not to be come at without
the toil of the hands and sweat of the brows. Providence furnishes materials, but expects that we should
work them up ourselves. The earth must be laboured
before it gives its increase, and when it is forced into
its several products, how many hands must they pass
through before they are fit for use? Manufactures,
trade, and agriculture, naturally employ more than
nineteenth parts of the species in twenty; and as for
those who are not obliged to labour, by the condition

in which they are born, they are more miserable than the rest of mankind, unless they indulge themselves in that voluntary labour which goes by the name of exercise.

My friend Sir Roger has been an indefatigable man in business of this kind, and has hung several parts of his house with the trophies of his former labours. The walls of his great hall are covered with the horns of several kinds of deer that he has killed in the chace, which he thinks the most valuable furniture of his house, as they afford him frequent topics of discourse, and shew that he has not been idle. At the lower end of the hall, is a large otter's skin stuffed with hay, which his mother ordered to be hung up in that manner, and the knight looks upon it with great satisfaction, because it seems he was but nine years old when his dog killed him. A little room adjoining to the hall is a kind of arsenal filled with guns of several sizes and inventions, with which the knight has made great havoc in the woods, and destroyed many thousands of pheasants, partridges and woodcocks. His stable doors are patched with noses that belonged to foxes of the knight's own hunting down. Sir Roger shewed me one of them that for distinction's sake has a brass nail stuck through it, which cost him about fifteen hours' riding, carried him through half a dozen counties, killed him a brace of geldings, and lost about half his dogs. This the knight looks upon as one of the greatest exploits of his life. The perverse widow, whom I have given some account of, was the death of several foxes; for

Sir Roger has told me that in the course of his
amours he patched the western door of his stable.
Whenever the widow was cruel, the foxes were sure
to pay for it. In proportion as his passion for the 100
widow abated and old age came on, he left off fox-
hunting ; but a hare is not yet safe that sits within
ten miles of his house.

There is no kind of exercise which I would so recommend to my readers of both sexes as this of riding, 105
as there is none which so much conduces to health,
and is every way accommodated to the body, according to the idea which I have given of it. Dr. Sydenham is very lavish in its praises ; and if the English
reader will see the mechanical effects of it described 110
at length, he may find them in a book published not
many years since, under the title of " Medicina Gymnastica." For my own part, when I am in town, for
want of these opportunities, I exercise myself an hour
every morning upon a dumb-bell that is placed in 115
a corner of my room, and pleases me the more because it does everything I require of it in the most
profound silence. My landlady and her daughters
are so well acquainted with my hours of exercise, that
they never come into my room to disturb me whilst 120
I am ringing.

When I was some years younger than I am at present, I used to employ myself in a more laborious
diversion, which I learned from a Latin treatise of
exercises that is written with great erudition : It is 125
there called the σκιομαχία, or the fighting with a
man's own shadow, and consists in the brandishing

of two short sticks grasped in each hand, and loaden
with plugs of lead at either end. This opens the
chest, exercises the limbs, and gives a man all the 13c
pleasure of boxing without the blows. I could wish
that several learned men would lay out that time
which they employ in controversies and disputes
about nothing, in this method of fighting with their
own shadows. It might conduce very much to evap- 135
orate the spleen, which makes them uneasy to the
public as well as to themselves.

   To conclude, as I am a compound of soul and body,
I consider myself as obliged to a double scheme of
duties ; and I think I have not fulfilled the business 14c
of the day when I do not thus employ the one in
labour and exercise, as well as the other in study and
contemplation.

L.

CHAPTER VII.

[No. 117.

THE COVERLEY WITCH.

———*Ipsi sibi somnia fingunt.*
—Virg.

There are some opinions in which a man should
stand neuter, without engaging his assent to one side
or the other. Such a hovering faith as this, which re-
fuses to settle upon any determination, is absolutely
necessary to a mind that is careful to avoid errors   5
and prepossessions. When the arguments press
equally on both sides in matters that are indifferent

to us, the safest method is to give up ourselves to neither.

It is with this temper of mind that I consider the subject of witchcraft. When I hear the relations that are made from all parts of the world, not only from Norway and Lapland, from the East and West Indies, but from every particular nation in Europe, I cannot forbear thinking that there is such an intercourse and commerce with evil spirits, as that which we express by the name of witchcraft. But when I consider that the ignorant and credulous parts of the world abound most in these relations, and that the persons among us, who are supposed to engage in such an infernal commerce, are people of a weak understanding and a crazed imagination, and at the same time reflect upon the many impostures and delusions of this nature that have been detected in all ages, I endeavour to suspend my belief till I hear more certain accounts than any which have yet come to my knowledge. In short, when I consider the question, whether there are such persons in the world as those we call witches, my mind is divided between the two opposite opinions; or rather (to speak my thoughts freely) I believe in general that there is and has been such a thing as witchcraft; but at the same time can give no credit to any particular instance of it.

I am engaged in this speculation, by some occurrences that I met with yesterday, which I shall give my reader an account of at large. As I was walking with my friend Sir Roger by the side of one of his woods, an old woman applied herself to me for my charity. Her dress and figure put me in mind of the following description in Otway.   40

> *In a close lane, as I pursued my journey,*
> *I spied a wrinkled hag, with age grown double,*
> *Picking dry sticks, and mumbling to herself.*
> *Her eyes with scalding rheum were gall'd and red,*
> *Cold palsy shook her head; her hands seemed wither'd;*   45
> *And on her crooked shoulders had she wrap't*
> *The tatter'd remnants of an old striped hanging,*
> *Which served to keep her carcass from the cold:*
> *So there was nothing of a piece about her.*
> *Her lower weeds were all o'er coarsely patch'd*   50
> *With diff'rent-colour'd rags, black, red, white, yellow,*
> *And seemed to speak variety of wretchedness.*

As I was musing on this description, and comparing it with the object before me, the knight told me that this very old woman had the reputation of a witch   55 all over the country, that her lips were observed to be always in ·motion, and that there was not a switch about her house which her neighbours did not believe had carried her several hundreds of miles.   If she chanced to stumble, they always found sticks or   60 straws that lay in the figure of a cross before her. If she made any mistake at church, and cried Amen in the wrong place, they never failed to conclude that she was saying her prayers backwards.   There was not a maid in the parish that would take a pin of her,   65 though she would offer a bag of money with it.   She goes by the name of Moll White, and has made the country ring with several imaginary exploits which are palmed upon her.   If the dairy maid does not make

her butter come so soon as she would have it, Moll 70
White is at the bottom of the churn. If a horse
sweats in the stable, Moll White has been upon his
back. If a hare makes an unexpected escape from
the hounds, the huntsman curses Moll White. Nay,
(says Sir Roger) I have known the master of the pack, 75
upon such an occasion, send one of his servants to
see if Moll White had been out that morning.

This account raised my curiosity so far, that I begged my friend Sir Roger to go with me into her hovel,
which stood in a solitary corner under the side of the 80
wood. Upon our first entering Sir Roger winked to
me, and pointed at something that stood behind the
door, which, upon looking that way, I found to be an
old broom-staff. At the same time he whispered me
in the ear to take notice of a tabby cat that sat in the 85
chimney-corner, which, as the old knight told me,
lay under as bad a report as Moll White herself; for
besides that Moll is said often to accompany her in
the same shape, the cat is reported to have spoken
twice or thrice in her life, and to have played several 90
pranks above the capacity of an ordinary cat.

I was secretly concerned to see human nature in so
much wretchedness and disgrace, but at the same
time could not forbear smiling to hear Sir Roger,
who is a little puzzled about the old woman, advising 95
her as a justice of the peace to avoid all communication with the devil, and never to hurt any of her
neighbours' cattle. We concluded our visit with a
bounty, which was very acceptable.

In our return home, Sir Roger told me, that old 100

Moll had been often brought before him for making
children spit pins, and giving maids the night-mare ;
and that the country people would be tossing her into
a pond and trying experiments with her every day, if
it was not for him and his chaplain.   105

I have since found upon enquiry, that Sir Roger
was several times staggered with the reports that
had been brought him concerning this old woman,
and would frequently have bound her over to the
county sessions, had not his chaplain with much ado 110
persuaded him to the contrary.

I have been the more particular in this account,
because I hear there is scarce a village in England
that has not a Moll White in it. When an old
woman begins to doat, and grow chargeable to a 115
parish, she is generally turned into a witch, and fills
the whole country with extravagant fancies, imaginary distempers, and terrifying dreams. In the mean
time, the poor wretch that is the innocent occasion
of so many evils begins to be frighted at herself, 120
and sometimes confesses secret commerces and famil-
iarities that her imagination forms in a delirious old
age.   This frequently cuts off charity from the greatest objects of compassion, and inspires people with
a malevolence towards those poor decrepid parts of 125
our species, in whom human nature is defaced by
infirmity and dotage.

                                             L.

CHAPTER VIII.

[No. 121.

ON INSTINCT.

*——Equidem credo, quia sit Divinitus illis
Ingenium————.*
—Virg.

As I was walking this morning in the great yard that belongs to my friend's country house, I was wonderfully pleased to see the different workings of instinct in a hen followed by a brood of ducks. The young, upon the sight of a pond, immediately ran into it; while the step-mother, with all imaginable anxiety, hovered about the borders of it, to call them out of an element that appeared to her so dangerous and destructive. As the different principle which acted in these different animals cannot be termed reason, so, when we call it instinct, we mean something we have no knowledge of. To me, as I hinted in my last paper, it seems the immediate direction of Providence, and such an operation of the Supreme Being as that which determines all the portions of matter to their proper centres. A modern philosopher, quoted by Monsieur Bayle, in his learned dissertation on the souls of brutes, delivers the same opinion, though in a bolder form of words, where he says *Deus est animi brutorum*, God himself is the soul of brutes. Who can tell what to call that seeming sagacity in animals, which directs them to such food as is proper for them and makes them naturally avoid whatever is noxious or unwholesome? Tully has observed, that a lamb no

sooner falls from its mother, but immediately and of 25
its own accord it applies itself to the teat.   Dampier,
in his travels, tells us, that when seamen are thrown
upon any of the unknown coasts of America, they
never venture upon the fruit of any tree, how tempt-
ing soever it may appear, unless they observe that it 30
is marked by the peckings of birds, but fall on without any fear or apprehension where the birds have
been before them.

But notwithstanding animals have nothing like the
use of reason, we find in them all the lower parts of 35
our nature, the passions and senses, in their greatest
strength and perfection.   And here it is worth our
observation, that all beasts and birds of prey are wonderfully subject to anger, malice, revenge, and all the
other violent passions that may animate them in 40
search of their own proper food ; as those that are
incapable of defending themselves, or annoying
others, or whose safety lies chiefly in their flight, are
suspicious, fearful and apprehensive of everything
they see or hear ; whilst others that are of assistance 45
and use to man have their natures softened with something mild and tractable, and by that means are
qualified for a domestic life.   In this case the passions
generally correspond with the make of the body.   We
do not find the fury of a lion in so weak and defence- 50
less an animal as a lamb, nor the meekness of a lamb
in a creature so armed for battle and assault as the
lion.   In the same manner, we find that particular
animals have a more or less exquisite sharpness
and sagacity in those particular senses which most 55

turn to their advantage, and in which their safety and welfare is the most concerned.

Nor must we here omit that great variety of arms with which nature has differently fortified the bodies of several kinds of animals, such as claws, hoofs and horns, teeth and tusks, a tail, a sting, a trunk or a proboscis. It is likewise observed by naturalists, that it must be some hidden principle distinct from what we call reason, which instructs animals in the use of these their arms, and teaches them to manage them to the best advantage ; because they naturally defend themselves with that part in which their strength lies, before the weapon be formed in it : as is remarkable in lambs, which though they are bred within doors, and never saw the actions of their own species, push at those who approach them with their foreheads, before the first budding of a horn appear.

I shall add to these general observations an instance which Mr. Locke has given us of Providence, even in the imperfections of a creature which seems the meanest and most despicable in the whole animal world. " We may," says he, " from the make of an oyster, or a cockle, conclude that it has not so many nor so quick senses as a man, or several other animals ; nor if it had, would it, in that state and incapacity of transferring itself from one place to another, be bettered by them. What good would sight and hearing do to a creature that cannot move itself to or from the object, wherein at a distance it perceives good or evil ? And would not quickness of sensation be an inconvenience to an animal that must be still

where chance has once placed it, and these receive
the afflux of colder or warmer, clean or foul water,
as it happens to come to it?"

I shall add to this instance out of Mr. Locke 90
another out of the learned Dr. More, who cites it from
Cardan, in relation to another animal which Providence has left defective, but at the same time has
shown its wisdom in the formation of that organ in
which it seems chiefly to have failed. "What is more 95
obvious and ordinary than a mole? and yet what more
palpable argument of Providence than she? the members of her body are so exactly fitted to her nature
and manner of life; for her dwelling being under
ground, where nothing is to be seen, nature has so 100
obscurely fitted her with eyes, that naturalists can
hardly agree whether she have any sight at all or no.
But for amends, what she is capable of for her defence and warning of danger, she has very eminently
conferred upon her; for she is exceeding quick of 105
hearing. And then her short tail and short legs, but
broad fore feet armed with sharp claws, we see by the
event to what purpose they are, she so swiftly working herself under ground, and making her way so fast in
the earth, as they that behold it cannot but admire it. 110
Her legs therefore are short, that she need dig no
more than will serve the mere thickness of her body;
and her fore feet are broad that she may scoop away
much earth at a time; and little or no tail she has,
because she courses it not on the ground, like the rat 115
or the mouse, of whose kindred she is, but lives under

the earth, and is fain to dig herself a dwelling there. And she making her way through so thick an element, which will not yield easily, as the air or the water, it had been dangerous to have drawn so long a train 120 behind her ; for her enemy might fall upon her rear, and fetch her out, before she had completed or got full possession of her works."

I cannot forbear mentioning Mr. Boyle's remark upon this last creature, who, I remember, somewhere 125 in his works observes, that though the mole be not totally blind (as it is commonly thought) she has not sight enough to distinguish particular objects. Her eye is said to have but one humour in it, which is supposed to give her the idea of light, but of nothing 130 else, and is so formed that this idea is probably painful to the animal. Whenever she comes up into broad day, she might be in danger of being taken, unless she were thus affected by a light striking upon her eye, and immediately warning her to bury herself in her 135 proper element. More sight would be useless to her, as none at all might be fatal.

I have only instanced such animals as seem the most imperfect works of nature ; and if Providence shows itself even in the blemishes of these creatures, 140 how much more does it discover itself in the several endowments which it has variously bestowed upon such creatures as are more or less finished and completed in their several faculties, according to the condition of life in which they are posted. 145

I could wish our Royal Society would compile a body of natural history, the best that could be gathered

together from books and observations.   If the several
writers among them took each his particular species,
and gave us a distinct account of its original, birth,   150
and education ; its policies, hostilities and alliances,
with the frame and texture of its inward and outward
parts, and particularly those that distinguish it from
all other animals, with their peculiar aptitudes for the
state of being in which Providence has placed them,   155
it would be one of the best services their studies could
do mankind, and not a little redound to the glory of
the all-wise Contriver.

It is true, such a natural history, after all the disquisitions of the learned, would be infinitely short and   160
defective.   Seas and deserts hide millions of animals
from our observation.   Innumerable artifices and
stratagems are acted in the howling wilderness and
in the great deep, that can never come to our knowledge.   Besides that there are infinitely more species   165
of creatures which are not to be seen without, nor indeed with the help of the finest glasses, than of such
as are bulky enough for the naked eye to take hold
of.   However, from the consideration of such animals
as lie within the compass of our knowledge, we might   170
easily form a conclusion of the rest, that the same
variety of wisdom and goodness runs through the
whole creation, and puts every creature in a condition
to provide for its safety and subsistence in its proper
station.   175
Tully has given us an admirable sketch of natural
history, in his second book concerning the Nature of
the Gods ; and that in a style so raised by metaphors

and descriptions, that it lifts the subject above raillery
and ridicule, which frequently fall on such observa- 180
tions when they pass through the hands of an ordinary writer.

L.

CHAPTER IX.

SIR ROGER AT THE ASSIZES.

Comes jucundus in via pro vehiculo est.
—Pub. Syr. Frag.

A man's first care should be to avoid the reproaches
of his own heart; his next, to escape the censures of
the world; if the last interferes with the former, it
ought to be entirely neglected; but otherwise there
cannot be a greater satisfaction to an honest mind, 5
than to see those approbations which it gives itself
seconded by the applauses of the public : a man is
more sure of his conduct, when the verdict which he
passes upon his own behaviour is thus warranted and
confirmed by the opinion of all that knew him. 10

My worthy friend Sir Roger is one of those who is
not only at peace within himself, but beloved and
esteemed by all about him. He receives a suitable
tribute for his universal benevolence to mankind, in
the returns of affection and good-will, which are paid 15
him by every one that lives within his neighbourhood.
I lately met with two or three odd instances of that
general respect which is shewn to the good old knight.
He would needs carry Will Wimble and myself with

him to the county assizes. As we were upon the road,   20
Will Wimble joined a couple of plain men who rode
before us, and conversed with them for some time;
during which my friend Sir Roger acquainted me with
their characters.

"The first of them," says he, "that has a spaniel   25
by his side, is a yeoman of about an hundred pounds
a year, an honest man : he is just within the game-
act, and qualified to kill an hare or a pheasant : he
knocks down a dinner with his gun twice or thrice a
week ; and by that means lives much cheaper than   30
those who have not so good an estate as himself.
He would be a good neighbour if he did not destroy
so many partridges : in short he is a very sensible
man ; shoots flying ; and has been several times fore-
man of the petty jury.   35

"The other that rides along with him is Tom
Touchy, a fellow famous for taking the law of every
body. There is not one in the town where he lives
that he has not sued at a quarter-sessions. The
rogue had once the impudence to go to law with the   40
widow. His head is full of costs, damages, and
ejectments ; he plagued a couple of honest gentlemen
so long for a trespass in breaking one of his hedges,
till he was forced to sell the ground it inclosed to
defray the charges of the prosecution : his father left   45
him fourscore pounds a year ; but he has cast and
been cast so often, that he is not now worth thirty.
I suppose he is going upon the old business of the
willow tree."

As Sir Roger was giving me this account of Tom   50

Touchy, Will Wimble and his two companions stopped short until we came up to them. After having paid their respects to Sir Roger, Will told him that Mr. Touchy and he must appeal to him upon a dispute that arose between them. Will, it seems, had been giving his fellow-traveller an account of his angling one day in such a hole ; when Tom Touchy, instead of hearing out his story, told him, that Mr. such an one, if he pleased, might *take the law of him* for fishing in that part of the river. My friend Sir Roger heard them both upon a round trot ; and after having paused some time, told them, with the air of a man who would not give his judgment rashly, that *much might be said on both sides.* They were neither of them dissatisfied with the knight's determination, because neither of them found himself in the wrong by it ; upon which we made the best of our way to the assizes.

The court was set before Sir Roger came ; but notwithstanding all the justices had taken their places upon the bench, they made room for the old knight at the head of them ; who, for his reputation in the country, took occasion to whisper in the judge's ear, that he was glad his lordship had met with so much good weather in his circuit. I was listening to the proceedings of the court with much attention, and infinitely pleased with that great appearance and solemnity which so properly accompanies such a public administration of our laws, when, after about an hour's sitting, I observed to my great surprise, in the midst of a trial, that my friend Sir Roger was

getting up to speak. I was in some pain for him till
I found he had acquitted himself of two or three
sentences, with a look of much business and great
intrepidity.   85

Upon his first rising the court was hushed, and a
general whisper ran among the country people that
Sir Roger was up. The speech he made was so little
to the purpose, that I shall not trouble my readers
with an account of it ; and I believe was not so much   90
designed by the knight himself to inform the court,
as to give him a figure in my eye, and keep up his
credit in the country.

I was highly delighted, when the court rose, to see
the gentlemen of the country gathering about my old   95
friend, and striving who should compliment him
most ; at the same time that the ordinary people
gazed upon him at a distance, not a little admiring
his courage, that was not afraid to speak to the
judge.   100

In our return home we met with a very odd accident, which I cannot forbear relating, because it
shows how desirous all who know Sir Roger are of
giving him marks of their esteem. When we were
arrived upon the verge of his estate, we stopped at a   105
little inn to rest ourselves and our horses. The man
of the house had, it seems, been formerly a servant
in the knight's family ; and to do honour to his old
master, had some time since, unknown to Sir Roger,
put him up in a sign-post before the door ; so that   110
"The Knight's Head" had hung out upon the road
about a week before he himself knew anything of the

matter.   As soon as Sir Roger was acquainted with
it, finding that his servant's indiscretion proceeded
wholly from affection and good-will, he only told him 115
that he had made him too high a compliment ; and
when the fellow seemed to think that could hardly be,
added with a more decisive look, that it was too great
an honour for any man under a duke ; but told him
at the same time, that it might be altered with a very 120
few touches, and that he himself would be at the
charge of it.   Accordingly, they got a painter by the
knight's directions to add a pair of whiskers to the
face, and by a little aggravation of the features to
change it into " The Saracen's Head."   I should not 125
have known this story, had not the innkeeper, upon
Sir Roger's alighting, told him in my hearing, that his
honour's head was brought back last night with the
alterations that he had ordered to be made in it.
Upon this my friend with his usual cheerfulness re- 130
lated the particulars above-mentioned, and ordered
the head to be brought into the room.   I could not
forbear discovering greater expressions of mirth than
ordinary upon the appearance of this monstrous face,
under which, notwithstanding it was made to frown 135
and stare in a most extraordinary manner, I could
still discover a distant resemblance of my old friend.
Sir Roger, upon seeing me laugh, desired me to tell
him truly if I thought it possible for people to know
him in that disguise. I at first kept my usual silence ; 140
but upon the knight conjuring me to tell him whether
it was not still more like himself than a Saracen, I
composed my countenance in the best manner I could,

and replied that, *much might be said on both sides.*

These several adventures, with the knight's beha- 145
viour in them, gave me as pleasant a day as ever I
met with in any of my travels.

L.

CHAPTER X.

[No. 123.

THE STORY OF AN HEIR.

Doctrina sed vim promovet insitam,
Rectique cu'tus pectora roborant;
Utcunque defecere mores,
Dedecorant bene nata culpæ.
—Hor.

As I was yesterday taking the air with my friend
Sir Roger, we were met by a fresh-coloured ruddy
young man, who rid by us full speed, with a couple
of servants behind him.   Upon my inquiry who he
was, Sir Roger told me that he was a young gentle-   5
man of a considerable estate, who had been educated
by a tender mother that lived not many miles from the
place where we were.   She is a very good lady, says my
friend, but took so much care of her son's health,
that she has made him good for nothing.   She   10
quickly found that reading was bad for his eyes, and
that writing made his head ache.   He was let loose
among the woods as soon as he was able to ride on
horseback, or to carry a gun upon his shoulder.   To
be brief, I found, by my friend's account of him, that   15
he had got a great stock of health, but nothing else ;

and that if it were a man's business only to live, there would not be a more accomplished young fellow in the whole country.

The truth of it is, since my residing in these parts I have seen and heard innumerable instances of young heirs and elder brothers, who either from their own reflecting upon the estates they are born to, and therefore thinking all other accomplishments unnecessary, or from hearing these notions frequently inculcated to them by the flattery of their servants and domestics, or from the same foolish thought prevailing in those who have the care of their education, are of no manner of use but to keep up their families, and transmit their lands and houses in a line to posterity.

Eudoxus and Leontine began the world with small estates. They were both of them men of good sense and great virtue. They prosecuted their studies together in their earlier years, and entered into such a friendship as lasted to the end of their lives. Eudoxus, at his first setting out in the world, threw himself into a court, where by his natural endowments and his acquired abilities he made his way from one post to another, till at length he had raised a very considerable fortune. Leontine, on the contrary, sought all opportunities of improving his mind by study, conversation, and travel. He was not only acquainted with all the sciences, but with the most eminent professors of them throughout Europe. He knew perfectly well the interests of its princes, with the customs and fashions of their courts, and could scarce meet with the name of an extraordinary person in the *Gazette* whom he had not either talked to or seen. In short, he had so well mixed and digested his knowledge of men and books, that he made one of the most accomplished persons of his age. During the whole course of his studies and travels he kept up a punctual correspondence with Eudoxus, who often made himself acceptable to the principal men about court by the intelligence which he received from Leontine. When they were both turned of forty (an age in which, according to Mr. Cowley, there is no dallying with life) they determined, pursuant to the resolution they had taken in the beginning of their lives, to retire, and pass the remainder of their days in the country. In order to this, they both of them married much about the same time. Leontine, with his own and his wife's fortune, bought a farm of three hundred a year, which lay within the neighbourhood of his friend Eudoxus, who had purchased an estate of as many thousands. They were both of them fathers about the same time, Eudoxus having a son born to him, and Leontine a daughter; but to the unspeakable grief of the latter, his young wife (in whom all his happiness was wrapt up) died in a few days after the birth of her daughter. His affliction would have been insupportable, had not he been comforted by the daily visits and conversations of his friend. As they were one day talking together with their usual intimacy, Leontine, considering how incapable he was of giving his daughter a proper education in his own house, and Eudoxus reflecting on the

ordinary behaviour of a son who knows himself to be
the heir of a great estate, they both agreed upon an 80
exchange of children, namely, that the boy should be
bred up with Leontine as his son, and that the girl
should live with Eudoxus as his daughter, till they
were each of them arrived at years of discretion. The
wife of Eudoxus, knowing that her son could not be so 85
advantageously brought up as under the care of Leontine, and considering at the same time that he would
be perpetually under her own eye, was by degrees
prevailed upon to fall in with the project. She therefore took Leonilla, for that was the name of the girl, 90
and educated her as her own daughter. The two
friends on each side had wrought themselves to such
an habitual tenderness for the children who were
under their direction, that each of them had the real
passion of a father, where the title was but imaginary. 95
Florio, the name of the young heir that lived with
Leontine, though he had all the duty and affection
imaginable for his supposed parent, was taught to
rejoice at the sight of Eudoxus, who visited his friend
very frequently, and was dictated by his natural affec- 100
tion, as well as by the rules of prudence, to make
himself esteemed and beloved by Florio. The boy
was now old enough to know his supposed father's
circumstances, and that therefore he was to make his
way in the world by his own industry. This consi- 105
deration grew stronger in him every day, and produced so good an effect, that he applied himself with
more than ordinary attention to the pursuit of every
thing which Leontine recommended to him. His

natural abilities, which were very good, assisted by 110
the directions of so excellent a counsellor, enabled
him to make a quicker progress than ordinary through
all the parts of his education.   Before he was twenty
years of age, having finished his studies and exercises
with great applause, he was removed from the univer- 115
sity to the Inns of Court, where there are very few
that make themselves considerable proficients in the
study of the place, who know they shall arrive at
great estates without them.   This was not Florio's
case ; he found that three hundred a-year was but a 120
poor estate for Leontine and himself to live upon ; so
that he studied without intermission, till he gained a
very good insight into the constitution and laws of his
country.

I should have told my reader, that whilst Florio 125
lived at the house of his foster-father, he was always
an acceptable guest in the family of Eudoxus, where
he became acquainted with Leonilla from her infancy.
His acquaintance with her by degrees grew into love,
which in a mind trained up in all the sentiments of 130
honour and virtue became a very uneasy passion. He
despaired of gaining an heiress of so great a fortune,
and would rather have died than attempted it by any
indirect methods. Leonilla, who was a woman of the
greatest beauty, joined with the greatest modesty, 135
entertained at the same time a secret passion for
Florio, but conducted herself with so much prudence
that she never gave him the least intimation of it.
Florio was now engaged in all those arts and improvements that are proper to raise a man's private fortune, 140

and give him a figure in his country, but secretly tor-
mented with that passion, which burns with the
greatest fury in a virtuous and noble heart, when he
received a sudden summons from Leontine to repair
to him in the country, the next day. For it seems 145
Eudoxus was so filled with the report of his son's reputation, that he could no longer withhold making
himself known to him. The morning after his arrival
at the house of his supposed father, Leontine told him
that Eudoxus had something of great importance to 150
communicate to him ; upon which the good man embraced him, and wept.   Florio was no sooner arrived
at the great house that stood in his neighbourhood,
but Eudoxus took him by the hand, after the first
salutes were over, and conducted him into his closet. 155
He there opened to him the whole secret of his pa-
rentage and education, concluding after this manner :
" I have no other way left of acknowledging my gratitude to Leontine, than by marrying you to his
daughter. He shall not lose the pleasure of being 160
your father by the discovery I have made to you.
Leonilla too shall still be my daughter ; her filial
piety, though misplaced, has been so exemplary, that
it deserves the greatest reward I can confer upon it.
You shall have the pleasure of seeing a great estate 165
fall to you, which you would have lost the relish of,
had you known yourself born to it. Continue only
to deserve it in the same manner you did before you
were possessed of it. I have left your mother in the
next room. Her heart yearns towards you. She is 170
making the same discoveries to Leonilla which I have

made to yourself." Florio was so overwhelmed with this profusion of happiness, that he was not able to make a reply, but threw himself down at his father's feet, and amidst a flood of tears kissed and embraced 175 his knees, asking his blessing, and expressing in dumb show those sentiments of love, duty, and gratitude, that were too big for utterance. To conclude, the happy pair were married, and half Eudoxus's estate settled upon them. Leontine and Eudoxus 180 passed the remainder of their lives together, and received in the dutiful and affectionate behaviour of Florio and Leonilla the just recompense, as well as the natural effects, of that care which they had bestowed upon them in their education.   185

L.

CHAPTER XI

[No. 125.

ON PARTY SPIRIT.

Ne pueri, ne tanta animis assuescite bella :
Neu patriæ validas in viscera vertite vires.
—Virg.

· My worthy friend Sir Roger, when we are talking of the malice of parties, very frequently tells us an accident that happened to him when he was a schoolboy, which was at a time when the feuds ran high between the Roundheads and Cavaliers. This worthy   5 knight, being then but a stripling, had occasion to inquire which was the way to St. Anne's Lane, upon **which the** person whom he spoke to, instead of answering his question, called him a young Popish cur, and asked him who had made Anne a saint! The boy, being in some confusion, inquired of the next he met, which was the way to Anne's Lane, but was called a prick-eared cur for his pains, and instead of being shewn the way, was told, that she had been a saint before he was born, and would be one after he was hanged. Upon this, says Sir Roger, I did not think fit to repeat the former question, but going into every lane of the neighbourhood, asked what they called the name of that lane. By which ingenious artifice he found out the place he inquired after, without giving offence to any party. Sir Roger generally closes this narrative with reflections on the mischief that parties do in the country, how they spoil good neighbourhood, and make honest gentlemen hate one another; besides that they manifestly tend to the prejudice of the land-tax and the destruction of the game.

There cannot a greater judgment befall a country than such a dreadful spirit of division as rends a government into two distinct people, and makes them greater strangers and more averse to one another, than if they were actually two different nations. The effects of such a division are pernicious to the last degree, not only with regard to those advantages which they give the common enemy, but to those private evils which they produce in the heart of almost every particular person. This influence is very fatal both to men's morals and their understandings; it sinks the virtue of a nation, and not only so, but destroys even common sense. 40

A furious party-spirit, when it rages in its full violence, exerts itself in civil war and bloodshed ; and when it is under its greatest restraints, naturally breaks out in falsehood, detraction, calumny, and a partial administration of justice. In a word, it fills a 45 nation with spleen and rancour, and extinguishes all the seeds of good nature, compassion, and humanity.

Plutarch says very finely, that a man should not allow himself to hate even his enemies, because, says he, " if you indulge this passion on some occasions, 50 it will rise of itself in others ; if you hate your enemies, you will contract such a vicious habit of mind, as by degrees will break out upon those who are your friends, or those who are indifferent to you." I might here observe how admirably this precept of morality 55 (which derives the malignity of hatred from the passion itself, and not from its object) answers to that great rule which was dictated to the world about an hundred years before this philosopher wrote; but instead of that, I shall only take notice, with a real 60 grief of heart, that the minds of many good men among us appear soured with party-principles, and alienated from one another in such a manner, as seems to me altogether inconsistent with the dictates either of reason or religion. Zeal for a public cause 65 is apt to breed passions in the hearts of virtuous persons, to which the regard of their own private interest would never have betrayed them.

If this party-spirit has so ill an effect on our morals,

it has likewise a very great one upon our judgments. 70
We often hear a poor insipid paper or pamphlet cried
up, and sometimes a noble piece depreciated, by
those who are of a different principle from the author.
One who is actuated by this spirit is almost under an
incapacity of discerning either real blemishes or beau- 75
ties. A man of merit in a different principle is
like an object seen in two different mediums, that appears crooked or broken, however straight and entire
it may be in itself. For this reason there is scarce a
person of any figure in England who does not go by 80
two contrary characters, as opposite to one another
as light and darkness. Knowledge and learning
suffer in a particular manner from this strange prejudice, which at present prevails amongst all ranks and
degrees of the British nation. As men formally be- 85
came eminent in learned societies by their parts and
acquisitions, they now distinguish themselves by the
warmth and violence with which they espouse their
respective parties. Books are valued upon the like
considerations : an abusive scurrilous style passes 90
for satire, and a dull scheme of party notions is called
fine writing.

There is one piece of sophistry practised by both
sides, and that is the taking any scandalous story,
that has been ever whispered or invented of a private 95
man, for a known undoubted truth, and raising suitable speculations upon it. Calumnies that have been
never proved, or have been often refuted, are the
ordinary postulations of these infamous scribblers,
upon which they proceed as upon first principles 100

granted by all men, though in their hearts they know they are false, or at best very doubtful. When they have laid these foundations of scurrility, it is no wonder that their superstructure is every way answerable to them. If this shameless practice of the present age endures much longer, praise and reproach will cease to be motives of action in good men.

There are certain periods of time in all governments when this inhuman spirit prevails. Italy was long torn in pieces by the Guelfes and Gibellines: and France by those who were for and against the league: but it is very unhappy for a man to be born in such a stormy and tempestuous season. It is the restless ambition of artful men, that thus breaks a people into factions, and draws several well-meaning persons to their interest by a specious concern for their country. How many honest minds are filled with uncharitable and barbarous notions, out of their zeal for the public good? What cruelties and outrages would they not commit against men of an adverse party, whom they would honour and esteem, if instead of considering them as they are represented, they knew them as they are? Thus are persons of the greatest probity seduced into shameful errors and prejudices, and made bad men even by that noblest of principles, the love of their country. I cannot here forbear mentioning the famous Spanish proverb, " If there were neither fools nor knaves in the world all people would be of one mind."

For my own part, I could heartily wish that all honest men would enter into an association, for the support of one another against the endeavours of those whom they ought to look upon as their common enemies, whatsoever side they may belong to. Were there such an honest body of neutral forces, we should 135 never see the worst of men in great figures of life, because they are above practising those methods which would be grateful to their faction. We should then single every criminal out of the herd and hunt him down, however formidable and overgrown he might 140 appear : on the contrary, we should shelter distressed innocence, and defend virtue, however beset with contempt or ridicule, envy or defamation. In short, we should not any longer regard our fellow-subjects as Whigs or Tories, but should make the man of merit 145 our friend, and the villain our enemy.

C.

CHAPTER XII.

[No. 126.

PARTY SPIRIT—*Continued.*

Tros Ratu'usve fuat, nullo discrimine habebo.
—Virg.

In my yesterday's paper I proposed, that the honest men of all parties should enter into a kind of association for the defence of one another, and the confusion of their common enemies. As it is designed this neutral body should act with a regard to nothing but truth 5 and equity, and divest themselves of the little heats and prepossessions that cleave to parties of all kinds, I have prepared for them the following form of an asso-

ciation, which may express their intentions in the most
plain and simple manner :   10

We, whose names are hereunto subscribed, do so-
lemnly declare, that we do in our consciences believe
two and two make four ; and that we shall adjudge
any man whatsoever to be our enemy who endeavours
to persuade us to the contrary. We are likewise ready   15
to maintain with the hazard of all that is near and
dear to us, that six is less than seven in all times and
all places ; and that ten will not be more three years
hence than it is at present. We do also firmly declare,
that it is our resolution as long as we live to call black   20
black, and white white. And we shall upon all occasions oppose such persons that upon any day of the year
shall call black white, or white black, with the utmost
peril of our lives and fortunes.

Were there such a combination of honest men, who   25
without any regard to places would endeavour to ex-
tirpate all such furious zealots as would sacrifice one-
half of the country to the passion and interest of the
other ; as also such infamous hypocrites, that are for
promoting their own advantage under colour of the   30
public good ; with all the profligate immoral retainers
to each side, that have nothing to recommend them
but an implicit submission to their leaders ; we should
soon see that furious party-spirit extinguished, which
may in time expose us to the derision and contempt   35
of all the nations about us.

A member of this society, that would thus carefully
employ himself in making room for merit, by throwing down the worthless and depraved part of mankind

from those conspicuous stations of life to which they
have been sometimes advanced, and all this without
any regard to his private interest, would be no small
benefactor to his country.

I remember to have read in Diodorus Siculus an
account of a very active little animal, which I think
he calls Ichneumon, that makes it the whole business
of his life to break the eggs of the crocodile, which he
is always in search after. This instinct is the more
remarkable, because the Ichneumon never feeds upon
the eggs he has broken, nor any other way finds his
account in them. Were it not for the incessant labours
of this industrious animal, Egypt, says the historian,
would be over-run with crocodiles; for the Egyptians
are so far from destroying those pernicious creatures,
that they worship them as gods.

If we look into the behaviour of ordinary partizans,
we shall find them far from resembling this disinterested animal; and rather acting after the example of
the wild Tartars, who are ambitious of destroying a
man of the most extraordinary parts and accomplishments, as thinking that upon his decease, the same
talents, whatever posts they qualified him for, enter of
course into his destroyer.

As in the whole train of my speculations, I have
endeavoured as much as I am able to extinguish that
pernicious spirit of passion and prejudice, which rages
with the same violence in all parties, I am still the
more desirous of doing some good in this particular,
because I observe that the spirit of party reigns more
in the country than in the town. It here contracts a

kind of brutality and rustic fierceness, to which men of a politer conversation are wholly strangers. It extends itself even to the return of the bow and the hat; and at the same time that the heads of parties preserve towards one another an outward show of good breeding, and keep up a perpetual intercourse of civilities, their tools that are dispersed in these outlying parts will not so much as mingle together at a cock-match. This humour fills the country with several periodical meetings of Whig jockeys and Tory foxhunters; not to mention the innumerable curses, frowns, and whispers it produces at a quarter-sessions.

I do not know whether I have observed in any of my former papers, that my friends Sir Roger de Coverley and Sir Andrew Freeport are of different principles, the first of them inclined to the *landed*, and the other to the *moneyed* interest. This humour is so moderate in each of them, that it proceeds no farther than to an agreeable raillery, which very often diverts the rest of the club. I find, however, that the knight is a much stronger Tory in the country than in the town, which, as he has told me in my ear, is absolutely necessary for the keeping up his interest. In all our journey from London to his house, we did not so much as bait at a Whig inn; or if by chance the coachman stopped at a wrong place, one of Sir Roger's servants would ride up to his master full speed, and whisper to him that the master of the house was against such an one in the last election. This often betrayed us into hard beds and bad cheer; for we were not so inquisitive about the inn as the innkeeper; and provided our landlord's principles were sound, did not take any notice of the staleness of his provisions. This I found still the more inconvenient, because 105 the better the host was, the worse generally were his accommodations ; the fellow knowing very well that those who were his friends would take up with coarse diet and hard lodging. For these reasons, all the while I was upon the road, I dreaded entering into an 110 house of any one that Sir Roger had applauded for an honest man.

Since my stay at Sir Roger's in the country, I daily find more instances of this narrow party humour. Being upon a bowling-green at a neighbouring mar- 115 ket-town the other day (for that is the place where the gentlemen of one side meet once a week), I observed a stranger among them of a better presence and genteeler behaviour than ordinary ; but was much surprised, that notwithstanding he was a very 120 fair better, nobody would take him up. But upon inquiry, I found that he was one who had given a disagreeable vote in a former parliament, for which reason there was not a man upon that bowling-green who would have so much correspondence with him 125 as to win his money of him.

Among other instances of this nature, I must not omit one which concerns myself. Will Wimble was the other day relating several strange stories that he had picked up, nobody knows where, of a certain 130 great man ; and upon my staring at him, as one that was surprised to hear such things in the country,

which had never been so much as whispered in the
town, Will stopped short in the thread of his discourse, and after dinner asked my friend Sir Roger 135
in his ear, if he was sure that I was not a fanatic.

It gives me a serious concern to see such a spirit
of dissension in the country, not only as it destroys
virtue and common sense, and renders us in a manner barbarians towards one another, but as it per- 140
petuates our animosities, widens our breaches, and
transmits our present passions and prejudices to our
posterity.   For my own part, I am sometimes afraid
that I discover the seeds of a civil war in these our
divisions ; and therefore cannot but bewail, as in 145
their first principles, the miseries and calamities of
our children.

C.

CHAPTER XIII.

[No. 130.

THE COVERLEY GIPSIES.

> *Semperque recentes*
> *Convectare juvat prædas, et vivere rapto.*
> *—*Virg.

As I was yesterday riding out in the fields with my
friend Sir Roger, we saw at a little distance from us a
troop of gipsies.   Upon the first discovering of them,
my friend was in some doubt whether he should not
exert justice of the peace upon such a band of lawless 5
vagrants ; but not having his clerk with him, who is a
necessary counsellor on those occasions, and fearing
that his poultry might fare the worse for it, he let the

thought drop; but at the same time gave me a particular
account of the mischiefs they do in the country, in   10
stealing people's goods and spoiling their servants.
" If a stray piece of linen hangs upon an hedge,"
says Sir Roger, " they are sure to have it ; if a hog
loses his way in the fields, it is ten to one that he
becomes their prey ; our geese cannot live in peace   15
for them ; if a man prosecutes them with severity,
his hen-roost is sure to pay for it. They generally
straggle into these parts about this time of the year,
and set the heads of our servant-maids so agog for
husbands, that we do not expect to have any business   20
done as it should be whilst they are in the country.
I have an honest dairy-maid who crosses their hands
with a piece of silver every summer, and never fails
being promised the handsomest young fellow in the
parish for her pains.   Your friend the butler has been 25
fool enough to be seduced by them ; and, though he
is sure to lose a knife, a fork, or a spoon every time
his fortune is told him, generally shuts himself up in
the pantry with an old gipsy for above half an hour,
once in a twelvemonth. Sweethearts are the things   30
they live upon, which they bestow very plentifully
upon all those that apply themselves to them. You
see now and then some handsome young jades among
them ; the sluts have very often white teeth and black
eyes."   35

Sir Roger observing that I listened with great attention to his account of a people who were so entirely new to me, told me, that if I would they should
tell us our fortunes. As I was very well pleased with

the knight's proposal, we rid up and communicated our hands to them. A Cassandra of the crew, after having examined my lines very diligently, told me, that I loved a pretty maid in a corner, that I was a good woman's man, with some other particulars which I do not think proper to relate. My friend Sir Roger alighted from his horse, and exposing his palm to two or three of them that stood by him, they crumpled it into all shapes, and diligently scanned every wrinkle that could be made in it ; when one of them who was elder and more sunburnt than the rest, told him, that he had a widow in his line of life ; upon which the knight cried, " Go, go, you are an idle baggage ; " and at the same time smiled upon me. The gipsy finding he was not displeased in his heart, told him after a further inquiry into his hand, that his true love was constant, and that she should dream of him to-night : my old friend cried, " Pish," and bid her go on. The gipsy told him that he was a bachelor, but would not be so long ; and that he was dearer to somebody than he thought ; the knight still repeated that she was an idle baggage, and bid her her go on. "Ah, master," says the gipsy, " that roguish leer of yours makes a pretty woman's heart ache ; you ha'n't that simper about the mouth for nothing." The uncouth gibberish with which all this was uttered like the darkness of an oracle, made us the more attentive to it. To be short, the knight left the money with her that he had crossed her hand with, and got up again on his horse.

As we were riding away, Sir Roger told me, that

he knew several sensible people who believed these gipsies now and then foretold very strange things; and for half an hour together appeared more jocund than ordinary. In the height of his good humour, meeting a common beggar upon the road who was no conjuror, as he went to relieve him, he found his pocket was picked ; that being a kind of palmistry at which this race of vermin are very dexterous.

I might here entertain my reader with historical remarks on this idle profligate people, who infest all the countries in Europe, and live in the midst of governments in a kind of commonwealth by themselves. But instead of entering into observations of this nature I shall fill the remaining part of my paper with a story which is still fresh in Holland, and was printed in one of our monthly accounts about twenty years ago. "As the Trekschuyt, or the hackney boat, which carries passengers from Leyden to Amsterdam, was putting off, a boy running along the side of the canal desired to be taken in, which the master of the boat refused, because the lad had not quite money enough to pay the usual fare. An eminent merchant, being pleased with the looks of the boy, and secretly touched with compassion towards him, paid the money for him, and ordered him to be taken on board. Upon talking with him afterwards, he found that he could speak readily in three or four languages, and learned upon further examination that he had been stolen away when he was a child by a gipsy, and had rambled ever since with a gang of

these strollers up and down several parts of Europe.
It happened that the merchant, whose heart seems
to have inclined towards the boy by a secret kind of
instinct, had himself lost a child some years before.
The parents, after a long search for him, gave him 105
for drowned in one of the canals with which that
country abounds ; and the mother was so afflicted at
the loss of a fine boy, who was her only son, that she
died for grief of it. Upon laying together all particulars, and examining the several moles and marks 110
by which the mother used to describe the child when
he was first missing, the boy proved to be the son of
the merchant whose heart had so unaccountably
melted at the sight of him. The lad was very well
pleased to find a father who was so rich, and likely 115
to leave him a good estate ; the father, on the other
hand, was not a little delighted to see a son return
to him, whom he had given for lost, with such a
strength of constitution, sharpness of understanding,
and skill of languages." Here the printed story 120
leaves off ; but if I may give credit to reports, our
linguist, having received such extraordinary rudi-
ments towards a good education, was afterwards
trained up in everything that becomes a gentleman ;
wearing off by little and little all the vicious habits 125
and practices that he had been used to in the course
of his peregrinations. Nay, it is said that he has
since been employed in foreign courts upon national
business, with great reputation to himself and honour
to those who sent him, and that he has visited seve- 130

ral countries as a public minister, in which he formerly wandered as a gipsy.

C.

CHAPTER XIV.

[No. 131.

A SUMMONS TO LONDON.

————*Ipsæ rursum concedite Sylvæ.*
—Virg.

It is usual for a man who loves country sports to
preserve the game on his own grounds, and divert
himself upon those that belong to his neighbour. My
friend Sir Roger generally goes two or three miles
from his house, and gets into the frontiers of his   5
estate, before he beats about in search of a hare or
partridge, on purpose to spare his own fields, where
he is always sure of finding diversion when the worst
comes to the worst. By this means the breed about
his house has time to increase and multiply, besides   10
that the sport is more agreeable where the game is
the harder to come at, and where it does not lie so
thick as to produce any perplexity or confusion in
the pursuit. For these reasons the country gentleman, like the fox, seldom preys near his own home.   15
In the same manner, I have made a month's excursion out of town, which is the great field of game
for sportsmen of my species, to try my fortune in the
country, where I have started several subjects, and
hunted them down, with some pleasure to myself,   20
and, I hope, to others. I am here forced to use a

great deal of diligence before I can spring anything
to my mind, whereas in town, whilst I am following
one character, it is ten to one but I am crossed in my
way by another, and put up such a variety of odd
creatures of both sexes, that they foil the scent of
one another, and puzzle the chase. My greatest
difficulty in the country is to find sport, and in town
to choose it. In the meantime, as I have given a
whole month's rest to the cities of London and Westminster, I promise myself abundance of new game
upon my return thither.

It is indeed high time for me to leave the country,
since I find the whole neighbourhood begin to grow
very inquisitive after my name and character; my
love of solitude, taciturnity, and particular way of
life, having raised a great curiosity in all these parts.

The notions which have been framed of me are
various ; some look upon me as very proud, some as
very modest, and some as very melancholy. Will
Wimble, as my friend the butler tells me, observing
me very much alone, and extremely silent when I am
in company, is afraid I have killed a man. The
country people seem to suspect me for a conjurer ;
and some of them, hearing of the visit which I made
to Moll White, will needs have it that Sir Roger has
brought down a cunning man with him, to cure the
old woman, and free the country from her charms.
So that the character which I go under in part of
the neighbourhood is what they here call a white
witch.

A justice of peace, who lives about five miles off,

and is not of Sir Roger's party, has, it seems, said twice or thrice at his table, that he wishes Sir Roger does not harbour a Jesuit in his house ; that he thinks the gentlemen of the country would do very well to make me give some account of myself.

On the other side, some of Sir Roger's friends are afraid the old knight is imposed upon by a designing fellow ; and as they have heard that he converses very promiscuously when he is in town, do not know but he has brought down with him some discarded Whig, that is sullen, and says nothing because he is out of place.

Such is the variety of opinions which are here entertained of me, so that I pass among some for a disaffected person, and among others for a Popish priest ; among some for a wizard, and among others for a murderer ; and all this for no other reason, that I can imagine, but because I do not hoot and hollow and make a noise. It is true my friend Sir Roger tells them that it is my way, and that I am only a philosopher ; but this will not satisfy them. They think there is more in me than he discovers, and that I do not hold my tongue for nothing.

For these and other reasons I shall set out for London to-morrow, having found by experience that the country is not a place for a person of my temper, who does not love jollity, and what they call good neighbourhood. A man that is out of humour when an unexpected guest breaks in upon him, and does not care for sacrificing an afternoon to every chance comer,—that will be the master of his own time, and the pursuer of his own inclinations,—makes but a very unsociable figure in this kind of life. I shall therefore retire into the town, if I may make use of that phrase, and get into the crowd again as fast as I can, in order to be alone. I can there raise what speculations I please upon others without being observed myself, and at the same time enjoy all the advantages of company with all the privileges of solitude. In the meanwhile, to finish the month, and conclude these my rural speculations, I shall here insert a letter from my friend Will Honeycomb, who has not lived a month for these forty years out of the smoke of London, and rallies me after his way upon my country life.

" DEAR SPEC,

" I suppose this letter will find thee picking up daisies, or smelling to a lock of hay, or passing away thy time in some innocent country diversion of the like nature. I have, however, orders from the club to summon thee up to town, being all of us cursedly afraid thou wilt not be able to relish our company, after thy conversations with Moll White and Will Wimble. Pr'ythee don't send up any more stories of a cock and a bull, nor frighten the town with spirits and witches. Thy speculations begin to smell confoundedly of woods and meadows. If thou dost not come up quickly, we shall conclude that thou art in love with one of Sir Roger's dairy-maids. Service to the knight. Sir Andrew is grown the cock of the club since he left us, and if he does not return quickly, will make every mother's son of us commonwealth's men.

> "Dear Spec.,
> "Thine eternally,
> "WILL HONEYCOMB."

C.

CHAPTER XV.

[No. 269.

SIR ROGER IN LONDON.

> ————*Ævo rarissima nostro*
> *Simplicitas*————.
> —Ovid.

I was this morning surprised with a great knocking at the door, when my landlady's daughter came up to me, and told me that there was a man below desired to speak with me. Upon my asking her who it was, she told me it was a very grave elderly person, but that she did not know his name. I immediately went down to him, and found him to be the coachman of my worthy friend Sir Roger de Coverley. He told me that his master came to town last night, and would be glad to take a turn with me in Gray's Inn walks. As I was wondering in myself what had brought Sir Roger to town, not having lately received any letter from him, he told me that his master was come up to get a sight of Prince Eugene, and that he desired I would immediately meet him.

I was not a little pleased with the curiosity of the old knight, though I did not much wonder at it,

having heard him say more than once in private discourse, that he looked upon Prince Eugenio (for so
the knight always calls him) to be a greater man than 20
Scanderbeg.

I was no sooner come into Gray's Inn walks, but
I heard my friend upon the terrace hemming twice
or thrice to himself with great vigour, for he loves to
clear his pipes in good air (to make use of his own 25
phrase), and is not a little pleased with any one who
takes notice of the strength which he still exerts in
his morning hems.

I was touched with a secret joy at the sight of the
good old man, who, before he saw me, was engaged 30
in conversation with a beggar man that had asked an
alms of him. I could hear my friend chide him for
not finding out some work ; but at the same time
saw him put his hand into his pocket and give him
sixpence. 35

Our salutations were very hearty on both sides,
consisting of many kind shakes of the hand, and several affectionate looks which we cast upon one another.
After which the knight told me, my good friend his
chaplain was very well, and much at my service, and 40
that the Sunday before he had made a most incomparable sermon out of Dr. Barrow. " I have left,"
says he, " all my affairs in his hands, and being willing to lay an obligation upon him, have deposited
with him thirty merks, to be distributed among his 45
poor parishioners."

He then proceeded to acquaint me with the welfare
of Will Wimble. Upon which he put his hand into

his fob, and presented me in his name with a tobacco-
stopper, telling me, that Will had been busy all the
beginning of the winter in turning great quantities
of them ; and that he made a present of one to every
gentleman in the country who has good principles,
and smokes. He added, that poor Will was at
present under great tribulation, for that Tom Touchy
had taken the law of him for cutting some hazel
sticks out of one of his hedges.

Among other pieces of news which the knight
brought from his country seat, he informed me that
Moll White was dead ; and that about a month after
her death the wind was so very high, that it blew
down the end of one of his barns. " But for my own
part," says Sir Roger, " I do not think that the old
woman had any hand in it."

He afterwards fell into an account of the diversions which had passed in his house during the holidays ; for Sir Roger, after the laudable custom of his
ancestors, always keeps open house at Christmas.
I learned from him, that he had killed eight fat hogs
for this season ; that he had dealt about his chines
very liberally amongst his neighbours ; and that in
particular he had sent a string of hog's-puddings with
a pack of cards to every poor family in the parish.
" I have often thought," says Sir Roger, " it happens
very well that Christmas should fall out in the middle
of winter. It is the most dead and uncomfortable
time of the year, when the poor people would suffer
very much from their poverty and cold, if they had
not good cheer, warm fires, and Christmas gambols

to support them. I love to rejoice their poor hearts 80
at this season, and to see the whole village merry in
my great hall. I allow a double quantity of malt to
my small beer, and set it a running for twelve days
to every one that calls for it. I have always a piece
of cold beef and a mince pie upon the table, and am 85
wonderfully pleased to see my tenants pass away a
whole evening in playing their innocent tricks, and
smutting one another. Our friend Will Wimble is as
merry as any of them, and shows a thousand roguish
tricks upon these occasions." 90

I was very much delighted with the reflection of
my old friend, which carried so much goodness in it.
He then launched out into the praise of the late act of
parliament for securing the Church of England, and
told me, with great satisfaction, that he believed it 95
already began to take effect, for that a rigid dissenter,
who chanced to dine at his house on Christmas day
had been observed to eat very plentifully of his
plum-porridge.

After having despatched all our country matters, 100
Sir Roger made several enquiries concerning the club,
and particularly of his old antagonist Sir Andrew
Freeport. He asked me, with a kind of smile, whether
Sir Andrew had not taken the advantage of his absence to vent among them some of his republican 105
doctrines ; but soon after, gathering up his countenance into a more than ordinary seriousness, " Tell
me truly," says he, " don't you think Sir Andrew had
a hand in the Pope's procession"--but without giving
me time to answer him, " Well, well," says he, " I 110

know you are a wary man, and do not care for talking of public matters."

The knight then asked me if I had seen Prince
Eugenio, and made me promise to get him a stand
in some convenient place where he might have a full 115
sight of that extraordinary man, whose presence does
so much honour to the British nation. He dwelt very
long on the praises of this great general; and I found
that, since I was with him in the country, he had
drawn many observations together out of his reading 120
in Baker's *Chronicle*, and other authors, who always
lie in his hall window, which very much redound to
the honour of this prince.

Having passed away the greatest part of the morning in hearing the knight's reflections, which were 125
partly private and partly political, he asked me if I
would smoke a pipe with him over a dish of coffee at
Squire's. As I love the old man, I take delight in
complying with every thing that is agreeable to him,
and accordingly waited on him to the coffee-house, 130
where his venerable aspect drew upon us the eyes of
the whole room. He had no sooner seated himself
at the upper end of the high table, but he called for a
clean pipe, a paper of tobacco, a dish of coffee, a wax-
candle, and the Supplement, with such an air of 135
cheerfulness and good humour, that all the boys in
the coffee-room (who seemed to take pleasure in serv-
ing him) were at once employed on his several
errands, insomuch that nobody else could come at a
dish of tea, till the knight had got all his conveni- 140
ences about him.

L.

CHAPTER XVI.

SIR ROGER IN WESTMINSTER ABBEY.

Ire tamen restat, Numa quo devenit, et Ancus.
                                        —Hor.

My friend Sir Roger de Coverley told me the other
night, that he had been reading my paper upon Westminster Abbey, "in which," says he, " there are a great
many ingenious fancies." He told me at the same time
that he observed that I had promised another paper   5
upon the tombs, and that he should be glad to go and
see them with me, not having visited them since he
had read history.   I could not at first imagine how
this came into the knight's head, till I recollected
that he had been very busy all last summer upon   10
Baker's *Chronicle*, which he has quoted several times
in his dispute with Sir Andrew Freeport since his
last coming to town.   Accordingly, I promised to call
upon him the next morning, that we might go together to the Abbey.   15
I found the knight under his butler's hand, who
always shaves him.   He was no sooner dressed than
he called for a glass of the Widow Trueby's water,
which he told me he always drank before he went
abroad.   He recommended to me a dram of it at the   20
same time, with so much heartiness, that I could not
forbear drinking it.   As soon as I had got it down, I
found it very unpalatable ; upon which the knight,
observing that I had made several wry faces, told me

that he knew I should not like it at first, but that it was the best thing in the world against the stone or gravel.

I could have wished, indeed, that he had acquainted me with the virtues of it sooner; but it was too late to complain, and I knew what he had done was out of good will. Sir Roger told me further, that he looked upon it to be very good for a man whilst he stayed in town, to keep off infection, and that he got together a quantity of it upon the first news of the sickness being at Dantzic: when, of a sudden, turning short to one of his servants who stood behind him, he bid him call a hackney-coach, and take care it was an elderly man that drove it.

He then resumed his discourse upon Mrs. Trueby's water, telling me that the Widow Trueby was one who did more good than all the doctors and apothecaries in the country; that she distilled every poppy that grew within five miles of her; that she distributed her water gratis among all sorts of people; to which the knight added, that she had a very great jointure, and that the whole country would fain have it a match between him and her; "and truly," says Sir Roger, "if I had not been engaged, perhaps I could not have done better."

His discourse was broken off by his man's telling him he had called a coach. Upon our going to it, after having cast his eye upon the wheels, he asked the coachman if his axle-tree was good. Upon the fellow's telling him he would warrant it, the knight

turned to me, told me he looked like an honest man, 55
and went in without further ceremony.

We had not gone far, when Sir Roger, popping out
his head, called the coachman down from his box,
and upon his presenting himself at the window, asked
him if he smoked ; as I was considering what this 60
would end in, he bid him stop by the way at any
good tobacconist's and take in a roll of their best Virginia.   Nothing material happened in the remaining
part of our journey, till we were set down at the west
end of the Abbey. 65

As we went up the body of the church, the knight
pointed at the trophies upon one of the new monuments, and cried out, "A brave man, I warrant
him !" Passing afterwards by Sir Cloudesley Shovel,
he flung his hand that way, and cried, " Sir Cloudesley 70
Shovel, a very gallant man !" As we stood before
Busby's tomb, the knight uttered himself again after
the same manner. " Dr. Busby, a great man ! he
whipped my grandfather ; a very great man ! I
should have gone to him myself, if I had not been a 75
blockhead ; a very great man !"

We were immediately conducted into the little
chapel on the right hand. Sir Roger planting himself at our historian's elbow, was very attentive to
everything he said, particularly to the account he 80
gave us of the lord who cut off the king of Morocco's
head. Among several other figures, he was very well
pleased to see the statesman Cecil upon his knees ;
and concluding them all to be great men, was conducted to the figure which represents that martyr to 85

good housewifery, who died by the prick of a needle. Upon our interpreter's telling us that she was a maid of honour to Queen Elizabeth, the knight was very inquisitive into her name and family ; and after having regarded her finger for some time, "I wonder," says he, "that Sir Richard Baker has said nothing of her in his *Chronicle*."

We were then conveyed to the two Coronation chairs, where my old friend, after having heard that the stone underneath the most ancient of them, which was brought from Scotland, was called Jacob's pillar, sat himself down in the chair ; and looking like the figure of an old Gothic king, asked our interpreter : "What authority they had to say, that Jacob had ever been in Scotland ?" The fellow, instead of returning him an answer, told him, that he hoped his honour would pay his forfeit. I could observe Sir Roger a little ruffled upon being thus trepanned ; but our guide not insisting upon his demand, the knight soon recovered his good humour, and whispered in my ear that if Will Wimble were with us, and saw those two chairs, it would go hard but he would get a tobacco-stopper out of one or the other of them.

Sir Roger, in the next place, laid his hand upon Edward the Third's sword, and leaning upon the pommel of it, gave us the whole history of the Black Prince ; concluding, that in Sir Richard Baker's opinion, Edward the Third was one of the greatest princes that ever sat upon the English throne.

We were then shewn Edward the Confessor's tomb ; upon which Sir Roger acquainted us, that he was the

first who touched for the evil ; and afterwards Henry
the Fourth's, upon which he shook his head, and told
us that there was fine reading in the casualties of
that reign.   120

Our conductor then pointed to that monument
where there is the figure of one of our English kings
without an head : and only giving us to know, that
the head, which was of beaten silver, had been stolen
away several years since ; " Some Whig, I'll warrant 125
you," says Sir Roger ; " you ought to lock up your
kings better ; they will carry off the body too, if you
don't take care."

The glorious names of Henry the Fifth and Queen
Elizabeth gave the knight great opportunities of 130
shining, and of doing justice to Sir Richard Baker,
" who," as our knight observed with some surprise,
" had a great many kings in him, whose monuments
he had not seen in the Abbey."

For my own part, I could not but be pleased to see 135
the knight shew such an honest passion for the glory
of his country, and such a respectful gratitude to the
memory of its princes.

I must not omit, that the benevolence of my good
old friend, which flows out towards every one he con- 140
verses with, made him very kind to our interpreter,
whom he looked upon as an extraordinary man, for
which reason he shook him by the hand at parting,
telling him, that he should be very glad to see him at
his lodgings in Norfolk Buildings, and talk over these 145
matters with him more at leisure.

L.

CHAPTER XVII.

SIR ROGER AT THE PLAY.

Respicere exemplar vitæ morumque jubebo
Doctum imitatorem, et veras hinc ducere voces.
—Hor.

My friend Sir Roger de Coverley, when we last met
together at the club, told me that he had a great mind
to see the new tragedy with me, assuring me at the
same time, that he had not been at a play these twenty
years. "The last I saw," said Sir Roger, "was *The*   5
Committee, which I should not have gone to neither,
had not I been told before-hand that it was a good
Church of England comedy." He then proceeded to
inquire of me who this *Distressed Mother* was ; and
upon hearing that she was Hector's widow, he told me   10
that her husband was a brave man, and that when he
was a school-boy he had read his life at the end of the
Dictionary. My friend asked me, in the next place,
if there would not be some danger in coming home
late, in case the Mohocks should be abroad. "I assure   15
you," says he, "I thought I had fallen into their hands
last night ; for I observed two or three lusty black
men that followed me half way up Fleet Street, and
mended their pace behind me in proportion as I put
on to get away from them. You must know," con-   20
tinued the knight, with a smile, "I fancied they had
a mind to hunt me ; for I remember an honest gentleman in my neighbourhood, who was served such a

trick in King Charles II.'s time, for which reason he has not ventured himself in town ever since. I might have shewn them very good sport, had this been their design ; for as I am an old fox-hunter, I should have turned and dodged, and have played them a thousand tricks they had never seen in their lives before." Sir Roger added, that if these gentlemen had any such intention, they did not succeed very well in it ; " for I threw them out," says he, " at the end of Norfolk Street, where I doubled the corner, and got shelter in my lodgings before they could imagine what was be- come of me. " However," says the knight, " if Cap- tain Sentry will make one with us to-morrow night, and if you will both of you call upon me about four o'clock, that we may be at the house before it is full, I will have my coach in readiness to attend you, for John tells me he has got the forewheels mended."

The Captain, who did not fail to meet me there at the appointed hour, bid Sir Roger fear nothing, for that he had put on the same sword which he made use of at the battle of Steenkirk. Sir Roger's servants, and among the rest, my old friend the butler, had, I found, provided themselves with good oaken plants, to attend their master upon this occasion. When we had placed him in his coach, with myself at his left hand, the Captain before him, and his butler at the head of his footmen in the rear, we convoyed him in safety to the play-house, where, after having marched up the entry in good order, the Captain and I went in with him, and seated him betwixt us in the pit. As soon as the house was full, and the candles lighted,

my old friend stood up and looked about him with that
pleasure which a mind seasoned with humanity naturally feels in itself, at the sight of a multitude of people who seem pleased with one another, and partake
of the same common entertainment. I could not but
fancy myself, as the old man stood up in the middle
of the pit, that he made a very proper centre to a tra-
gic audience. Upon the entering of Pyrrhus, the
knight told me that he did not believe the king of
France himself had a better strut. I was indeed very
attentive to my old friend's remarks, because I looked
upon them as a piece of natural criticism, and was
well pleased to hear him, at the conclusion of almost
every scene, telling me that he could not imagine how
the play would end. One while he appeared much
concerned for Andromache, and a little while after as
much for Hermione ; and was extremely puzzled to
think what would become of Pyrrhus.

When Sir Roger saw Andromache's obstinate refusal to her lover's importunities, he whispered me in
the ear, that he was sure she would never have him ;
to which he added, with a more than ordinary vehemence, " You can't imagine, Sir, what it is to have to
do with a widow." Upon Pyrrhus his threatening afterwards to leave her, the knight shook his head and
muttered to himself, " Ay, do if you can." This part
dwelt so much upon my friend's imagination, that at
the close of the third act, as I was thinking of something else, he whispered in my ear, " These widows,
Sir, are the most perverse creatures in the world. But
pray," says he, " you that are a critic, is this play ac-

cording to your dramatic rules, as you call them? Should your people in tragedy always talk to be understood ? Why, there is not a single sentence in this play that I do not know the meaning of."

The fourth act very unluckily began before I had time to give the old gentleman an answer : " Well," says the knight, sitting down with great satisfaction, " I suppose we are now to see Hector's ghost." He then renewed his attention, and, from time to time, fell a-praising the widow. He made, indeed, a little mistake as to one of her pages, whom at his first entering he took for Astynax : but he quickly set himself right in that particular, though, at the same time, he owned he should have been very glad to have seen the little boy ; " who," said he, " must needs be a very fine child by the account that is given of him." Upon Hermione's going off with a menace to Pyrrhus, the audience gave a loud clap, to which Sir Roger added, " On my word, a notable young baggage ! "

As there was a very remarkable silence and stillness in the audience during the whole action, it was natural for them to take the opportunity of these intervals between the acts, to express their opinion of the players and their respective parts. Sir Roger hearing a cluster of them praise Orestes, struck in with them, and told them that he thought his friend Pylades was a very sensible man. As they were afterwards applauding Pyrrhus, Sir Roger put in a second time : "and let me tell you," says he, " though he speaks but little, I like the old fellow in whiskers as well as any of them." Captain Sentry seeing two or three wags who sat near us, lean with an attentive ear towards Sir Roger, and fearing lest they should smoke the knight, plucked him by the elbow, and whispered something in his ear, that lasted till the opening of 120 the fifth act. The knight was wonderfully attentive to the account which Orestes gives of Pyrrhus his death, and at the conclusion of it told me, it was such a bloody piece of work, that he was glad it was not done upon the stage. Seeing afterwards Orestes in 125 his raving fit, he grew more than ordinary serious, and took occasion to moralize (in his way) upon an evil conscience, adding, that Orestes, in his madness, looked as if he saw something.

As we were the first that came into the house, so 130 we were the last that went out of it ; being resolved to have a clear passage for our old friend, whom we did not care to venture among the jostling of the crowd. Sir Roger went out fully satisfied with his entertainment, and we guarded him to his lodgings in 135 the same manner that we brought him to the playhouse ; being highly pleased, for my own part, not only with the performance of the excellent piece which had been presented, but with the satisfaction which it had given to the good old man. 140

CHAPTER XVIII.

[No 383.

SIR ROGER AT VAUXHALL.

Criminibus debent hortos.
                    —Juv.

As I was sitting in my chamber, and thinking on a subject for my next *Spectator*, I heard two or three irregular bounces at my landlady's door ; and upon the opening of it, a loud cheerful voice inquiring whether the philosopher was at home.   The child who went to the door answered very innocently, that he did not lodge there.   I immediately recollected that it was my good friend Sir Roger's voice, and that I had promised to go with him on the water to Spring Garden, in case it proved a good evening.   The knight put me in mind of my promise from the bottom of the staircase, but told me, that if I was speculating, he would stay below till I had done.   Upon my coming down, I found all the children of the family got about my old friend, and my landlady herself, who is a notable prating gossip, engaged in a conference with him ; being mightily pleased with his stroking her little boy upon the head, and bidding him be a good child, and mind his book.

We were no sooner come to the Temple stairs, but we were surrounded with a crowd of watermen, offering us their respective services.   Sir Roger, after having looked about him very attentively, spied one

with a wooden leg, and immediately gave him orders
to get his boat ready. As we were walking towards
it, " You must know," says Sir Roger, " I never
make use of anybody to row me that has not either
lost a leg or an arm. I would rather bate him a few
strokes of his oar than not employ an honest man
that has been wounded in the Queen's service. If I
was a lord or a bishop, and kept a barge, I would
not put a fellow in my livery that had not a wooden
leg."

My old friend, after having seated himself and
trimmed the boat with his coachman, who, being a
very sober man, always serves for ballast on these
occasions, we made the best of our way for Vauxhall.
Sir Roger obliged the waterman to give us the history
of his right leg, and hearing that he had left it at La
Hogue, with many particulars which passed in that
glorious action, the knight, in the triumph of his
heart, made several reflections on the greatness of
the British nation ; as, that one Englishman could
beat three Frenchmen ; that we could never be in
danger of Popery so long as we took care of our fleet ;
that the Thames was the noblest river in Europe ;
that London bridge was a greater piece of work than
any of the seven wonders of the world ; with many
other honest prejudices which naturally cleave to the
heart of a true Englishman.

After some short pause, the old knight, turning
about his head twice or thrice, to take a survey of
this great metropolis, bid me observe how thick the
city was set with churches, and that there was scarce

a single steeple on this side Temple Bar. "A most 55
heathenish sight!" says Sir Roger. "There is no
religion at this end of the town. The fifty new
churches will very much mend the prospect ; but
church work is slow, church work is slow."

I do not remember I have anywhere mentioned, 60
in Sir Roger's character, his custom of saluting
everybody that passes by him with a good morrow
or a good night. This the old man does out of the
overflowings of his humanity, though at the same
time it renders him so popular among all his country 65
neighbours, that it is thought to have gone a good
way in making him once or twice knight of the shire.
He cannot forbear this exercise of benevolence even
in town, when he meets with any one in his morning
or evening walk. It broke from him to several boats 70
that passed by upon the water ; but to the knight's
great surprise, as he gave the good night to two or
three young fellows a little before our landing, one of
them, instead of returning the civility, asked us what
queer old put we had in the boat, and whether he was 75
not ashamed to go a-wenching at his years ? with a
great deal of the like Thames ribaldry. Sir Roger
seemed a little shocked at first, but at length assuming a face of magistracy, told us that if he were a
Middlesex justice, he would make such vagrants 80
know that her Majesty's subjects were no more to be
abused by water than by land.

We were now arrived at Spring Garden, which is
exquisitely pleasant at this time of the year. When
I considered the fragrancy of the walks and bowers, 85

with the choirs of birds that sung upon the trees,
and the loose tribe of people that walked under the
shades, I could not but look upon the place as a kind
of Mahometan paradise. Sir Roger told me it put
him in mind of a little coppice by his house in the 90
country, which his chaplain used to call an aviary of
nightingales. "You must understand," says the
knight, "there is nothing in the world that pleases a
man in love so much as your nightingale. Ah, Mr.
Spectator! the many moonlight nights that I have 95
walked by myself, and thought on the widow by the
music of the nightingale!" He here fetched a deep
sigh, and was falling into a fit of musing, when a
mask, who came behind him, gave him a gentle tap
upon the shoulder, and asked him if he would drink 100
a bottle of mead with her? But the knight, being
startled at so unexpected a familiarity, and displeased
to be interrupted in his thoughts of the widow, told
her she was a wanton baggage, and bid her go about
her business. 105

We concluded our walk with a glass of Burton ale
and a slice of hung beef. When we had done eating
ourselves, the knight called a waiter to him, and bid
him carry the remainder to the waterman that had
but one leg. I perceived the fellow stared upon him 110
at the oddness of the message, and was going to be
saucy; upon which I ratified the knight's commands
with a peremptory look.

As we were going out of the garden, my old friend,
thinking himself obliged, as a member of the *quorum*, 115
to animadvert upon the morals of the place, told the

mistress of the house, who sat at the bar, that he should be a better customer to her garden if there were more nightingales, and fewer improper persons.

120

L.

————

[As year followed year, Addison seems to have felt the maintenance of the *Spectator*, unexampled as had been its success, an increasing burden, and to have cast about for the means of handsomely bringing it to a close.   One obvious expedient was to kill off, or otherwise dispose of, the   5
members of the Club.   We find mention accordingly, in No. 513, of the Clergyman as lying on his death-bed, and four numbers later the incomparable Sir Roger himself is made to succumb to fate.   On the whole, Addison's management of the character had been little interfered with by the   10
other contributors.   In a paper (No. 174), probably written by Steele, the knight holds an entertaining argument with Sir Andrew Freeport on the merits of trade ; and in one by Budgell (No. 359), he is made to discourse on *beards* in a style neither edifying nor witty.   A slight mention of him   15
occurs in No. 359.   But about a month after the appearance of Addison's paper, just printed, describing Sir Roger's visit to Vauxhall, Steele introduced him (No. 410) as the hero of a questionable and unseemly adventure, in which the reader is presented with the disagreeable alternative of considering   20
the poor old knight either as a knave or a fool.   He is described as falling in with a girl called Sukey ir the Temple cloisters, with whose appearance and manners he is so much taken that he gives her a dinner at a tavern, invites her to come to his lodgings, and promises that if she comes down   25
to the country she shall be encouraged.   This made Addison very angry ; he is said to have had a sharp altercation with

Steele,* and he resolved to send the darling of his imagination to the land where the " wicked cease from troubling," and no rude hand could mar the sweet image of simplicity and goodness which he desired should be the final result, in the minds of thousands of readers, of the contemplation of Sir Roger's character.　We are thus brought to the following paper.]

CHAPTER XIX.

[No. 517.

DEATH OF SIR ROGER.

Heu pietas! heu prisca fides!
　　　　　　—Virg.

We last night received a piece of ill news at our club, which very sensibly afflicted every one of us.　I question not but my readers themselves will be troubled at the hearing of it.　To keep them no longer in suspense, Sir Roger de Coverley *is dead*.　He departed this life at his house in the country, after a few weeks' sickness.　Sir Andrew Freeport has a letter from one of his correspondents in those parts, that informs him the old man caught a cold at the county-sessions, as he was very warmly promoting an address of his own penning, in which he succeeded according to his wishes.　But this particular comes from a Whig justice of the peace, who was always Sir Roger's enemy and antagonist.　I have letters both from the chaplain and Captain Sentry, which mention nothing of it, but are

---

* Life by Dr. Johnson.

filled with many particulars to the honour of the good
old man.　I have likewise a letter from the butler,
who took so much care of me last summer when I
was at the knight's house.　As my friend the butler
mentions, in the simplicity of his heart, several cir-　20
cumstances the others have passed over in silence,
I shall give my reader a copy of his letter, without any
alteration or diminution.

"HONOURED SIR,

"Knowing that you was my master's good friend,　25
I could not forbear sending you the melancholy news
of his death, which has afflicted the whole country, as
well as his poor servants, who loved him, I may say,
better than we did our lives.　I am afraid he caught
his death the last county-sessions, where he would go　30
to see justice done to a poor widow woman, and her
fatherless children, that had been wronged by a neighbouring gentleman ; for you know, sir, my good master was always the poor man's friend.　Upon his coming home, the first complaint he made was, that he　35
had lost his roast-beef stomach, not being able to
touch a sirloin, which was served up according to custom ; and you know he used to take great delight in
it. From that time forward he grew worse and worse,
but still kept a good heart to the last.　Indeed we were　40
once in great hope of his recovery, upon a kind message that was sent him from the widow lady whom he
had made love to the forty last years of his life, but
this only proved a lightning before death.　He has bequeathed to this lady, as a token of his love, a great　45

pearl necklace, and a couple of silver bracelets set with jewels, which belonged to my good old lady his mother ; he has bequeathed the fine white gelding, that he used to ride a hunting upon, to his chaplain, because he thought he would be kind to him, and he has left you all his books. He has, moreover, bequeathed to the chaplain a very pretty tenement with good lands about it. It being a very cold day when he made his will, he left for mourning, to every man in the parish, a great frieze-coat, and to every woman a black riding-hood. It was a most moving sight to see him take leave of his poor servants, commending us all for our fidelity, whilst we were not able to speak a word for weeping. As we most of us are grown grey-headed in our dear master's service, he has left us pensions and legacies, which we may live very comfortably upon the remaining part of our days. He has bequeathed a great deal more in charity, which is not yet come to my knowledge, and it is peremptorily said in the parish, that he has left money to build a steeple to the church ; for he was heard to say some time ago that if he lived two years longer, Coverley church should have a steeple to it. The chaplain tells everybody that he made a very good end, and never speaks of him without tears. He was buried, according to his own directions, among the family of the Coverleys, on the left hand of his father Sir Arthur. The coffin was carried by six of his tenants, and the pall held up by six of the *quorum ;* the whole parish followed the corpse with heavy hearts, and in their mourning suits, the men in frieze, and the women in riding-hoods. Captain Sentry, my master's nephew, has taken possession of the Hall-house, and the whole estate When my old master saw him a little before his death, he shook him by the hand, and wished him joy of the estate which was falling to him, desiring him only to make a good use of it, and to pay the several legacies, and the gifts of charity which he told him he had left as quit-rents upon the estate. The Captain truly seems a courteous man, though he says but little. He makes much of those whom my master loved, and shews great kindnesses to the old house-dog, that you know my poor master was so fond of. It would have gone to your heart to have heard the moans the dumb creature made on the day of my master's death. He has never joyed himself since; no more has any of us. 'Twas the melancholiest day for the poor people that ever happened in Worcester-shire. This is all from,

" Honoured Sir, your most sorrowful servant,

" EDWARD BISCUIT."

" P.S.—My master desired, some weeks before he died, that a book which comes up to you by the car-rier should be given to Sir Andrew Freeport, in his name."

This letter, notwithstanding the poor butler's man-ner of writing it, gave us such an idea of our good old friend, that, upon the reading of it, there was not a dry eye in the club. Sir Andrew, opening the book, found it to be a collection of acts of parliament. There was in particular the Act of Uniformity, with some pas-

sages in it marked by Sir Roger's own hand.   Sir
Andrew found that they related to two or three points
which he had disputed with Sir Roger the last time
he appeared at the club.   Sir Andrew, who would have 110
been merry at such an incident on another occasion,
at the sight of the old man's hand-writing, burst into
tears, and put the book into his pocket.   Captain Sentry informs me that the knight has left rings and
mourning for every one in the club.   115

O.

[In the following number Will Honeycomb is disposed
of; his sprightliness and knowledge of the town will be at
the service of the Club no more.   Captain Sentry succeeds
to the estate of his uncle Sir Roger de Coverley, and we are   5
to suppose that he will not often be seen in town for the future.   He almost says as much in a letter introduced in No.
544, probably written by Steele, in which also he takes occasion to protest that the passage in No. 410 relating to Sir
Roger's behaviour to the girl whom he met at the Temple   10
cloisters had been misunderstood, and that not the slightest
reflection on the knight's moral character had been intended.
In No. 541 we are told that the Templar has determined
upon "a closer pursuit of the law," which seems to be a way
of saying that he will not any longer frequent the club.]   15

R

NOTES TO THE DE COVERLEY PAPERS.

CHAPTER II.

"Spectator," No. 106.—Monday, July 2nd, 1711.
Hor. 1. Od. xvii. 14.

> Here plenty's liberal horn shall pour
> Of fruits for thee a copious shower,
> Rich honors of the quiet plain.

2 A month, July of 1711.

6 Sir Roger. Notwithstanding the difficulty into which it was known the *Tatler* had been drawn by describing real characters, and the express statement of the *Spectator*, in No. 262, that his writings were not "aimed at private persons," many futile attempts have been made to identify the original of Sir Roger De Coverley, as well as the other characters of the *Spectator*.

In 1783, Mr. Tyers, in his *Historical Essays on Mr. Addison*, named Sir John Packington, of Westwood, Worcestershire, as the prototype of Sir Roger; but, as Mr. Wills has pointed out, the assertion is untenable, for Sir John was twice married, an ardent politician and a barrister, while Sir Roger was a bachelor, and not greatly interested in either politics or law.

"The name of Roger of Coverley (Cuvèrley) applied to a *contre-danse* (i.e. a dance in which partners stand in opposite rows) anglicised, Country Dance, was ascribed to the house of Calverley, in Yorkshire, by an ingenious member thereof, Ralph Thoresby, who has left a MS. account of the family, written in 1717. Mr. Thoresby has it that Sir Roger of Calverley, in the time of Richard I. had a harper which was the composer of this tune; his evidence being, apparently, that persons of the name of Harper had lands in the neighborhood of Calverley. Mr. W. Chappell, who repeats this statement in his 'Popular Music of the Olden Time,' says that in a MS. of the beginning of the last century, this tune is called 'Old Roger of Coverlay, for evermore.' A Lancashire Hornpipe. In the Dancing Master of 1696, it is called 'Roger of Coverly.'   Mr. Chappell quotes also, in illustration of the familiar knowledge of this tune and its name in Addison's time, from the History of Robert Powell the Puppet Showman (1715), that upon the Preludis being ended, each party fell to bawling and calling for particular tunes.   The hobnail'd fellows, whose breeches and lu gs seem'd to be of the same leather, cried out for Cheshire Rounds, Roger of Coverly, &c."—Morley.

7 Humour. See note on Chap. vi. l. 29, also, on *D. V.* l. 33.

22 Valet-de-chambre. Words from foreign languages should not be used when it is possible to express the idea intended by any from our own.

27 Pad. For the knight's further treatment of this old horse, see Chapter xix.

33 Ancient. Still used in this sense in French.

39 Tempered = intermingled.   *Temper* and *distemper* were once used technically in the theory of medicine explained in the note on Chap. vi. l. 29, being applied to the mixture of the different humours.

57 In the nature of = in the capacity of.

59 Conversation -- behavior, deportment.
Cf. 1 Peter ii. 12 :—" Having your conversation honest among the Gentiles."

70 This cast, &c. This sentence is not properly constructed, as *This cast of mind* has no verb.   Arrange it correctly.

77 Insulted with Latin, &c. The fox-hunting squires of England at this time possessed but little learning or literary taste.   Yet it must not be supposed that literature was not cultivated in the country.   The great attention which was given to both poetical and prose composition, and the activity of literary men, both as scholars in their Colleges and as publishers of newspapers and pamphlets, sufficiently shews that in the political, religious and purely literary world there was not wanting a large number of prolific and able writers, and that they could command no mean audience. But compared with modern times, when railway and postal communication have made all England as accessible as the City of London then was, the means of general information was very small.

89 If he outlives, &c. As to how Sir Roger kept his promise, see Chapter xix.

97 Apply themselves. Not now used reflexively in this sense.

111 Bishop of St. Asaph. Lloyd, one of the Seven Bishops

who refused to read James II.'s Declaration of Indulgence. Mr.
Arnold thinks that Dr. Fleetwood, who then occupied the See,
or his predecessor, Beveridge, is meant.

112 Dr. South (1643—1716), called the "wittiest churchman" of the day, was one of the most bigoted defenders of the
doctrine of passive obedience. He often preached before Charles
II., and was much admired by the Court. He was a perfect
master of English prose ; his style being easy, vigorous and rhyth-
mical.

115 Archbishop Tillotson (1630—1694), next to Barrow, was
the most popular preacher of his time : he rendered himself conspicuous by his strong Puritan sympathies. His published sermons
fill fourteen volumes 8vo.   His style is easy, even to familiarity.

115 Bishop Saunderson (1587—1663), "one of the most
celebrated of the High-Church Divines, wrote works on casu-
istry, and sermons distinguished by great learning."—Shaw.

116 Dr. Barrow (1630—1677) was a man of almost universal
acquirements.   He was one of the greatest mathematicians of his
age, surpassed only by his pupil, Newton.   In science, he was
nearly as well versed as in mathematics.   His eloquence in the
pulpit was irresistible.   His sermons are laden with thought, and
filled with the powerful reasonings of a giant intellect.   Chatham
recommended Barrow to his son as the finest model of eloquence.

116 Dr. Calamy (1600—1666), originally a clergyman of the
Church of England, but afterwards a dissenting minister in London.   He took part in the *Smectymnuus*.   He opposed the execution of Charles I., and aided in bringing about the Restoration.   He became chaplain to Charles II. ; but the Act of Uniformity made him again a seceder.

130 Handsome elocution=A pleasing delivery.

CHAPTER III.

"Spectator," No. 108.—Wednesday, July 4th, 1711.

Phaedr. Fab. v. 2.

Out of breath to no purpose, and very busy about nothing.

This paper affords an excellent example of the method by
which the *Spectator* labored to correct the abuses and follies of
the period.   It is not by railing at what is wrong, but by taking

a particular case of the reprehensible custom, and so presenting it as, with quiet sly humor, to expose it to ridicule.

Will Wimble, like most of the *Spectator's* characters, has been traced to a supposed original. It has been said that he was a Mr. Thomas Morecraft, the younger son of a Yorkshire baronet. Mr. Steele was acquainted with him in early life and introduced him to Mr. Addison, from whom he received assistance. As Mr. Wills has pointed out, Will Wimble's is a continuation of the character of Mr. Thomas Gules (of No. 256 of the *Tatler*), who, " according to the principles of all younger brothers of his family, had never sullied himself with business, but had chosen rather to starve like a man of honour than to do anything beneath his quality. He produced several witnesses that he had never employed himself beyond the twisting of a whip, or the making of a pair of nut-crackers, in which he only worked for his diversion, in order to make a present now and then to his friends."

10 **Jack**, Fr. *Jaques*, James, is a term familiarly applied to a great variety of objects. Here a common pike.

25 **Quality**=rank. The word is now often used colloquially as a term of concealed contempt.

27 **Baronet.** The next title below a baron, and above a knight, and the lowest which is hereditary in England; instituted by James I. in 1611.

37 **Officious.** Lat. *ob* and *facio*, I do. Here, obliging. At present it means too obliging, intruding one's services where they are not wanted.

39 **Correspondence**=intercourse. It is now confined chiefly to intercourse by letter.

41 **Tulip-root.** The cultivation of particular species of flowers was begun in Europe by the Dutch in the seventeenth century. In 1636–7, a wonderful flower mania, chiefly about tulips, prevailed in Holland; the bulbs rose to an enormous price, and men speculated in them as wildly as in South-Sea shares. A single bulb sold for 13,000 florins. After the craze passed away many people were involved in financial ruin. The fashion of raising special flowers passed into England also, and is referred to in the text.

46 **Setting-dog,** often 'called *setter*, is a sporting dog of the same species as the spaniel, trained to sit or crouch to the game he finds.

Made=trained.

67 **No sooner . . but.** A comparative is now followed by *than*.

85 Particularities = particulars. Cf. Swift's *Journal*, Mar. 11, 1711 :—"I have a mind to write and publish an account of all the particularities of this fact,"

89 Quail pipe. A pipe used by fowlers for alluring quails.

105 Had rather. This seems to be an irregular construction for *would rather*. As it stands, *had* may be regarded as an incomplete verb with *rather* for its complement.

113 Accordingly, &c. Sir Andrew Freeport is the representative of the class of Englishmen who, having made large fortunes in trade, purchased landed estates. He, however, was not a "younger son," but had risen from the ranks by "honest industry." The foolish prejudices which Mr. Addison here derides, have not yet been given up, although many young scions of noble families do at present engage in commerce.

121 Improper = unqualified, unsuited.

CHAPTER IV

" Spectator," No. 110.—Friday, July 6th, 1711.

Virg. Æn. ii. 755.

> All things are full of horror and affright,
> And dreadful ev'n the silence of the night. —*Dryden.*

This paper is in Addison's plainest style. There is little ornament, no attempt at effect by inversions, unusual collocations or witticisms ; but a simple, direct and easy description of the old abbey walk, intermingled with quiet, but pointed reflections that do not fail to accomplish the evident design of making the superstitions of the time appear ridiculous.

10 Feedeth the young ravens.—Psalm cxlvii. 9.

13 It lies under. This form is now become colloquial, and is scarcely ever found in good authorities except with the prepositions "to," or "of."

42 Awfulness = solemnity.

46 Mr. Locke (1632-1704), who saw much of the vicissitudes of public life while following the fortunes of his patron, the Earl of Shaftesbury, was an original thinker and voluminous writer. The greatest of his works is his *Essay on the Human Understanding*, the object of which is to prove that all our ideas arise either from Sensation or Reflection.

67 Trivial is derived, according to Trench, from Lat. *tres*, three, and *via*, roads; and has its meaning from the trifling matters discussed by persons meeting at crossings. It is more probable that it is from Gr. πρειβω, to rub ; hence the worn or beaten path. As what comes out of the road is common or of little value, so *trivial* has that meaning.

85 Exorcised. Gr. ἐξορκίζω, to exorcise, (from ἐκ, from and, ὅρκος, an oath ;) Lat. *exorcizo*. To drive away, as evil spirits, by certain forms of conjuration.

Observe that superstitions linger longest among the most ignorant classes. The servants are very superstitious, Sir Roger is not quite free from the charge, while Mr. Spectator and the chaplain rise entirely above anything so foolish.

The folly of believing in "spirits and apparitions," and the ill effects of filling children's minds with ghost stories, are the subject of issue No. 12 of the *Spectator*.

103 Lucretius, a Roman poet who lived in the first century before Christ. His chief work is a didactic poem entitled *De Rerum Natura*.

CHAPTER V.

" Spectator," No. 112. Monday, July 9th, 1711.

Pythag.
> First, in obedience to thy country's rites,
> Worship th' immortal gods.

Mr. Wills says that the "church close to which Addison was born and where his father ministered may have supplied some of the traits to the exquisite picture of a rural Sabbath which this chapter presents.

" The parish church of Milston is a modest edifice, situated in a combe or hollow of the Wiltshire downs, about two miles northwest of Amesbury. In the parsonage house—now an honored ruin—on the 1st of May, 1672, Joseph Addison was born. It is only separated from the grave-yard by a hawthorn fence, and must have been, when inhabited, the beau-ideal of a country parsonage. It has a spacious garden, rich glebe, and commands a pretty view, bounded by the hill on which stands the church of Darrington.

" Milston church remains nearly in the same state as during the first twelve years of his life which Addison passed under its shadow. As no benevolent parishioner took the hint conveyed in Sir Roger's will, it is still without tower or steeple ; the belfry being nothing more than a small louvered shed. Within, the church is partitioned off by tall, worm eaten pews, and is scarcely capable of holding a hundred persons. At the east end stands the communion-table ' railed in.' It was once lighted by a stained-glass window ; but of this it was deprived by the cupidity of a deceased incumbent. The same person was guilty of a worse act : to oblige a friend—'a collector'—he actually tore out the leaf of the parish register which contained the entry of Joseph Ad lison's birth.

" Milston church does not display the texts of Scripture a'tri- buted to the Coverley edifice. If any existed when Addison wrote, they must have been since effaced by whitewash."

3 **Were** is here used as the supposition is contrary to the truth.

4 **Could have been thought of.** Observe the force of the tense.

5 **The polishing of.** The tendency at present is to omit both *the* and *of.*

10 **Habits**=clothes. Cf. French *habit.*

9 **Village.** Collective nouns may have their verbs and pronouns either singular or plural. The plural brings into prom- inence the individuals who compose the whole ; the singular, the whole which the individuals make up.

18 **Eye of the Village.** A very neat and expressive figure, or rather combination of figures. *Village* for villagers, by *Metonymy*, and the *eye* stands for the esteem which the villagers feel as a resu't of what they see, the instrument for the effect produced in the mind—*Metonymy.*

32 **Hassock.** Sw. *hwass*, a rush and A. S. *sacc*, a sack. A thick mat to kneel on at church.

47 **Particularities**=peculiarities.

60 **For** governs the phrase *being an idle fellow.* When the'par- ticiple of a verb of incomplete predication is used as a noun, i. e., as the name of a state or condition, it requires a noun or adjec- tive to complete it in the same way as any other part of the verb.

65 **Polite** is now chiefly used actively as *polished* is passively.

71 **As soon as** = when.

82 **Bible** is in the objective case the subject of *to be given,* which is a Complementary Infinitive completing the object *Bible.*

84 Flitch. A. S. *flicce.*

86 Place = salary of the place—*Metonymy*

95 Parson. Lat. *persona,* a mask ; from *per,* through and *sono,* I speak, or sound. In old Latin plays the actors all wore masks ; hence first the part and next the actor, was called *persona.* The *parson* is the chief *person* of a parish.

95 Squire. See note on *Garden* l. 815.

100 Tithe-stealers. Tithes (A. S. *teotha,* a tenth) were instituted in England by the Saxon Kings, and have continued to be paid in some form till the present time. They were for many centuries paid in kind, i. e. the tenth lamb, pig, sheaf, &c. The inconvenience of this method often led to the substitution of a money payment ; and in 1838, it was finally decided by Act of Parliament that tithes in all cases should be commuted into a rent charge. The old system gave much room for dispute and dishonesty.

113 Very hardly = with great difficulty.

115 How—soever. An example of *Tmesis,* the separation of the part of a compound word.

This charming essay exhibits the great beauty of Addison's style, so easy, so apparently artless, so genial in spirit, so kindly in reproof, so well adapted to induce the reader insensibly to adopt the opinions of the writer. The pious zeal of the old knight whom we, like his tenants and servants, are beginning to love and admire in spite of his little singularities, is quaintly depicted with a tender mixture of admiration and humor.

CHAPTER VI.

"Spectator," No. 115, Friday, July 13th, 1711.

Juv. Sat. x. 356 :—
Pray for a sound mind in a sound body.

15 This description, &c. This sentence has a looseness and obscurity very rare in the clear and limpid style of these papers. *Which* refers to *muscle* and *ligature,* and *that* to *bowels, bones, &c.*

The metaphor of *tubes and pipes* of *glands and strainers,* is no less obscure than the "system" which it is intended to explain. at least, to us who have given up as exploded the theory of "humors."

29 **Ferments the humours.** In the sixteenth century, as chemistry became a science, its principles were combined with those of physiology, and gave rise to a new school of chemical physicians. They considered that diseases were referrible to certain fermentations which took place in the blood, and that certain *humors* were naturally acid and others naturally alkaline, and according as one or the other of these predominated, so certain specific diseases were the result, which were to be removed by the exhibition of remedies of an opposite nature to that of the disease. This school was followed by the mathematical. See note on *D. V.* l. *33*.

41 **Spleen.** The *spleen* used to be regarded as the reservoir of all the peccant humors of the body ; and just as the liver was supposed to be the seat of the erotic passions, and the heart is still spoken of as that of the affections, so ' the spleen' came to mean anger, ill-humour, melancholy. In Addison's time the *spleen* and the *vapors* (the former applied to men and the latter to women) were terms much in vogue to indicate a state of nervous weakness and consequent depression of spirits, under which the images of the brain float with a visible distinctness before the patient. It is now called hypochondriasis.

42 **Vapours.** See above.

47 **As necessarily, &c.** *As* has here the force of a relative pronoun.

47 **It is so ordered—without it.** This repetition of *it* so near and in two senses is objectionable.

57 **Brows.** Commonly used in the singular, except in the compound eye-brow. Perhaps this is an imitation of the Latin *templa.* The figure is called *Enallage.*

60 **Forced into its several products** = forced to yield its several products.

67 **Indulge themselves** = indulge.

75 **Which he thinks.** *Which* is here connective, and as it is so far from its antecedent *horns,* the sentence would be easier if it was replaced by *and this.*

He—his—him. Arrange so as to remove the ambiguity in the pronouns.

90 **Distinction's sake.** We now write *for the sake of distinction.*

91 **Cost,** is intransitive.

96 Some account of. See papers 113, 118.

101 Left off Fox-hunting. Paper 116 informs us how Sir Roger made up for the loss of this exercise.

108 Dr. Sydenham (1624-1689) was the most distinguished English physician of the 17th century. He was educated at Oxford and Montpellier and practised at Westminster. He inclined in theory to the chemical school. His writings, *Opera Medica*, were once very popular.

110 Will see = wishes to see.

112 Medicini Gymnastica, or, a Treatise Concerning the Power of Exercise. By Francis Fuller, M.A.

124 Latin Treatise of Exercises. "Artis Gymnastica apud Antiquas," in Libri VI. (Venice, 1569). By Hieronymus Mercurialis, who died at Forli, in 1606. He speaks of the shadow-fighting in Lib. IV. cap. 5, and Lib. V. Cap. 2.—Morley.

128 Loaden, now laden or loaded.

136 Uneasy = troublesome.

"The favourite occupations of the country gentry were field-sports. These amusements, though they somewhat changed their character, do not appear to have at all diminished during the first half of the eighteenth century, and it was in this period that Gay, and especially Somerville, published the most considerable sporting poems in the language. Hawking, which had been extremely popular in the beginning of the seventeenth century, and which was a favourite sport of Charles II., almost disappeared in the beginning of the eighteenth century. Stag-hunting declined with the spread of agriculture, but hare-hunting still held its ground, and fox-hunting greatly increased. Cricket had apparently just risen."—Lecky's *England in the Eighteenth Century*, vol. 1, page 604.

110 Guelfes and Gibellines. "Two great parties, whose conflicts make up the history of Italy and Germany from the eleventh to the fourteenth century. Guelph is the Italian form of *Welfe*, and Gibelline of *Waiblingen*, and the origin of these two words are this: At the battle of Weinsberg in Suabia (1114), Conrad, duke of Franconia, rallied his followers with the war-cry *Hie Waiblingen*, while Henry the Lion, duke of Saxony, used the cry of *Hie Welfe* (the family names of the rival chiefs). The former were the supporters of the imperial authority in Italy, and the latter were the anti-imperialists."—Brewer.

CHAPTER VII.

" Spectator," No. 117.   Saturday, July 14th, 1711.
  Virg. Ecl. viii. 108 :—
  With voluntary dreams they cheat their minds.

3 **Hovering faith.**   This metaphor is drawn from the manner in which some birds, when about to descend to the ground, *hover* in the air as if undecided where to alight.   It is still further carried out in the word *settle*.   Mr. *Spectator* was not alone, among even the best and most enlightened classes of English society, in holding this "hovering faith."

13 **Every particular nation** = every individual nation.

20 **Infernal commerce** = intercourse with evil spirits.

23 Before **reflect** understand *when I*.   The clause is adverbial to *endeavour*.

27 **Whether there are, &c.**   This is a noun clause in apposition to *question*.

35 **Which .... of.**   This colloquial form of expression is almost always employed in the *Spectator*.   The more formal usage of placing the preposition before the relative would not be in *keeping* with the easy and familiar style of these essays.   The relative *that* never admits the preposition before it.   See *that I met with* in the same line.

41 **In a close lane, &c.**   This quotation is from the *Orphan* (act ii.), by Thomas Otway (1651—1685).   Otway was the son of a clergyman.   After leaving Oxford, he tried, but without success, the profession of an actor.   He produced a number of dramatic pieces, which were performed on the stage, some with great success.   The best are the *Orphan* and *Venice Preserved*.   According to Sir Walter Scott, his talents in the scenes of passionate affection " rival, at least, and sometimes excel, those of Shakspeare : more tears have been shed, probably, for the Sorrows of Belvidera and Monimia than for those of Juliet and Desdemona."

49 **Of a piece.**   Explain.

50 **All** is an adverb qualifying *o'er*.

69 **If the dairy-maid, &c.**   The student should notice the effect of *variety* in the length of the sentences.   If one or more short ones are introduced after others of greater length, the mo-

notony is broken and the mind relieved of the strain caused by following long and complicated statements. Clearer, and consequently deeper, impressions are made by stating the condition first, as in these sentences.

85 Whispered me in the ear = whispered in my ear. This use of the dative is now obsolete in prose.

88 Besides is a preposition, showing the relation between *is reported* and *that*. That is a demonstrative pronoun, and the noun clause.

88 Moll is said, &c., is in apposition to it.

89 To have spoken. This is a noun infinitive, and represents the retained object after the passive voice.

96 As = in the capacity of.

This advice shews that the old knight had a lurking suspicion that witchcraft was a reality in this "particular instance." He evidently was not able to rise as far above the superstition of his age as his chaplain, for, like Mr. *Spectator*, whose humanity prevents him from condemning any individual, he "believes, in general, that there is, and has been, such a thing as witchcraft," if he does not go further and actually believe that Moll White is a veritable witch.

113 Scarce a. *Scarce* is an adverb, modifying **a** = one.

121 Commerces = intercourse.

By the statute of Elizabeth, in 1562, witchcraft was first made in itself a capital crime in England. The crime was still more minutely defined by the Act of James VI. (Anno I, cap. 12), which was in full force at the time the *Spectator* was published. By it, death was decreed to whoever dealt with evil or wicked spirits, or invoked them to or for any purpose whatever. Under this Act a vast number of persons, chiefly aged women, fell victims to the murderous fanaticism of the times. During the sittings of the Long Parliament, which was probably the period that witnessed the largest numbers of executions : no less than three thousand persons perished by legal executions, besides many more who were put to death by the mob. Even so great a man as Sir Mathew Hale, one of the wisest and best men of his time, was so misled by the superstition of his day that he tried and condemned two women for bewitching children ; and Sir Thomas Browne, who had written a work on *Popular Fallacies*, was present at the trial and gave his opinion against the prisoners. Chief Justices North and Holt were among the first persons occupying high positions who had the humanity and courage to set themselves against this delusion. The year after this essay was written Jane Wenham was prosecuted by Sir Henry Chauncey and the incumbent of the parish of Walkerne, in which she lived. She was found guilty, but was reprieved by Judge Powel. In 1716, a Mrs. Hicks and her daughter, aged nine, were hanged at Huntingdon for selling their souls to the devil, and raising a storm by pulling off their stockings and making a lather of soap. With this crowning atrocity the catalogue in England closes. The Witch Act was repealed in the tenth year of George II.

CHAPTER VIII.

"Spectator" No. 121, Thursday, July 19th, 1711.

Vir. Georg. i. 415:

> I deem their breasts inspired—
> With a divine sagacity—

3 Instinct. Instinct, according to Bain, is "untaught ability." Archdeacon Paley, *Nat. Theol.*, ch. 18, explains it to be "a propensity prior to experience and independent of instrucstruction." See also Darwin's *Descent of Man*, pt. I, ch. 2 and 3.

17 Bayle. "Bayle's Dictionary, here quoted, first appeared in English in 1701. Pierre Bayle himself had first produced it in two folio vols. in 1695-6, and was engaged in controversies caused by it until his death in 1706, at the age of 59. He was born at Carlat, educated at the universities of Puylaurens and Toulouse, was professor of philosophy successively at Sedan and Rotterdam till 1693, when he was deprived for scepticism. He is said to have worked fourteen hours a day for forty years, and has been called 'the Shakespeare of dictionary makers.'"—Morley.

24 Tully. Marcus Tullius Cicero, the great Roman orator, (B.C. 166-43.)

26 Dampier, a celebrated buccaneer and explorer, was born in 1652. After his buccaneering expedition, he was sent out by the government to explore. He published *a voyage round the world*, and several other works giving an account of his travels.

74 Locke. Essay on the Human Understanding, Bk ii. ch. 9, s. 13. See note on.

91 Dr. More, (1730-1802) a Scotch physician, is the author of a number of works on various subjects, travels, medicine, and fiction.

92 **Cardan** (1501-1576), a famous mathematician, naturalist and physician, was born at Pavia. He was a very voluminous writer, having composed 122 treatises on physic, mathematics, astronomy, rhetoric, history, medicine, &c,

124 **Boyle.** Robert Boyle (1627-1691), one of the greatest natural philosophers of his age, was the seventh son of the Earl of Cork. He devoted his life to the furtherance of science, and published a vast number of volumes containing his researches. The first complete edition of his works was that by Dr. Birch in five vols. folio, in 1744. He was one of the founders of the Royal Society.

146 **Royal Society,** an association for the promotion of mathematical and physical science, was incorporated by act of Parliament in 1662. Its members are elected by ballot, fifteen being elected each year out of those who have been previously proposed. To be elected a member is now considered the highest scientific honor an Englishman can receive; the *Philosophical Transactions* of the Society have been published every year since 1665, and form a complete history of the progress of science.

159 **After**=Notwithstanding.

CHAPTER IX.

"Spectator," No. 122. Friday, July 20th, 1711.

Pub. Syr. Frag :—

An agreeable companion upon the road is as good as a coach.

This paper is one of the most characteristic as well as the most interesting of the selection, and will amply repay the closest study. Mr. Addison never appears to more advantage than when planning his own observations or quietly unfolding some picture from his rich imagination. His mild, but insinuating tones, his lively fancy and sterling common sense, his clear relation and limpid description, never fail to attract attention and profit the reader; while his kindly humor scarcely breaking into satire spreads through the whole a charming warmth and geniality. The character of the old knight receives in this essay some of its finest touches. His benevolence scarcely appears till it is dashed with ancestral class distinction; our respect for him rises as his love of peace and "good neighborhood" awakens his shrewdness in settling Tom Touchy's dispute, but wavers as his vanity prompts him "to whisper in the ear of the judge"; once more, we admire him who is so much beloved and esteemed by all his people, though he makes a purposeless speech, but turns again to smile at the gentle hint that his burly face that covers a heart in which even the inn-keeper finds a place, is so easily transformed into a Saracen's head.

3 Last = latter.

19 Needs. See note on *Garden*.

26 Yeoman, i.e., a freeholder. At the Revolution, it has been estimated, the average annual income of a temporal lord was 2,800*l.*, that of a baronet 880*l.*, that of esquires and other gentlemen 450*l.* and 280*l.*, respectively, while there were 40,000 yeomen having 91*l.* each, a year, and 120,000 with 55*l.* annual income.

29 Dinner. *Metonymy.*

34 Shoots flying. The *Ellipsis* makes the expression ambiguous, but the author's meaning will scarcely be mistaken.

39 Sued is from Lat. *sequor*, I follow ; Fr. *suis.* Hence, to follow a person *into a court of justice.*

39 Quarter Sessions, in England, is a court or meeting of justices of the peace, or magistrates of the county, who assemble every quarter of the year for judicial and miscellaneous business. The jurisdiction of this court includes all criminal offences except the highest class. The chief officer is called the *custos rotulorum*, or keeper of the records. He is always one of the justices of the county. In this paper he is called the judge.

43 So long. *That* is now used to denote consequence.

46 Cast and been cast. Won his suit in the court at one time and lost at another.

55 Arose = had arisen.

64 They neither of them were = Neither of them was.

68 Assizes strictly means the periodical session of the judges of the superior courts of Common Law, held in the various counties of England, chiefly for the purpose of gaol delivery and trying causes at *Nisi Prius :* but as the term is often loosely applied, it probably stands for the quarter-sessions here.

69 Was sat - had began its sitting.

70 All the justices, &c. This is a noun clause after the pre·position *notwithstanding.*

72 For = for the purpose of maintaining.

77 Great appearance and solemnity = a very solemn and dignified appearance.

92 A figure, &c. If we credit the knight with shrewdness in understanding human nature, we must also admit a little vanity —pardonable though it be.

99 That was not, &c. This clause is adjectival to *his,*

109 Unknown to Sir Roger. This phrase is absolute and forms an adverbial extension of the predicate *put.*

110 Him = a likeness of him.—*Metonymy.*

116 Made . . compliment. *Paid* is now used.

133 Discovering = exhibiting. It is not used now causa·tively.

147 Met, i.e., have met. The present perfect tense and not the imperfect, is used when the period of time in which the event occurred, extends up to, and includes the present.

CHAPTER **X.**

" Spectator," No. 123.—Saturday, July 21st, 1711.

Hor. 4 Od. iv. 33 :—

> Yet the best blood by learning is refined,
> And virtue arms the solid mind ;
> Whilst vice will stain the noblest race,
> And the paternal stamp efface.—*Oldisworth.*

In the vast variety of subjects which flowed from the fertile imagination of the authors of the *Spectator*, the power of the tale to interest the general reader was not overlooked. At intervals, stories and visions are introduced throughout the whole course of its publication, not regularly, but probably, when it seemed desirable to reawaken a more general interest. Like the one before us, they all manifest a double purpose ; the interest they arouse is always utilized to impress some important moral or socail lesson. No amount of censure or reprehension could have been nearly so effectual, in exposing or correcting the mistaken methods of educating young people or of introducing a more prudent system, not to speak of the charming pleasure afforded every reader.

3 Rid. This form is always used in the *Spectator*. It is now obsolete.

Novel. Addison calls this story of Eudoxus and Leontine a novel, or fictitious story. The novel in its modern form did not exist till the latter part of the century. Richardson's *Pamela*, usually considered the first example of the modern domestic novel, was not published till 1746. De Foe's *Robinson Crusoe* was published in 1719.

116 Inns of Court. "The four voluntary societies which have the exclusive right of calling to the bar. They are the Inner Temple, the Middle Temple, Lincoln's Inn, and Gray's Inn. Each is governed by a board of benchers."—Brewer.

CHAPTER XI.

"Spectator," No. 125. Tuesday, July 24th, 1711.

Virgil Æn. vi. 832 :—

This thirst of kindred blood, my sons, detest,
Nor turn your face against your country's breast.
—Dryden.

6 Stripling. The termination *ling* is a double diminutive formed of *el* and *ing*. To the idea of diminution, it usually adds that of contempt as *lordling*, witling, underling. This, however, is not the case in foundling.

7 St. Anne's Lane. Of the two lanes of this name, Mr. Cunningham thinks, the one turning out of Great Peter Street, Westminster, is meant.

8 Upon which, &c. This is a principal clause.

15 A Saint before hanged. This is an example before structure, i.e., the different parts of the sentence are made similar in form. There is also combined with it, in this case, a species of antithesis or contrast in the meaning of the two clauses.

24 Honest. See note on *Garden*, l. 746.

26 Land-tax and game.

As the representative of the *landed-interest*, Sir Roger considered the keeping up the land-tax and securing the game the two all-important duties of the Government.

41 **A furious party spirit.** At no period in English History has party spirit raged more fiercely than at the time when these papers were written. The strong ground taken by the contending factions had driven them to the opposite poles. Religious rancour added to the bitterness of political division. The religio-political sermons of Dr. Sacheverell had awakened intense feeling. The cry that the church was in danger had, through the earnest efforts of the High Church clergy, been one of the most potent means by which the overwhelming Tory majority of 1710 was returned. The Whigs saw that the continuance of the war was the only chance for their retaining power, and used every means, fair and unfair, for attaining that end. But the machinations of the Tories were more than a match for their intriguing. Mrs. Masham supplanted the Duchess of Marlborough in the Queen's favor, and the Duke was forced to give up the command of the armies. These questions, the church and the war, along with succession, wrought the country to a white heat of partizan fury, that had all the injurious results described in these papers. Mr. Addison himself was deprived of all his employments, and Steele lost his office of Gazetteer. But even these days had bright gleams of beauty and sunshine. Had it been possible for Steele to continue his political pamphleteering or had Addison thought it would avail anything to ply his satire on the stolid Tory voting majority of six to one, they would have both continued at their work, and it is quite possible that they would never have turned their attention to the composition of these Social Essays, and the *Spectator* would have been an ardent defender of Whig politics, like the *Whig Examiner*, in which Addison strongly worked for his party before and during the election of 1710, or the *Freeholder*, in which he returned to the task of weakening his opponents as soon as their divisions and mistakes had laid them open to attack.

CHAPTER XII.

"Spectator," No. 126. Wednesday, July 25th, 1711.

Virgil Æn. x. 108 :—

Rutulians, Trojans, are the same to me.—Dryden.

44 **Diodorus Siculus,** a Greek historian who spent thirty

years in writing a history of the world in forty books. The work was written some time after the death of Julius Cæsar.

86 Sir Andrew Freeport is the character who, in the plan of *Spectator*, represents the moneyed-interest in England. Ever since the reign of Henry VII. the commerce of England had been rapidly increasing. In 1688, Gregory King estimated there were 2,000 eminent merchants with an income of 400*l*. each, 8,000 lesser merchants with 200*l*. each. Some of them became immensely wealthy, and in many instances, like Sir Andrew, withdrew their money from commerce and invested it in the purchase of land, and thus gradually gave rise to a new landed aristocracy, rivalling in wealth the most ancient houses of England.

96 Bait = take refreshments.

125 Correspondence = intercourse.

126 As to. See *How to parse*, par. 479.

136 Fanatic. A dissenter.

138 As = because.

146 First principles = beginnings.

CHAPTER XIII.

"Spectator," No. 130. Monday, July 30th, 1711.

Virgil Æn. vii. 748 :—

> A plundering race, still eager to invade,
> On spoil they live, and make of theft a trade.

3 Gipsies. "The English name ' Gipsy' and the Hungarian ' Pharaoh-nepet' (Pharaoh's people, applied to this race, testify to the popular (but erroneous) belief that they are of Egyptian origin. They were proscribed by Stat. 22 Hen. viii. c. 10 (1530) as the 'outlandish people calling themselves Egyptians.' There is a legend that they were expelled for having refused hospitality to Joseph and Mary, with the infant Saviour, on the banks of the Nile ; and it is stated that when they first appeared in Europe *circ.* 1418, they were led by one who styled himself ' Duke Michael of Little Egypt.' But in Egypt itself, where they are numerous, they are regarded as strangers quite as much as in Europe ; and their language affords ample proof that they are in reality of Indian origin. One of their names for themselves is *Sinte*, as coming from Sind i.e. India ; and the

Turks called them 'Tchingani,' from a tribe still existing near the mouth of the Indus (*Tshin-calo*, black Indians). They much resemble the Nuls or Bazegurs, a wandering race in Hindostan, of very low repute among the other Hindoos ; and it is conjectured that they belonged to the Soudras, a very low Indian caste, which were expelled by the Timour Beg c. 1390. In Feb., 1856, Sir H. Rawlinson read before the Royal Geographical Society of London a paper on the migrations of the Gypsies, tracing them distinctly from the Indus, through Paris and Syria, and Asia Minor, to the Bosphorus, whence they passed into Europe in the fourteenth century (see 'Athenæum,' 1856, p. 312). The earliest circumstantial account of the Gipsies in England is 'The Art of Juggling or Leger-demain by s. R., [Samuel Rid], Lond. 1612, 4to. This author states that they arrived in England about the year 1512. (Notes and Queries, 1st ser., xi. 826)."— Griffith.

14 **It is ten to one but,** i.e. it is ten chances to one chance if—not. *But* performs the double function of conjunction and negative adverb.

24 **Young fellow.** Fellow is in the objective case, the Retained Object after *promised.* See *How to Parse*, par. 123.

30 **Sweethearts.** This is an example of simulated derivation i. e., the word appears to be derived from *sweet* and *heart;* but it really comes from *sweet* and the Gothic Suffix *ard.*

40 **Communicated**—presented to be inspected. We now *communicate* intelligence, &c.

41 **Cassandra,** i.e., a prophetess. Using a proper name instead of a common is called *Antonomosia.*

Cassandra, the daughter of Priam, King of Troy, was gifted with the power of prophecy ; but Apollo, whom she had offended, brought it to pass that no one believed her predictions.

51 **Line of life.** The line in the palm which passes around nearest the thumb ; when deep it is said to indicate long life, and *vice versa.*

77 **Palmistry.** Note the *Pun.* The word usually signifies the pretended science of telling fortunes by the lines in the *palm* of the hand. It is here used for the action of the hand by which pockets are picked.

CHAPTER XIV.

" Spectator." No. 131.—Tuesday, July 31st. 1711.

Virgil Ecl. x. 63 :—

Once more, ye woods, adieu.

6 Beats about. *Beat*, A. S. *beatan*, properly signifies to strike often. Hence to beat about, is to go about striking the shrubbery to "put up" the game, to search for it.

That it may be explained by supposing that it was originally regarded as a demonstrative pronoun having the sentence following in apposition to it.

It is now considered pleonastic.

16 In the same manner, &c. This sentence is very loosely constructed, the phrase *to try, &c.*, is not well placed and the clause *where I, &c.*, hangs heavily at the close. The student should arrange properly.

16 A month's excursion. The first paper from Coverley Hall, was published on July 2nd, of this year.

19 Several subjects. Witches, widows, gipsies, &c.

25 Put up. = I start up.

36 Taciturnity. See Author's Preface.

36 Particular way of life. Describe.

47 Cunning. Literally knowing. Here, one who possesses some secret knowledge or art.

50 White witch. It was believed that there were three classes of witches—white, black and gray. The first helped, but could not hurt ; the second the reverse ; and the third did both.

55 Jesuit. Jesuits or Society of Jesus is a celebrated religious order in the Roman Catholic Church. It was founded by Ignatius Loyola in 1554. Its motto is *ad majorem Dei gloriam* (To God's greater glory), and the members in addition to the threefold obligations of all Catholic religious orders, of chastity, poverty and obedience, take a fourth, binding themselves to go as missionaries wherever the Pope may desire them. Here Jesuit is used for any priest of the Catholic Church.

As the Act of Conformity and the Test Act were not sufficient to gratify the intolerance of the Parliament of William III., in

1698, a still more stringent and disgraceful law was passed, enacting that "any person apprehending and prosecuting to conviction any such bishop, priest, or Jesuit, for saying mass, or exercising any priestly unction, is to receive a reward of a hundred pounds. The punishment for such convicted persons, or for a papist keeping a school, is to be perpetual imprisonment. Every person educated in the popish religion, upon attaining the age of eighteen, to take the oath of allegiance and supremacy and subscribe the declaration against transubstantiation and the worship of saints, and in default of such oath and subscription, is declared incapable of purchasing lands, or of inheriting lands under any devise or limitation, the next of kin, being a protestant, to enjoy such devised lands during life."—Knight's *History of England*, p. 681.

60 Converses, &c. i.e., has intercourse with a great variety of people.

62 Discarded Whig. The Tory party was returned to parliament at the election of 1710, and Mr. Addison lost his post of Chief Secretary for Ireland.

70 But because = than because.

87 The crowd . . . alone. An *Epigram*, "a figure which rouses the mind by a conflict between the form of the language and the meaning really conveyed,

94 Will Honeycomb. See Chapter I.

106 Pr'ythee=I pray thee.

CHAPTER XV.

"Spectator," No. 269. January 8th, 1712.

Ovid, Ars Am. I. 241.
Most rare is now our old simplicity.—*Dryden*.

9 Came. A proper sequence of tenses requires *had come*.

10 Gray's Inn walks. Gray's Inn Gardens were long a fashionable promenade. They are now a pent up retreat for poverty. The upper walk was the *terrace*. In this was placed a sundial on a stone pedestal, around which, on one side, a number of seats were arranged in a semi-circle.

14 Prince Eugene (1663-1736), a great general and statesman, was first intended for the Church, but, on account of the banishment of his mother, he renounced his country, France, and entered the service of the Emperor Leopold, as a volunteer against the Turks. In the war of the Spanish Succession, he was appointed president of the Council of War, and with Marlborough gained the important victories of Blenheim and Oudenarde.

The object of his present mission to England, was to urge the prosecution of the war against France and have Marlborough restored to his position as commander-in-chief of the English forces. The Whigs and the people who alike desired the continuance of the war, idolized the prince. The Tories also and the Queen received him on his arrival with every mark of favour, but when they found that he could not be induced to abandon the fallen Duke, they heaped every indignity upon him. He arrived in England on the 5th of January, three days before this paper appeared, and left on the 17th of March, without having accomplished his object.

21. Scanderbeg (1414-1467) the famous chief of Epirus was, in 1423, given a hostage to the Turks for the obedience of the Albanian Chiefs. His beauty and intelligence so pleased the Sultan that he had him brought up as his own son. After some service in the Sultan's armies, he deserted, returned to his own country, gathered around him his fellow-countrymen and defeated the Turkish armies sent against him. After twenty-four years of incessant toil, he died at Alessio, having defeated the Turks in twenty-two pitched battles.

38. One another. Is this strictly correct?

41. A most incomparable sermon. Sir Roger's appreciation of Dr. Barrow does credit to his intellectual ability and literary taste, as well as to the liberality of his religious sentiments.

70. Chines. Lat. *spina;* Fr. *échine;* Bret. *kein,* the back. Properly the back-bone or spine of an animal. Here, a piece of the back.

88. Smutting one another. Cf. *D. V.* l. 27.

93. The Act of Parliament. This Act is usually called the Occasional Conformity Bill. Its object was to exclude the Dissenters from all Government positions of power, profit or dignity. The Act of Uniformity had been evaded by Nonconformists, by occasionally attending the Established Church and communing in it. Many Dissenters had risen to important positions, and thus provoked the opposition of the High Church party. In 1702, 1703 and 1704, measures were passed in the

Commons, but rejected in the Lords, for suppressing Occasional Conformity. After the election of 1710, which turned upon Church questions, and in which the Whig party was defeated, largely through the Sacheverell agitation, the question was revived. A few of the extreme Tory party joined with the Whigs to defeat the peace of Utrecht, making it a condition that the Non-conformists should be abandoned. Accordingly, the Bill was passed in 1711. It provided that all persons holding positions of trust or profit and all common councilmen who attended any Non-conformist place of worship, should forfeit their office and pay a fine of £40. It had but little effect, as the Non-conformists who held office refrained entirely from going to church during the time it was in force, and held worship in their own houses.

109. Pope's procession. " Each anniversary of Queen Elizabeth's accession (Nov. 17th), was for many years celebrated by citizens of London in a manner expressive of their detestation of the Church of Rome. A procession—at times sufficiently attractive for royal spectators—paraded the principal streets, the chief figure being an effigy of

' The Pope, that pagan full of pride :'

well executed it was and expensively adorned with robe and tiara. He was accompanied by a train of Cardinals and Jesuits, and at his car stood a buffoon in the likeness of a horned devil. After having been paraded through divers streets, his holiness was exultingly burned opposite the Whig Club near the Temple gate, in Fleet Street. After the discovery of the Rye-house Plot, the Pope's Procession was discontinued ; but was resuscitated on the acquittal of the Seven Bishops and the dethronement of James II. Sacheverell's trial had added a new interest to the ceremony ; and on the occasion referred to by Sir Roger, besides a popular dread of the church being—from the listlessness of the ministers and the machinations of the Pretender—in danger, there was a very general opposition to the peace with France, for which the Tories were intriguing. The party cry of " No peace" was shouted in the same breath with " No Popery." The Whigs were determined, it was said, to give significance and force to these watchwords by getting up the anniversary show of 1711 with unprecedented splendor. No good Protestant, no honest hater of the French, could refuse to subscribe his guinea for such an object ; and it was said, upwards of a thousand pounds were collected for the effigies and their dresses and decorations alone, independent of a large fund for incidental expenses. The Pope, the devil, and the Pretender were, it was asserted, fashioned in the likeness of the obnoxious Cabinet Ministers. The procession was to take place at night, and 'a thousand mob' were to be hired to carry flambeaux at a crown a-piece, and as much beer and brandy as would inflame them for mischief. The pageant was to open with 'twenty-four bagpipes marching four and four, and playing the memorable tune of Lillibulero.' The remainder of the procession was to be formed with equal display, and the whole carried out in the most imposing manner. The Tories, who feared the consequences of a popular demonstration, spread the most exaggerated reports of these preparations, and asserted that the real intention was to prolong the war and maltreat the Ministers ; for this reason they sent a posse of constables to Drury Lane to destroy and carry off the images and entire paraphernalia. Swift, in his Journal, says, the images were not worth forty pounds ; yet to the public he either gave or superintended an account of the affair which was simply a string of all the mendacious exaggerations then wilfully put about by his patrons. Such were the party tactics of Sir Roger's time."—Wills.

114. To get him a stand, &c. This was highly necessary, for, whenever the prince appeared in public, he was immediately surrounded by immense crowds.

121. Baker's Chronicle. Sir Richard Baker (1568-1645), author of the *Chronicle of the Kings of England*, and several pious works, was educated at Oxford. For debts contracted by his wife's family, he was thrown into the Fleet prison, where he wrote his works. His *Chronicle* was, notwithstanding its many errors, greatly esteemed among the country gentry, and considered an authority on all matters of English history.

128. Squire's. Squire's Coffee House was situated in Fulwood's Rents, which led to Gray's Inn Gardens. It was frequented by benchers and students of Gray's Inn. The house was very roomy and had a wide staircase. See Timbs' *Clubs and Club Life*.

135. Supplement. One of the newspapers of the time. The first Daily in England was begun in 1702. See Grant's *Newspaper Press*.

CHAPTER XVI.

"Spectator," No. 329. Tuesday, March 18th, 1712.

Hor. i. Ep. vi. 27 :—

> With Ancus, and with Numa, kings of Rome,
> We must descend into the silent tomb.

2. My paper upon Westminster Abbey. *Spectator*, No. 26. It contains brief remarks upon the epitaphs, some reflections on seeing a grave dug, a stricture on Sir Cloudesley Shovel's monument, and closes with some further thoughts inspired by the place.

18. Widow Trueby's Water. One of the many fashionable drinks of the time. Such mixtures were considered good for the vapors and the spleen. Mr. Addison is said to have been fond of these draughts, although he professes to dislike the taste of this one. These disguised forms of ardent spirits are advertised in several numbers of the *Spectator*.

35. Sickness being at Dantzic. A plague raged there in 1709.

35. When of a sudden, &c. A sentence should possess unity, i. e., the parts should form one whole. Hence, this clause should commence a new sentence.

45. Jointure. An estate settled on a wife to be enjoyed after her husband's death. It is here used in a general sense for income or fortune.

48. Engaged. This must have taken place since Mr. *Spectator* was out in the country in July of the preceding year.

62. Virginia. It is believed that the use of tobacco was introduced into England about the time of Queen Elizabeth. James I. issued a *Counter-blaste to Tobacco*, in which he described its use as "a custom loathsome to the eye, hateful to the nose, harmful to the brain, dangerous to the lungs, and in the black, stinking fume thereof nearest resembling the horrible stygian smoke of the pit that is bottomless." The opinions both of kings and people had changed before Sir Roger's day.

69. Sir Cloudesley Shovel rose from being a cabin boy to the rank of admiral of a fleet. When returning from an unsuccessful attack on Toulon, his fleet was wrecked (1707). His body was found and buried in the sand by some fishermen. A ring which they took off discovered his quality—and he was afterwards removed to Westminster Abbey. The monument is in the South aisle of the choir. It was designed by F. Bird. In the number of the *Spectator* above referred to, Mr. Addison says: "This monument has very often given me great offence; instead of the brave rough English admiral, which was the distinguishing character of that plain, gallant man, he is represented on his tomb by a figure of a beau, dressed in a long periwig, and reposing himself upon velvet cushions under a canopy of state."

73. Dr. Busby. (1606-1695.) The most celebrated of English schoolmasters was headmaster of Westminster school from 1640 till his death. He has the reputation of having "bred up the largest number of learned scholars that ever adorned any age or nation." His monument, sculptured by Bird, stands near that of Sir Cloudesley Shovel.

83. Cecil. "In the Chapel of St. Nicholas. This tomb was erected by the great Lord Burleigh, in the reign of Queen Elizabeth, to the memory of his wife Mildred and their daughter Anne, whose effigies lie under a carved arch. 'At the base of the monument, within Corinthian columns, are kneeling figures of Lord Cecil, their son and three grand-daughters. The inscription is in Latin, very long and tiresome.' Peter Cunningham's *Westminster Abbey*."—Wills.

85. Martyr, &c. "Described in Murray's *London* as an alabaster statue of Elizabeth Russell, of the Bedford family—foolishly shown for many years as the lady who died by the prick of a needle."—Arnold.

93. Two Coronation chairs. These stand in the chapel of Edward the Confessor. One, the King's chair, encloses the stone referred to in the note on *Jacob's pillar*, l. 96, the other the Consort's chair, was constructed for the coronation of Mary, wife of William III. Both are still used at Coronations.

96 Jacob's Pillar. "This is the stone enclosed in our coronation chair, which was brought from Scone by Edward I., and said to be the stone on which the patriarch Jacob laid his head when he dreamt about the ladder reaching to heaven. This stone was originally used in Ireland as a coronation stone. It was called 'Innisfoil,' or stone of fortune."—Brewer.

103 Trepanned = entrapped. In this sense, it is said by Skinner to be derived from Trapani, a part of Sicily where, in the reign of Queen Elizabeth, some English ships were invited, with great show of friendship, and then detained. It is more probable that it comes from A. S. *treppe*, a trap; *treppan*, to snare. In this sense it is usually spelt *trapan*. *Trepan*, an instrument for removing portions of bone, is from Gr. $\tau\rho\upsilon\pi\acute{\alpha}\omega$, to bore.

117 Touched for the evil. The kings of England, like those of France, were long believed to have the power of curing the struma, or scrofulous tumors, by their touch. The English kings were supposed to have inherited the power from Edward the Confessor, and retained, except in the case of William III., till Queen Anne. No amount of profligacy, immorality on the part of the king, nor even the Reformation, shook the popular faith in the efficacy of the royal touch. With the burst of enthusiasm that heralded in the Restoration, the superstition was revived, and Charles II. is said to have touched 100,000 persons in the course of his reign. The apostacy of James did not deprive him of the virtue, and in Anne's reign the belief was reawakened by the high-church clergy for the purpose of strengthening the Tory party ; and so far were religious feelings carried during the Sachaverell agitation, that if the queen had died then there is little doubt that the Pretender would have been at once recalled to the throne. The service which had been previously printed separately was in Anne's reign inserted in the prayer-book, and the privy council issued proclamations stating that the queen would perform the miracle. On a single day in 1712 two hundred persons, among them Samuel Johnson, was touched, and the royal physician states that many of the cures were real.

123 Without an head. "This is the effigy of Henry V., which was of plated silver, except the head, and that was of solid metal. At the dissolution of the monasteries the figure was stripped of its plating and the head stolen."—Wills.

———

CHAPTER XVII.

"Spectator," No. 335, Tuesday, March 25th, 1712.

Hor. Ars Poet. 327 :—

> Keep Nature's great original in view,
> And thence the living images pursue.

3 New Tragedy. This was "The Distressed Mother," a drama by Ambrose ("Pastoral") Philips, a friend of Addison. He (1675-1749) was the author of some Pastorals, an epistle to the Earl of Dorset, a fragment of Sappho and three tragedies.

The "Distressed Mother" is Andromache, the widow of
Hector. At the fall of Troy, she and her son Astyanax fell to
the lot of Pyrrhus, king of Epirus. Pyrrhus fell in love with her
and wished to marry her, but she refused him. At length an
embassy from Greece, headed by Orestes, son of Agamemnon,
was sent to Epirus to demand the death of Astyanax, lest in
manhood he might seek to avenge his father's death. Pyrrhus
told Andromache he would protect her son, and defy all Greece,
if she would consent to marry him ; and she yielded. While the
marriage rites were going on, the Greek ambassadors fell on
Pyrrhus and murdered him. As he fell he placed the crown on
the head of Andromache, who thus became queen of Epirus,
and the Greeks hastened to their ships in flight. This play is
an English translation of Racine's *Andromaque* (1667)"—Brewer.

A few days before this paper appeared in No. 290 of the
Spectator, Mr. Addison had given a highly commendatory account of this tragedy—an account which, indeed, we can by no
means accept, but one which, like the present paper, most con-
clusively shows that in the narrow, stinted and sentimental age
in which he lived, and by whose opinions he was too much
guided in his own dramatic writings, he had the discernment to
see what the comedy should be, as well as the courage to declare
his convictions.

5 " The *Committee*, or *the Faithful Irishman*, was written by
Sir Robert Howard soon after the Restoration, with for its heroes
two cavalier colonels, whose estates are sequestered, and their
man Teg (Teague), an honest blundering Irishman. The Cavaliers defy the Roundhead Committee, and ' the day may come.'
says one of them, ' when those that suffer for their consciences
and honour may be rewarded.' Nobody who heard this from
the stage in the days of Charles II., could feel that the day *had*
come. Its comic Irishman kept the Committee on the stage,
and in Queen Anne's time the thorough Tory still relished the
stage caricatures of the maintainers of the Commonwealth in Mr.
Day with his greed, hypocrisy, and private incontinence ; his wife,
who had been a cooksmaid to a gentleman, but takes all the
State matters on herself ; and their empty son Abel, who knows
parliament men and sequestrators, and whose ' profound contemplations' are caused by the consternation of his spirits for the
nation's good."—*Morley*.

This comedy was afterwards cut down to a farce by L. Knight,
and kept possession of the stage for a long time under the title of
The Honest Thieves.

6 **Not—neither** = not—either. Neither (either) is here adverbial. Cf. Shakes. *J. C.* I. 2.

15 **Mohocks**, " a class of ruffians who at one time infested the streets of London.   So called from the Indian Mohocks.   At the Restoration, the street bullies were called Muns and Tytre-Tus ; they were next called Hectors and Scorners ; later still, Nickers and Hawkabites ; and lastly Mohocks.   A full account of the proceedings of the Mohocks is given in No. 324 of the *Spectator*.   No. 332 contains a description of an adventure with the Sweaters, a similar set of " well-disposed savages."   An attempt was made to suppress the outrages of the Mohocks by a royal proclamation issued on the 18th March, but it had very little effect, for on the 25th Swift writes : " They go on still, and cut people's faces every night.   But they shan't cut mine : I like it better as it is."   See Timb's Club Life, p. 33-37.

35 **Captain Sentry**.   One of the members of the club, nephew and heir to Sir Roger.   See chaps. ii. and xix.

44 **Steenkirk**.   In August, 1692, William, who had been watching for an opportuninity to attack the forces of Luxembourg, found a spy in his camp.   He forced him to carry false information to his master, who thinking it strange news, still determined to trust it.   William accordingly attacked the French before daybreak, expecting an easy victory, but owing to the difficulty of getting the troops through the wood and past the fortifications and obstacles placed in the way by the enemy, the allies were repulsed with heavy loss—seven thousand are said to have fallen on each side.   The failure of the attack was attributed chiefly to the lack of tact on the part of General Solmes.   It led to great discontent in England, and parliament then for the first time asserted a right, which it has ever since exercised; of inquiring into military operations.   To commemorate the triumph of the French, the dandies of the time exchanged their elaborate cravats for a sort of loose necktie, which they called a *steenkirk*, to indicate the hurried dress in which the French general had defeated the English.   The fashion soon passed over to England where it continued for some years.

46 **Plants**.   A slang expression for canes or batons.

50 **Convoyed**.   Lat. *con*, with, and *via*, a way ; Fr. *voie*.

53 **Pit**.   When plays were first acted in England, the travelling companies that performed them, for want of better accommodation, generally used the yards of inns.   As these were also employed for the exhibition of cock-fighting, and called the cock-pit or yard, the name pit or yard was applied to the ground on which the common spectators stood ; and this was continued after the theatres were built.

54 **Candles.** Lighting by coal-gas was invented by Robert Murdoch about 1792. It was first used in the Soho workshops of Boulton and Watt, at Birmingham, where he fitted up an apparatus for manufacturing gas. It was not used in theatres till 1803, the Royal Lyceum being the first to adopt the invention.

74 **Pyrrhus his.** This use of the possessive case of this pronoun, which was once quite common, is thought by some to be the origin of what is called the Saxon possessive. This opinion is doubtless quite erroneous.

CHAPTER XVIII.

" Spectator," No. 383.   Tuesday, 20th, 1712.   By Addison.
   Juv. Sat. i. 75 :—
      A beauteous garden, but by vice maintain'd.

9 **Spring Garden** was situated in Lambeth, opposite Mill-bank, near the manor called Fulke's Hall (the residence of Fulke de Breanté, a follower of King John), from which it was called Fox Hall or Vauxhall.   It was called *Spring Garden* after the old public pleasure gardens of the reigns of James I. and Charles I., in which there was a playfully-contrived water-work, that, on being trodden upon, sprinkled the unsuspecting promenader. The spring was omitted in the new gardens.   They covered eleven acres, and were tastefully and artistically laid out in arbors, walks, shady groves, refreshment booths, and a dark walk. The company appears to have been of a very varied character, and the amusements equally diversified.   It continued for about two centuries to be the chief promenade for the upper and middle classes of London society.   The most prosperous period of its history was the fifty years (1732—1782), during which it was under the management of Mr. Jonathan Tyers.

12 **Speculating.** Meditating, studying.   The word now usually means incurring financial risks.

16 **Gossip, A. S.** *God* and *Sib*, akin ; originally, as still with the Hampshire peasantry, a name given to sponsors in baptism, because they were believed to become spiritually related to the child for whom they stood.   Sponsors were, by the act of common sponsorship, brought into familiarity with one another, and indulged first in familiar, then in idle, talk.

20 Temple Stairs. The chief rendezvous of the waterman on the Thames, situated just below the Temple, the residences of the legal profession.

28 Bate = abate (A. S. *beaten*, Fr. *abattre*), to beat down. Hence to abate, to lessen.

34 My old friend, &c. This sentence is ungrammatical. *Friend* stands without a verb. Arrange it correctly.

35 With = with the assistance of.

39 La Hogue. At La Hogue, the French Army, under Tourville, sent by Louis to assist in restoring James II., was totally defeated by Admiral Russell in 1692.

47 London Bridge. This bridge was finished in 1209, having been thirty-three years in course of erection. It was rebuilt in the early part of the present century, having stood for more than six hundred years.

48 Seven wonders of antiquity. (1) The Pryamids of Egypt ; (2) The Hanging Gardens of Babylon ; (3) The Tomb of Mausolose ; (4) The Temple of Diana at Ephesus ; (5) The Colossus of Rhodes; (6) The Statue of Zeus (Jupiter) by Phidias; (7) The Pharos of Egypt, or else the Palace of Cyprus, cemented with gold.

55 Temple Bar. An old dingy gateway of blackened Portland stone which separates the strand from Fleet street, the city from the Shire, and the Freedom of the city of London from the Liberty of the city of Westminster, was built by Sir Christopher Wren in the year 1670. It has recently been removed. For a full description, see Thornbury's *Haunted London*, pp. 4-24.

57 Fifty new churches. "The want of new churches in the growing suburbs of London had long been felt ; an address from Convocation on the subject was presented to the Queen in 1711, and this led to resolutions of the House of Commons, readily passed by the High Church and Tory majority, for building fifty new churches within the bills of mortality."—Arnold.

107 Hung beef. Dried-beef, jerked-beef.

CHAPTER XIX.

"Spectator," No 517, Thursday, Oct 23, 1712, by Addison.

Virg. Æn. vi. 878 : —

> Mirror of ancient faith !
> Undaunted worth !   Inviolable truth !—Dryden.

14 **Letters.**   See papers No. 544.

52 **The chaplain a very pretty tenement.**   See chap. iii.

68 **Steeple.**   See note on chap. v.

74 **Quorum.**   The justices of the peace for the county.

Goldsmith tells us that Mr. Addison killed Sir Roger lest some one else should mar his character, as Mr. Steele had apparently done in No. 410 ; Budgell asserts that it was done for the same reason as Cervantes killed his Don Quixote, and Shakespeare his Mercutio, lest he should be killed by him.   But the reason suggested by Chalmers is, doubtless, the correct solution. The work had become burthensome, and it seemed necessary to draw it to a close.   No better plan suggested itself than killing of and otherwise disposing of the members of the Club.   In No. 513 we are told that the clergyman is on his death-bed ; in this, 517, Sir Roger himself passes away ; in 530, Will Honeycomb writes to say that he has married a farmer's daughter, and will henceforth "make a vacancy in the Club ;" in 541, we learn that the Templar meditates "a closer pursuit of the law ;" in 544, Captain Sentry intimates that he will in future be required on his estate ; and in 549, Sir Andrew Freeport announces his withdrawal from the Club.   It is shortly after closed, and proposals made for the formation of a new Club.   The particulars about this are stated in part in 556, when the *Spectator* is revived, after having ceased publication for eighteen months.

84 **Quit-rents.**   A yearly rent, by the payment of which the tenant goes *quit* and free of all other services.

91 **Joyed**=enjoyed.

Coffee-houses in England, from the time of their commencement (1652), took the place, in part at least, of the modern newspapers, both as a disseminating point for news, and for political discussions.   In the days of Addison and Steele there was but or daily paper ; it was small in size, and conducted with little ability and energy, compared with the mammoth sheets of modern

times.   Every coffee-house had its special purpose.   At one met
the seekers for pleasure and frolic ; at another politicians ; at a
third physicians, and so on.   Those in which Mr. Spectator
says he was to be found, Will's, at No. 1, Bond Street, was the
meeting place for wits and poets ; Child's, in St. Paul's Churchyard, the resort of clergymen ; St. James's, the *Spectator's*
headquarters, at the end of Pall Mall, the rendezvous of politicians, as the Cocoa in St. James Street was of the Tories and
men of fashion ; the Grecian, in Devereux Court, the assembly
hall of the learned ; Jonathan's, in Change Alley, the general
mart for stock-jobbers.

" Clubs in England and France arose almost at the same time,
and from the same causes.   The barriers of rank were all-
powerful in ordinary life : and the clubs were a protest against,
and an evasion of, these barriers.   They were a necessary result
of the desire of men of intellect of the higher and middle classes
to meet on terms of equality.   Modifications were soon introduced.   One club became that of physicians, another that of
lawyers, another of Greek scholars, and so on : the political character of some clubs arising from the fact that each had some
leading member who had probably strong political opinions, and
who would gradually draw around him others of similar opinions.   Some few purely political clubs there were both in England and France."—Airy.

QUESTIONS FOR EXAMINATION.

THE DESERTED VILLAGE.

1. What is the main thesis of the *Deserted Village?*

2. To what variety of poetry does the *D. V.* belong? Give a list of poems belonging to this variety, with authors and dates.

3. Give a brief sketch of the person to whom the *D. V.* is dedicated.

4. State Lord Macaulay's criticism of the *D. V.* and inquire into its correctness.

5. To what place is the poet supposed to refer under the name *Auburn?*   Give the reasons for your answer.

6. What were the circumstances and engagements of the poet at the time of the production of the *D. V.?*.

7. How do the *Traveller* and *D. V.* compare as to plan and execution?

8. Contrast, after Goldsmith, the Village in its prosperity and decay.

9. In ll. 1-50, explain *labouring swain, decent, toil remitting, sleight of art, simply, mistrustless, tyrant's hand,* l. 40, *hollow sounding, unvaried crisis, spoiler's hand.*

10. Examine the statement contained in ll. 51-2.

11. Compare Goldsmith's apostrophe to "Retirement" (*D. V.* ll. 96-112) with that of Cowper (*Garden* ll. 675-701) (a) in sentiment, (b) diction, (c) pathos, (d) elevation.

12. In the *D. V.*, ll. 57-74, Goldsmith intimates that England once enjoyed a happiness that had passed away before his day ; and in the *Garden* ll. 75-107, Cowper declares that the virtue she once possessed, had likewise departed. State wherein this happiness and virtue con-

sisted, and inquire how far each statement is borne out by history.

13. Explain the position that Goldsmith holds in relation to the poetical literature of England.

14. How far was Goldsmith's belief in the decrease of the population of the country shared by the leading men of the day? How far was it actually correct?

15. In ll 52-192, write brief notes on *hastening ills*, *trade's unfeeling train*, l. 66, *tyrant's power*, l. 105, and ll. 187-8.

16. In ll. 113-136, the "village" is again presented in its prime and decay. Compare these pictures with those of the early part of the poem. What peculiarities of poetry are illustrated in these pictures?

17. Describe, after Goldsmith, the "village preacher." Quote in your description as many lines as you can of more than ordinary beauty, and state wherein that beauty consists.

18. Point out the different meanings in which the word, "Mansion" is used in the poem ; also, "Train."

19. Who are thought to have been the originals of the village preacher?

20. Compare this description of the parson with Cowper's (in the *Time-piece*, ll. 337-480.)

21. What other English poets have described "the parson"?

22. Where did Goldsmith borrow the simile with which his description of the parson closes?

23. Write in your own language a description of the 'village master.'

24. What are the excellencies and defects of Goldsmith's poetry?

25. Point out the poetic beauties in the picture of the 'master.'

26. Where did Goldsmith find the original of the 'master' and his school?

27. Draw, after Goldsmith, a picture of the inn and its company.

28. Where did the poet see the picture he has here drawn? Is the inn English or Irish?

29. By whom was the inn at Lissoy rebuilt? When? Why?

30. Explain in ll. 191-250, *straggling fence, unprofitably gay, boding tremblers, day's disaster, cipher, terms and tides, gauge, nut-brown draughts, parlour splendours, festive, double debt,* l. 233, l. 240, ll. 242-3, *mantling bliss,* l. 250.

31. Why does the poet prefer the " simple blessings " of the poor to the " toiling pleasure " of the great ?

32. How does the poet think wealth has been acquired ?

33. Point out the fundamental error of his theory.

34. Give some account of the great political economist who lived in Goldsmith's time, and briefly state the chief doctrines he taught.   Shew wherein they differ from Goldsmith's.

35. Shew the fallacy of the simile of the " fair female " as applied to England.   To Ireland.

36. Explain the cause of the effect produced by ll. 301-2 upon a reader whose judgment is convinced that as a matter of fact the statement is incorrect.

37. Inquire how far the poet's views as to the decrease of population are correct ; also, what are the real effects of the cause to which he attributes a decrease.

38. Characterize the poet's attack on luxury.

39. " Goldsmith's fallacy lies in identifying trade and luxury."   Examine the correctness of this statement.

40. Give some account of the " commons " in England and of the Enclosure Acts by which they have been limited.

41. How far is the poet's charge, that the " sons of wealth " have appropriated the commons " justifiable ?

42. Point out the poetic beauties of the lines that describe the reception of " poverty " at the city.

43. In ll. 251-340, explain *vacant mind, wanton,* l. 268, *freighted ore,* ll. 273-4, *needful product, solicitous to bless, vistas, artist, tumultuous grandeur, blazing square, idly.*

44. What crimes, in Goldsmith's days, were punished by the " black gibbet ? "

45. What do you understand by the terms " subjective poet," " objective poet," " realistic poetry," " idealistic poetry ? "   How would you class Goldsmith and Cowper and their poetry under these heads ?

46. What important effects had the school-boy days of Goldsmith and Cowper upon their mature life and upon their writings ?

47. Discuss Goldsmith's views on *trade ; luxury ; commerce ; emigration.*

48. Does Goldsmith use any particular word so often in the *D. V.* that it may be termed a mannerism ?

49. Mention any instances of poetic license in the *D. V.*

50. Quote the passages of the *D. V.* in which the author refers to himself.

51. What is the great charm of this poem ?

52. What were Goldsmith's motives for adopting literature as a profession ?

53. Is there any internal evidence in the *D. V.* which you could adduce to show approximately the period at which it was written ?

54. Explain in ll. 340-430, *convex world, gathers death around, tigers, seats, conscious virtue, sapped, Torno, equinoctial fervours, trade's proud empire.*

55. Quote the lines written by Dr. Johnson.

56. How far are the poet's views of the state of poetry in his time literally correct ?

57. Compare the actual condition of the immigrant in America with the poet's picture. Why does he exaggerate the happiness of the peasant at home and the misery of his situation in the New World ?

58. Point out the peculiarity of the construction of the last four lines. Examine the theory they propound.

59. What is the date of the publication of the *D. V. ?* By whom published ? The price ? How was it received ? How many editions were issued within two months ?

60. To whom was the poem dedicated ? How was the dedication received ?

61. To what extent can you trace Dr. Johnson's influence in the *D. V. ?*

62. Compare Goldsmith and Addison as dramatic writers, as prose writers, and as poets.

THE TASK.—BOOK III.

THE GARDEN.

1. How was Cowper led to undertake the *Task?*
2. What is the chief topic on which it dwells?
3. How long was Cowper engaged in writing it?
4. How does his theory of poetry differ from Pope's?
5. How far may Cowper lay claim to originality in poetry?
6. Name the Books of the *Task*, and outline the contents of each?
7. Give a minute account of the subjects treated of in the *Garden.*
8. What poets had most influence on Cowper?
9. Estimate the influence of Cowper's poetry upon subsequent poetical literature.
10. Account for Cowper's severe treatment of history and science.
11. What difference is there between the views held before and since Cowper's time, regarding the province and object of history?
12. In what state were geology and astronomy when the *Task* was written?
13. In what light did writers on theology regard science at that time?
14. When did the custom of going to London against which Cowper rails, come into fashion? What benefits did it confer on the country gentleman? What evil consequences had it?

15. Give the date of the publication of the *Task* and of Cowper's other chief works.

16. Define the term " school of poets."

17. Of what school was Cowper the founder?

18. Name the representative poets of the following schools: (*a*) Didactic, (*b*) Natural, (*c*) Lake, (*d*) Romantic, (*e*) Metaphysical, (*f*) Artificial.

19. Compare the leading features of modern poetical literature with those of the age of Goldsmith and of that of Cowper.

20. How does the *Garden* differ from the other books of the *Task*?

21. Show how the introductory lines (1-40) of the *Garden* connect it with the preceding book, *The Time-piece*.

22. Wherein does the chief interest of the *Garden* consist?

23. Point out the direct personal allusions the author makes to his own circumstances and history in the *Garden*.

24. Inquire into the effectiveness with which Cowper " cracked the satiric thong" in Book II. of the *Task*. To what rank among English satirists is he entitled by his first series of moral poems?

25. Briefly state the criticisms referred to in l. 35.

26. Quote parallel passages from the *D. V.* and the *Garden*.

27. Does l. 15 refer to the *Time-piece* or to the *Tirocinium*?

28. Explain l. 52, l. 63, *sharped* in l. 85, *fair* in l. 93, *soliciting* in l. 115, *other views* in l. 122, *contrive creation* in l. 156, *wielded the elements* in l. 170, *parallax* in l. 215.

29. Give the chief features of Cowper's poetic style as seen in the *Task*.

30. What were his motives for writing poetry?

31. Describe his Olney Hymns?

32. What rank does Cowper hold as a letter writer?

33. Give the substance of Southey's criticism on the *Task*.

34. Approximate the date of the authorship of the *Task* from internal evidence.

35. Give some account of Cowper's most intimate friends, and estimate their influence on his writings.

36. Compare Cowper's account of his conversion as given in the *Garden*, ll. 108-120 with the one he has left us in prose.

37. When did the custom of drinking "fragrant lymph" become common in England?

38. Give an account of the moral and religious condition of the different classes of society in Cowper's day.

39. Show how the religious movements of the eighteenth century affected Cowper's life and poetry.

40. Is the poet's attack on the pursuits of men prompted by censoriousness, or by a sincere desire to do his fellows good? Justify your answer.

41. On what grounds do Newton, Milton, and Hale gain the poet's approbation? Give some account of them.

42. Answer the question of ll. 277-289.

43. What are Cowper's opinions of sporting? What features of his character do they exhibit?

44. What were the chief out-door exercises at this period?

45. Give an account of the hare referred to in l. 334.

46. What are the poet's "various employments" as set forth in the *Garden*?

47. Make a brief sketch of "her who shared his pleasures and his heart" (l. 390.)

48. Describe, after the poet, the raising of cucumbers. Quote the lines you consider the best, state wherein their excellence consists.

49. Account for the long description of a garden and a green-house.

50. Explain *Castalian dew* in l. 251, *British Themis* in l. 257, *vanity* in l. 367, *compose* in l. 305, *jovial* in l. 333, *trim* in l. 357, *fragrant lymph* in l. 391, *the Mantuan bard* in l. 453, l. 457, *mats* in l. 525, *their sexes* in l. 537, *crape* in l. 802, *levee* in l. 822.

51. Examine the correctness of the poet's views of the moral advantages of rural life.

52. What are the respective advantages of rhyme and blank verse?

53. Why did Cowper write the *Task* in blank verse?

54. What causes contributed to the poetical activity of the latter part of the 18th century?

55. Was Cowper's malady induced by physical or religious causes?

56. Did Cowper sympathize with the American Revolutionists?

57. Did the French Revolution produce any appreciable effect on his poetry?

58. Name the leading poets contemporary with Cowper.

59. Compare Cowper and Addison as hymn writers.

60. Contrast Goldsmith's and Cowper's views of commerce, and of the causes that prevented the prosperity of the country.

61. Relate particular instances of the bribery referred to in ll. 795-800.

62. Quote the apostrophe to London.

63. Goldsmith and Cowper profess to have each an object specially dear to himself. Mention it, and dilate on the sincerity of the affection each bestowed upon it.

64. The poetry of Goldsmith differs widely from Cowper's, each has a charm peculiarly its own. Point out this difference ; fully state and illustrate the special beauties of each.

65. Trace the change which poetry underwent during the 18th century, and show clearly how Cowper came to found a new school of poetry.

66. Why does the poet prefer rural to city life?

67. Give, after the poet, the causes why people leave the country to take refuge in the city.

68. Was the rage for expensive improvements general or merely local? What opportunity had Cowper of seeing the "omnipotent magician's work"

69. How far is Cowper's character reflected in the *Task*?

70. "Cowper is eminently the poet of the domestic affections, and the exponent of the strong religious feeling of the latter part of the 18th century." Illustrate this statement from his poem on the *Garden*.

QUESTIONS FOR EXAMINATION.

THE DE COVERLEY PAPERS.

From the " Spectator."

1. How was the idea of the *Spectator* suggested ?
2. By whom was it first proposed ?
3. Give the dates and numbers of each consecutive part.
4. Describe its predecessor and successors.
5. What estimate has been made of its circulation ?
6. What was its price ?   What the cause of its ceasing to be published ?
7. Describe the plan of the *Spectator*.   How far was it carried out ?
8. What proportion of the papers were written by Addison ?   By Steele? By whom were the rest written ?
9.   What were the circumstances of Addison and Steele when they were engaged in writing the *Tatler, Spectator,* and *Guardian* ?
10. How are the papers written by Addison distinguished ? How those by Steele ?   Explain Addison's signature.
11. Name and characterize Addison's dramatic writings.
12. Who were Addison's chief contemporaries in poetry and prose ?
13. Sketch the life of Swift and compare his prose style with Addison's.
14. What are the common faults of prose ?   Which of them are found in Addison's writings ?
15. Distinguish between prose and poetry.
16. What are the chief elements of style ?   Treat the style of Addison under each head.
17. Point out the leading features of Addison's styl

18. Compare the style of Addison with that of Steele.

19. Account for the prose style of Queen Anne's reign.

20. Who is supposed to have been the original of Sir Roger? of Will Wimble? State the objections to these theories.

21. Where did the *Spectator* get the name Sir Roger De Coverley?

22. Write a short account of the originator of such papers as the *Spectator*.

23. Name Steele's works and newspapers.

24. How far does Sir Roger represent the actual squire of that time?

25. Describe the character of Sir Roger De Coverley.

26. In how many of the papers of the *Spectator* does Sir Roger occur? By whom are these papers written?

27. Give some account of the clubs and coffee-houses of the *Spectator's* day.

28. Give a short sketch of the rise of journalism in England.

29. What relation did the *Spectator* bear to the ordinary newspaper of the time?

30. What were the different classes of society in Sir Roger's time?

31. Tell what you know of the members of the Spectator Club.

32. Sketch the Life of Addison.

33. Describe the Augustan Age.

34. What public offices did Addison hold? Steele?

35. What relation does the *Spectator* bear to the modern "novel"?

36. Define that species of literature termed "The Novel," and discuss the claims of Addison, Defoe, Goldsmith and Richardson to being its originator.

Chap. II.—1. Derive and explain *humour, pad, ancient, conversation, digested, spirits, elocution,*

2. What impressions does this essay leave of the character of Sir Roger?

3. Write notes on the preachers in the chaplain's list.

4. Describe the chaplain.

5. Is *parsonage* used for an office or a building? (Cf. *tenement* in chap. XIX.)

Chap. III.—1. Point out the words in this paper that are obsolete or obsolescent, and give their modern equivalents.
2. What features of Addison's literary style and of his method of treating social subjects are illustrated in this essay?
3. Has his advice as to the training of "younger sons" been adopted in England yet?

Chap. IV.—1. Derive and explain *proper, awfulness, sprites, trivial, exorcised.*
2. Write notes on Locke, Josephus and Lucretius.
3. Examine how far Mr. Spectator himself is free from superstition.

Chap. V.—1. Give in your own words an account of the methods Sir Roger adopts to promote the religious interests of his people.
2 Derive and explain *habits, indifferent, flitch, parson, tithe-stealers.*
3. Tell what you know of the condition of the ' agricultural laborers in Queen Anne's reign.
4. Explain the tithing system of England and its modern management.

Chap. VI.—1. Explain *sedentary tempers, vapours, proper for it, refining those spirits.*
2. Select the sentences of this paper that violate the rules of grammar, and arrange them correctly.
3. When did fox-hunting become fashionable in England?

Chap. VII.—1. Give an account of the belief in witchcraft in Addison's time. When and why did it pass away?
2. Explain *hovering faith, intercourse and commerce, speculation, distemper, secret commerces, county sessions.*
3. Write a note on Otway.
4. Addison says, " The great aim of these

my speculations is to banish vice and ignorance out of the territories of Great Britain." What was their effect in that direction?

Chap. VIII.—1. Compare Mr. Addison's idea of instinct with that held by Darwin and Spencer.

2. Write short notes on the proper names in this paper and on the Royal Society.

3. There are in this paper several instances of variation from modern grammatical construction. Correct them.

4. Addison says, " Animals have nothing like the use of reason." What is your opinion? That of modern scientists?

Chap. IX.—1. What features of the old knight's character are brought out in this essay?

2. Explain *verdict, cast, appearance, discovering, assizes.*

3. Make brief notes on the state of the Game Act, on the administration of justice, and on the divisions of the rural population, in Sir Roger's day.

4. How does the construction of the first paragraph of this essay differ from Addison's usual style?

Chap. X.—1. Relate in your own language the story of Eudoxus and Leontine, imitating the style of Addison as well as you can. Then compare what you have written with his relation, and inquire wherein you have failed to equal it.

2. With what incident in Mr. Addison's life is the writing of this story connected?

Chap. XI.—1. What was the state of political parties in 1710-12?

2. Describe Addison as a politician and political writer.

3. What did Sir Roger consider the evils of party spirit?   Mr. Spectator?

4. On what questions were the English public divided when Sir Roger " was a school-boy ?"

Chap   XII.—1. Explain *account, politer conversation, Whig jockeys and Tory fox-hunters, landed and moneyed interest, bait, humour, correspondence, fanatic, first principles.*

2. Relate what is said of Sir Andrew Freeport in chap. I. What proportion of the population were engaged in commerce at the Revolution? How many had an income equal to that of a country squire?

3. On what questions were parties divided at the time this paper was written?

4. How had Addison and Steele suffered from party spirit?

Chap.   XIII.—1. Reproduce the matter of this paper, varying the language but following style.

2. Derive and explain *gipsies, sweethearts, bachelor, palmistry, line of life, exert, the justice of the peace.*

3. Parse *ten to one but he becomes, him to be taken on board, gave him for drowned.*

4. Point the words and phrases that have become obsolete or colloquial.

5. Give some account of the gipsies in England.

6. In what light does Sir Roger appear in this essay?

Chap.   XIV.—1. Explain *a month's excursion, several subjects, taciturnity, cunning, white-witch, converses, discarded whig, pr'ythee.*

U

2. Who was Will Honeycomb? Describe him from chap. I.
3. What is here meant by a Jesuit? Why were they objects of dislike in England at this time?
4. Under what social, political, and religious disabilities did the Catholics labor in Addison's time?
5. Compare the opinions of the *Spectator* and Cowper regarding the custom of going to London. Account for the difference.

Chap. XV.—1. Write notes on *Gray's Inn Walks, Prince Eugene, Scanderbeg, the late Act of Parliament, the Pope's procession, Baker's Chronicle, Squire's, the supplement.*
2. Describe the state of public feeling, political and religious, that is referred to in the different parts of this paper.
3. State your reasons for considering Sir Roger a person of some literary taste and culture.
4. What was the object of making Sir Roger idolize the Prince?
5. What is the antecedent of *which* in the clause *which very much redound, etc.?*
6. *Smutting, etc.* Quote a parallel passage from the *D. V.*

Chap. XVI.—1. Derive and explain *engaged, Virginia, trepanned, chines.*
2. Write explanatory notes on *my paper upon Westminster Abbey, Widow Trueby's water, the sickness at the Dantzic, the two Coronation Chairs, Jacob's pillar, the martyr to good housewifery,* and on the proper names in the essay.
3. When did Westminster become a burial place for the great?

Chap. XVII.—1. What was the particular object of this paper?

2. Why was Sir Roger taken to the theatre?

3. Describe the theatre after the Revolution.

4. Give some particulars about the two plays mentioned, and about their authors.

5. Who were the leading dramatic writers of the period?

6. When were theatres first lighted with gas?

Chap. XVIII.—1. Mention points of interest about *Spring Garden, Vauxhall, Temple Bar, La Hogue.*

2. Explain so as to show their meaning in the paper, *Seven wonders, Thames ribaldry, Mahometan paradise, bate, fifty new churches, Knight of the shire, a face of magistracy, hung beef, quorum.*

Chap. XIX.—1. What reasons have been assigned for the killing of Sir Roger?

2. In what quality of style does this paper excel?

3. Enumerate Sir Roger's bequests, and inquire whether they show his life to have been sincere.

4. Explain *roast beef stomach, a lightening before death, quit rents, Act of Uniformity.*